AF804165

Law's Hermeneutics: Other Investigations

Bringing together leading academics hailing from different cultural and scholarly horizons, this book revisits legal hermeneutics by making particular reference to philosophy, sociology and linguistics. On the assumption that theory has much to teach law, that theory motivates and enables, the writings of such intellectuals as Martin Heidegger, Hans-Georg Gadamer, Jacques Derrida, Paul Ricœur, Giorgio Agamben, Jürgen Habermas, Ronald Dworkin and Ludwig Wittgenstein receive special consideration. As it explores the matter of reading the law and as it inquires into the emergence of meaning within the dynamic between reader and text against the background of the reader's worldly finiteness, this collection of essays aims to contribute to an improved appreciation of the merits and limits of law's hermeneutics which, it argues, is emphatically not to be reduced to a simple tool for textual exegesis.

Simone Glanert is Senior Lecturer at Kent Law School and Director of the Kent Centre for European and Comparative Law.

Fabien Girard is Assistant Professor (*Maître de conférences*) at the Faculty of Law, Université Grenoble Alpes.

Law's Hermeneutics: Other Investigations

Simone Glanert
Fabien Girard

Routledge
Taylor & Francis Group
LONDON AND NEW YORK

First published 2017
by Routledge
2 Park Square, Milton Park, Abingdon, Oxon OX14 4RN

and by Routledge
711 Third Avenue, New York, NY 10017

Routledge is an imprint of the Taylor & Francis Group, an informa business

© 2017 selection and editorial matter, Simone Glanert and Fabien Girard; individual chapters, the contributors

The right of Simone Glanert and Fabien Girard to be identified as the authors of the editorial material, and of the authors for their individual chapters, has been asserted in accordance with sections 77 and 78 of the Copyright, Designs and Patents Act 1988.

All rights reserved. No part of this book may be reprinted or reproduced or utilised in any form or by any electronic, mechanical, or other means, now known or hereafter invented, including photocopying and recording, or in any information storage or retrieval system, without permission in writing from the publishers.

Trademark notice: Product or corporate names may be trademarks or registered trademarks, and are used only for identification and explanation without intent to infringe.

British Library Cataloguing in Publication Data
A catalogue record for this book is available from the British Library

Library of Congress Cataloging in Publication Data
Names: Glanert, Simone, 1973- editor. | Girard, Fabien, editor.
Title: Law's hermeneutics: other investigations / edited by Simone Glanert, Fabien Girard.
Description: New York, NY : Routledge, 2017. | Includes bibliographical references and index.
Identifiers: LCCN 2017001584| ISBN 9781138123724 (hardback) | ISBN 9781317301660 (adobe reader) | ISBN 9781317301653 (epub) | ISBN 9781317301646 (mobipocket)
Subjects: LCSH: Law—Interpretation and construction.
Classification: LCC K290 .L39 2017 | DDC 340/.1—dc23
LC record available at https://lccn.loc.gov/2017001584

ISBN: 978-1-138-12372-4 (hbk)
ISBN: 978-1-315-64865-1 (ebk)

Typeset in Galliard
by Keystroke, Neville Lodge, Tettenhall, Wolverhampton

MIX
Paper from responsible sources
FSC® C013604

Printed and bound by CPI Group (UK) Ltd, Croydon, CR0 4YY

Contents

Acknowledgements

The contributions to this volume were first presented at an international workshop entitled 'Law's Hermeneutics: Other Investigations' co-organized by the Kent Centre for European and Comparative Law and the Maison Française d'Oxford in Oxford on 5–6 June 2015, with the exception of Cristina Lafont's and Charles Taylor's chapters. These two texts were previously released and are included with permission of their authors and publishers. Revisions are stylistic only. The relevant bibliographical information is as follows:

Lafont, C. (2005) 'Hermeneutics', in H.L. Dreyfus and M.A. Wrathall (eds) *A Companion to Heidegger*, Oxford: Blackwell, pp. 265–84.

Taylor, C. (2002) 'Understanding the Other: A Gadamerian View on Conceptual Schemes', in J. Malpas, U. Arnswald and J. Kertscher (eds) *Gadamer's Century: Essays in Honor of Hans-Georg Gadamer*, Cambridge, MA: MIT Press, pp. 279–97.

We are grateful to the Maison Française d'Oxford for organizing and hosting the workshop. In addition, we wish to recognize the Centre de Recherches Juridiques, Université Grenoble Alpes, and in particular its co-directors, Michel Farge and Nicolas Kada, for providing financial assistance during the editorial process. At Kent Law School, Sarah Gilkes and Sarah Slowe gave generously of their time to make both the workshop and this editorial venture a success. We also wish to thank Okke Pollanen, who kindly facilitated the copy-editing of the initial drafts.

S.G. wants to record her deep appreciation to the Brown Foundation and to the Houston Museum of Fine Arts for the award of a residential fellowship at the Dora Maar House in Ménerbes, France, which allowed much of the editorial work to be conducted under optimal scholarly circumstances in the spring of 2016.

S.G. and F.G.

Notes on contributors

Dr Cosmin Sebastian Cercel is Assistant Professor of Law at the University of Nottingham. Dr Cercel completed his PhD dissertation on the nexus between law, politics and culture in communist Romania at the Sorbonne in 2012. His research focuses on genealogies of law and politics with specific reference to twentieth-century Continental legal history. Recent publications include 'Law Out of Bounds: Legal Picnolepsy, Intellectual Austerity and Romania's Legal Past', in C.S. Cercel, R. Mańko and A. Sulikowski (eds) *Law and Critique in Central Europe* (Counterpress, 2016); 'The Purloined Letter: Law, History and the Theory of Totalitarianism', in V. Breda and L. Rodak (eds) *Diverse Narratives of Legal Objectivity* (P. Lang, 2016); and 'The Enemy Within: Criminal Law and Ideology in Interwar Romania', in S. Skinner (ed.) *Fascism and Criminal Law* (Hart, 2015). On the occasion of the Critical Legal Conference in 2014 and 2015, Dr Cercel convened a series of panels dedicated to a critical reading of Giorgio Agamben's concept of the 'state of exception'. He is currently writing a monograph analyzing the jurisprudential aspects of state communism, to be published with Routledge.

Dr Fabien Girard is Assistant Professor (*Maître de conférences*) at the Faculty of Law, Université Grenoble Alpes, where he teaches philosophy of law, civil procedure and criminal justice. His PhD dissertation on the law of evidence in a cultural context was published with Presses Universitaires d'Aix-Marseille in 2013. While on secondment at the Maison Française d'Oxford (MFO) from 2014 to 2016, Dr Girard conducted a research programme on 'Theory of Law and Legal Anthropology'. Beyond his writings on biotechnologies and industrial property (*Biotechnologies végétales et propriété industrielle* (La Documentation Française, 2014), with Christine Noiville), he is particularly interested in the legal theory of Jeremy Bentham ('Bentham et l'esprit du Common Law', (2002) 2 *Revue de l'Institut Rhône-Alpin de sciences criminelles* 49) and in legal hermeneutics ('Prendre langue avec l'Étranger. La traduction: un modèle pour l'herméneutique juridique?' (2015) *Sens public*; www.sens-public.org/spip.php?article1137).

Dr Simone Glanert, a graduate of the Sorbonne and a former Rudolf B. Schlesinger Fellow at Cornell Law School, is a Senior Lecturer at Kent Law

School where she teaches comparative law, French public law and legal interpretation. She has repeatedly acted as visiting professor in Grenoble, Montreal, at the Sorbonne and at HBKU in Doha. Her research focuses on theoretical issues arising from the practice of comparison in the context of the globalization and Europeanization of laws. In this regard, Dr Glanert's monograph *De la traductibilité du droit* (Dalloz, 2011) critically assesses the possibilities and limits of legal translation from an interdisciplinary perspective. Having edited *Comparative Law: Engaging Translation* (Routledge, 2014), she has also acted as guest editor for a special issue on law and translation released by a leading translation-studies journal published by Routledge (*The Translator*, 2014). She is currently working on a book project provisionally entitled *Gadamer and Foreign Law*.

Jean Grondin is Professor of Philosophy at the Université de Montréal. The author of many influential books in the fields of hermeneutics and metaphysics which have been translated into 15 languages, Professor Grondin was a pupil, friend and close collaborator of Hans-Georg Gadamer of whom he wrote a landmark study, *Hans-Georg Gadamer: A Biography* (trans. J. Weinsheimer, Yale University Press, 2003). Some of his numerous contributions include *Introduction to Philosophical Hermeneutics* (trans. J. Weinsheimer, Yale University Press, 1994); *Introduction to Metaphysics* (trans. L. Soderstrom, Columbia University Press, 2012); *Paul Ricœur* (Presses Universitaires de France, 2013); *Du sens des choses: l'idée de la métaphysique* (Presses Universitaires de France, 2013). Professor Grondin's work has earned him numerous honours such as the Killam Prize, the Canada Council for the Arts Molson Prize and the Konrad-Adenauer-Award.

Cristina Lafont is Professor of Philosophy at Northwestern University. She is the author of *The Linguistic Turn in Hermeneutic Philosophy* (trans. J. Medina, MIT Press, 1999); *Heidegger, Language, and World-disclosure* (trans. G. Harman, Cambridge University Press, 2000); *Global Governance and Human Rights* (Spinoza Lecture Series) (Van Gorcum, 2012); and co-editor, with H. Brunkhorst and R. Kreide, of the *Habermas Handbuch* (J.B. Metzler, 2015). Her recent contributions include 'Was Heidegger an Externalist?' (2005) 48 *Inquiry* 507; 'Meaning and Interpretation: Can Brandomian Scorekeepers be Gadamerian Hermeneuts?' (2008) 3 *Philosophy Compass* 17; and 'Transcendental versus Hermeneutic Phenomenology in *Being and Time*', in S. Gardner and M. Grist (eds) *The Transcendental Turn* (Oxford University Press, 2015). In 2011, Professor Lafont held the Spinoza Chair at the University of Amsterdam. In 2012–13, she was a Fellow at the Institute for Advanced Study in Berlin. She directs the 'Program in Critical Theory' and co-directs the Research Group on 'Global Capitalism and Law' at Northwestern University.

Professor Pierre Legrand, a Rhodes Scholar and an Oxford graduate, teaches law at the Sorbonne. He writes in English and French, and his work on theoretical issues arising from comparative interventions in a glocalizing world has been translated into many languages. Representative publications include 'The Same and the Different', in P. Legrand and R. Munday (eds) *Comparative Legal Studies: Traditions and Transitions* (Cambridge University Press, 2003); 'Issues in the Translatability of Law', in S. Bermann and M. Wood (eds) *Nation, Language, and the Ethics of Translation* (Princeton University Press, 2005); 'On the Singularity of Law' (2006) 47 *Harvard International Law Journal* 517; 'Foreign Law: Understanding Understanding' (2011) 6/2 *Journal of Comparative Law* 67; and 'Negative Comparative Law' (2015) 10/2 *Journal of Comparative Law* 405. Professor Legrand's monograph *Negative Comparative Law* is forthcoming with Routledge.

François Ost is Professor of Law and Emeritus Vice-Chancellor at the Université Saint-Louis in Brussels and Visiting Professor at the University of Geneva. A member of the Royal Academies for Science and the Arts of Belgium, he edits the *Revue interdisciplinaire d'études juridiques* and co-chairs the European Academy of Legal Theory. With the late M. van de Kerchove, he co-authored *Le Droit ou les paradoxes du jeu* (Presses Universitaires de France, 1992); *Legal System Between Order and Disorder* (trans. I. Stewart, Oxford University Press, 1994); and *De la pyramide au réseau?* (FUSL, 2002). Professor Ost's contributions also include *Le Temps et le droit* (O. Jacob, 1999); *Raconter la loi* (O. Jacob, 2004); *Sade et la loi* (O. Jacob, 2005); *Traduire* (Fayard, 2009); *Shakespeare, la comédie de la loi* (Michalon, 2012); and *A quoi sert le droit* (Bruylant, 2016).

William Outhwaite, FAcSS, is Emeritus Professor of Sociology at Newcastle University. His research focuses on social theory (especially critical theory), philosophy of social science, history of social thought and contemporary Europe. Professor Outhwaite's publications include *Understanding Social Life: The Method Called* Verstehen (Allen and Unwin, 1975); *Concept Formation in Social Science* (Routledge, 1983); *New Philosophies of Social Science: Realism, Hermeneutics and Critical Theory* (Palgrave Macmillan, 1987); *The Future of Society* (Blackwell, 2006); *European Society* (Polity Press, 2008); *Habermas: A Critical Introduction*, 2nd edn (Polity Press, 2009); 'Legality and Legitimacy in the European Union', in C. Thornhill and S. Ashenden (eds) *Legality and Legitimacy: Normative and Sociological Approaches* (Nomos, 2010); *Critical Theory and Contemporary Europe* (Continuum, 2012); *Social Theory* (Profile, 2015); *Europe Since 1989* (Routledge, 2016); and *Contemporary Europe* (Routledge, 2017).

Professor Ralf Poscher directs the Institute for Philosophy of Law and manages the Centre for Security and Society at the University of Freiburg. He was Visiting Professor at the University of Osaka in 2007; a member of the Institute for Advanced Study in Princeton in 2007–08; a researcher within the 'Program in Law and Public Affairs' at Princeton University in 2012; and Fernand Braudel

Senior Fellow at the European University Institute in Florence in 2013. Recent writings in English include 'Ambiguity and Vagueness in Legal Interpretation', in L. Solan and P. Tiersma (eds) *The Oxford Handbook of Language and Law* (Oxford University Press, 2012); 'The Principle Theory: How Many Theories and What Is Their Merit?', in M. Klatt (ed.) *Institutionalized Reason: The Jurisprudence of Robert Alexy* (Oxford University Press, 2012); and 'Hermeneutics, Jurisprudence and Law', in J. Malpas and H.-H. Gander (eds) *The Routledge Companion to Hermeneutics* (Routledge, 2015). With G. Keil, he co-edited *Vagueness and Law* (Oxford University Press, 2016).

Julia Tanney is a philosopher who has written numerous articles in philosophy of mind and language, focusing especially on reason explanation, rule-following, self-knowledge and the nature of philosophical investigation. Her book *Rules, Reason, and Self-Knowledge* was published by Harvard University Press in 2013. She is an international expert on the philosophy of Gilbert Ryle and the later Wittgenstein. Having spent most of her career in the UK, she now works independently, dividing her time between Paris and the South of France.

Charles Taylor, a leading Canadian political philosopher, is Emeritus Professor of Philosophy at McGill University. A Rhodes Scholar, he acted as Chichele Professor of Social and Political Theory at the University of Oxford and Professor of Law and Philosophy at Northwestern University. Professor Taylor is the author of many influential works, including *Hegel and Modern Society* (Cambridge University Press, 1979); *Philosophical Papers*, 2 vols (Cambridge University Press, 1985); *Sources of the Self* (Harvard University Press, 1989); *The Ethics of Authenticity* (Harvard University Press, 1992); *A Secular Age* (Harvard University Press, 2007); *Dilemmas and Connections* (Harvard University Press, 2011); and *The Language Animal* (Harvard University Press, 2016). Professor Taylor is the recipient of many prestigious awards such as the Kyoto Prize, the Templeton Prize and the John W. Kluge Prize.

Paul Yowell is an Associate Professor in the Faculty of Law, University of Oxford, and Fellow and Tutor in Law at Oriel College. Prior to taking up his current post in 2012, he was Lecturer in Law at New College (2005–12) and a postdoctoral fellow with the Faculty of Law, University of Oxford, for the AHRC project 'Parliaments and Human Rights' (2010–11). He completed the BCL in European and Comparative Law and MPhil in Law at Balliol College, and the DPhil in Law at University College. His research interests are in legal philosophy, constitutional law and theory, EU law, and human rights. He has co-edited, with M. Hunt and H. Hooper, *Parliaments and Human Rights: Redressing the Democratic Deficit* (Hart, 2014); and, with N. Barber and R. Ekins, *Lord Sumption and the Limits of Law* (Hart, 2016).

List of cases

Hermeneuticizing the law

Simone Glanert and Fabien Girard

> In every genuine effort at research one needs to work out a consciousness of one's hermeneutical situation. Only in this way can one shed light on the basis of one's interests in it and on what supports one's standpoint of questioning. And of course one still must confess the endlessness of this task.
>
> Hans-Georg Gadamer (1993: 46)

The interpretation theory called 'hermeneutics' has made significant contributions to a better understanding of the matter of interpretation (Palmer 1969; Bruns 1992; Grondin 2008; Malpas and Gander 2014; Keane and Lawn 2016). For example, hermeneutics shows that, contrary to common assumptions, the meaning of a text cannot simply be discovered. Rather, the interpreter, a person situated in time and space, is actively involved in the creation of textual meaning using inscriptions as a beginning only. Further, hermeneutics demonstrates that neither an objective nor a subjective interpretation is possible. The interpreter, instead of adopting an Archimedean outlook or bringing to bear unfettered freedom, necessarily approaches the object of interpretation from a given perspective, which is inevitably informed by the historical tradition, including the language, to which she belongs. It follows that different interpreters might offer different interpretations of the 'same' text. Hermeneutics thus emphasizes that words do not have a fixed meaning. Accordingly, one never reaches a point where one is in a position to argue that everything that could possibly be said about a given text has been said. There is always more meaning to be generated; indeed, there will potentially be as many meanings being produced as there will be interpreters. Consequently, no method or rule of interpretation can lead the interpreter to the right or true meaning of a text.

It took several centuries for hermeneutics to clarify the modalities under which interpretation takes place. Against the background of Greek mythology where Hermes, the wing-footed messenger, acted as a mediator between immortal gods and human beings, hermeneutics was first introduced into philosophy through Aristotle's treatise *Peri Hermeneias*, commonly referred to by its Latin title,

De interpretatione (c. 350 BCE), which comprehensively examines the relationship between language and logic. However, it was not until the Middle Ages that genuine interpretative strategies were developed with a view to providing a theoretical framework for biblical exegesis. Beginning in the sixteenth century, hermeneutics, drawing on Greek antiquity, defined itself as the 'art' or 'science' of interpretation (Bruns 1992). In 1654, the word '*hermeneutica*' appeared in Johann C. Dannhauer's book *Hermeneutica sacra sive methodus exponendarum sacrarum litterarum*. The Latin neologism is rooted in the Greek noun '*hermeneia*' ('interpretation') and the verb '*hermeneuein*' ('to interpret'), both terms carrying three basic meanings: 'to express', 'to explain' and 'to translate' (Palmer 1969: 12).

Traditional hermeneutics aimed for the development of interpretative methods in order to minimize the arbitrariness and subjectivity in the interpretation of religious texts. In 1567, the Lutheran Matthias Flacius Illyricus offered a genuine hermeneutical theory within Protestantism in his *Clavis scripturæ sacræ*. Due to the inherent limits of Luther's principle '*sacra scriptura sui ipsius interpres*' ('The Holy Scriptures are their own interpreter'), Flacius suggested a *clavis* (key) allowing for the interpretation of ambiguous passages of the Bible based on the assumption that the individual parts draw their comprehensibility from the other parts and from the text as a whole.

> Here for the first time [. . .] essential rules of interpretation [. . .] were connected with a systematic doctrine, and this was done by means of the postulate that a universally valid understanding was to be reached through the orderly and skilful application of such rules.
>
> (Dilthey 1900: 243)

However, in the Renaissance, the Holy Scriptures were no longer regarded as indispensable to an understanding of the world, and it was not judged necessary to limit hermeneutics to the sphere of religious discourse. Specific hermeneutics were developed, for example, in law (Leyh 1992) and literary studies (Szondi 1975), in order to provide a distinctive set of interpretative methods for each type of text. But the era of specialization did not last very long.

The elaboration of a '*Kunstlehre*' or 'doctrine of art' by the German theologian and philosopher Friedrich Schleiermacher (1838), which cultivated understanding according to rigorous standards, constituted a decisive moment in the history of hermeneutics. His general and universal hermeneutics was to be applied without distinction to all fields of knowledge, an idea which was in fact already present in the earlier writings of Johann M. Chladenius (1742) and Georg F. Meier (1757). Schleiermacher, for whom 'hermeneutic rules must be [. . .] a method' (1838: 14), dealt with the problem of interpretation in a systematic manner. Understanding, he argued, takes the form of a reconstruction: 'every act of understanding is the inversion of a speech-act, during which the thought which was the basis of the speech must become conscious' (ibid.: 7). The interpreter has to 'understand the utterance at first just as well and then better than its author' (ibid.: 23). Schleiermacher emphasized that 'misunderstanding results as a matter of course and that understanding must be desired and sought at every point' (ibid.: 22, emphasis omitted). Aware of the central role of language in the interpretative process, he elaborated two hermeneutic methods: 'grammatical interpretation', which assumes knowledge of the grammatical and syntaxical specificities of the language used by the author, on the one hand, and 'psychological interpretation', which requires familiarity with the author's thinking, character and life, on the other. Both methods of interpretation are grounded in the 'hermeneutic circle' – that is, in the dynamic between the parts and the whole (ibid.: 30–157). Problematically, though, once the interpreter has exhausted the strategies of grammatical interpretation, she can only divine the experiences and thoughts that inform the text under consideration. Thus, it seems as if Schleiermacher 'may have slightly "misunderstood" himself when he placed his own hermeneutic project under the programme of a *Kunstlehre*, of a technique that would want to assign strict rules to understanding' (Grondin 1993: 94, emphasis original).

In the nineteenth century, some intellectuals, drawing on Schleiermacher's writings, conceived of hermeneutics principally as a methodological reflection on the scientific status of the human sciences. Most notably, the German philosopher Wilhelm Dilthey declared hermeneutics to be a methodology for the human sciences (1910). In fact, as Jean Grondin notes, 'the profound intuition of Dilthey, entailing important consequences, is that understanding and interpretation are not only "methods" specific to the human sciences but translate a search for meaning and for expression even more original than life itself' (2008: 26). Following Dilthey, Italian lawyer and legal historian Emilio Betti's massive 1955 *Teoria generale della interpretazione* (*General Theory of Interpretation*) held that the formulation of a general theory of interpretation was perfectly justified since all interpretative activities, such as historical research, philology, translation or the application of law, feature a common epistemological structure. Betti also aimed to make a strong case for objective interpretation. In his view, an interpreter cannot have access to another person's mind but must operate on the basis of the objective forms (say, language) through which the human mind expresses itself (Grondin 1991: 126).

Having been envisaged as an art of textual interpretation of texts and, later, as a methodology for the human sciences, hermeneutics progressively transformed itself into a philosophical approach to interpretation. Contrary to traditional hermeneutics, philosophical hermeneutics postulates that understanding does not obey rules and is not limited to texts but constitutes an essential feature of our historical and finite existence. In the early 1920s, in a lecture devoted to the hermeneutics of facticity, Martin Heidegger thus offered an existential approach to hermeneutics:

> Our theme is Dasein in its being-there for a while at the particular time. And our task: to bring this into view, have a look at it, and understand it in such

> a manner that in it itself basic characteristics of its being are able to be brought into relief.
>
> (1923: 37)

In other words, it is the role of hermeneutics to favour an explanatory interpretation of the 'human being'. Only a few years later, Heidegger emphasized in his *Being and Time* that the task of hermeneutics is to 'uncove[r] the meaning of Being and the basic structures of Dasein in general' (1927: 62). Heidegger's hermeneutics challenges traditional interpretation theory by showing how understanding is not an activity of consciousness but a condition of human existence or, in the philosopher's own terms, of 'Being-in-the-world' ('*In-der-Welt-sein*'). As Heidegger writes, '[t]he kind of Being which Dasein has, as potentiality-for-Being, lies existentially in understanding' (ibid.: 183). Understanding therefore amounts less to a theoretical and calculated exercise than a practical and unreflected ability. Although Heidegger allowed for a fundamental reconsideration of the interpretative process, he was not prepared to create modern hermeneutics. As he readily admitted in a letter dated 5 January 1973, '"philosophical hermeneutics" is Gadamer's business' (Pöggeler 1983: 395).

In 1960, at the age of 60, German philosopher Hans-Georg Gadamer, one of Heidegger's closest and most famous disciples, released his long-awaited book, *Truth and Method* (1986), which is commonly regarded as the cornerstone of modern philosophical hermeneutics (Palmer 1969; Warnke 1987; Grondin 1991; Davey 2006). Gadamer, rather than develop a method of interpretation, seeks to shed light on the process of understanding. 'My real concern', he writes, 'was and is philosophic: not what we do or what we ought to do, but what happens to us over and above our wanting and doing' (1986: xxv–xxvi). Gadamer's philosophical hermeneutics, which emphasizes the central role of tradition and language, demonstrates that interpretation is not something that individuals can rigorously and systematically master through recourse to rules of interpretation. Gadamer's work, which has been translated into many languages, has influenced a wide range of disciplines, not only literary theory, religious studies, translation studies and gender studies, but also law (Krajewski 2004; Malpas and Zabala 2010; Warnke 2016). Surprisingly, though, many lawyers still ignore the central features of philosophical hermeneutics and their relevance for the interpretation of law. In fact, even though Gadamer expressly devotes to law a number of pages within his book (1986: 321–36), his name is hardly ever mentioned in law school.

To the question 'What has hermeneutics to do with the law?', there is a ready answer: 'Everything' (Zimmermann 2015: 98). For lawyers, the postulates of contemporary hermeneutics are of the utmost importance. Legal texts, such as private contracts, notarial deeds, judicial decisions, statutes, constitutional provisions or international agreements, are never self-explanatory. Rather, in every instance they need to be *interpreted* and *applied* to a given situation. But what are the possibilities and limits of legal interpretation? Are lawyers neutral interpreters of legal texts? Can they ever become unprejudiced, say, through resort to a method? Are there words that can constrain the most activist of judges? Must even the adherent to the strongest form of judicial restraint accept that words carry inherent interpretative latitude? Does legal interpretation involve more than the simple application of the law to the facts? To what extent do economic, socio-political or religious factors influence the interpretation of law and how legitimately so? Ought the age and gender of the interpreter to play a determining role in the understanding of legal texts? Can rules of interpretation lead the interpreter to the correct meaning of the law? Is there the exact meaning of the law in any event? Further, one may ask whether it is not problematic that the interpretation of international legal texts should vary significantly from one country to another. For example, does one expect Chinese and Japanese judges to adopt the same approach to the legal interpretation of an international treaty? Can we at least assume that English and North American lawyers read legal texts in English in the same way? Is it possible to achieve a uniform interpretation of an international legal instrument across a great number of different countries or member states? As hermeneutics provides lawyers and laypersons alike with crucial insights into the interpretation of law, it offers sophisticated answers to all these questions and to many more also.

This collection of essays explores the matter of reading the law and inquires into the emergence of meaning within the dynamic between reader and text against the background of the reader's worldly finiteness. It wishes to contribute to an improved appreciation of the merits and limits of law's hermeneutics, which, it argues, is emphatically not to be reduced to a simple tool for textual exegesis. In this regard, the various chapters purport to supplement and update the body of work to be found in the available literature on legal hermeneutics, whether ancient (Lieber 1837) or recent (Betti 1955; Leyh 1992; Senn and Fritschi 2009; Omaggio and Carlizzi 2010; Kaspers 2014). More precisely, the contributions to this volume aim to revisit legal hermeneutics by making particular reference to such other disciplines as philosophy, sociology and linguistics.

The book is divided into three sections. The first part provides a matrix for a critical engagement with law's hermeneutics. In Chapter 1, Cristina Lafont offers a detailed analysis of the hermeneutic core of Martin Heidegger's *Being and Time*. Charles Taylor, in Chapter 2, discusses Gadamer's decisive contribution to modern interpretation theory by elucidating the conversational structure of understanding. Chapter 3 by Jean Grondin and Chapter 4 by Simone Glanert apply Gadamer's philosophical hermeneutics to legal interpretation and to the interpretation of foreign law respectively. The second part explores a number of broadly concurrent views. Taking Gadamer's philosophical hermeneutics as a touchstone, Fabien Girard critically assesses Paul Ricœur's contribution to legal hermeneutics in Chapter 5. In Chapter 6, Paul Yowell studies the influence of Gadamer's philosophical ideas on Ronald Dworkin's interpretative theory, with particular reference to Dworkin's influential book, *Law's Empire*. François Ost, in Chapter 7, then investigates the connections between narration and interpretation in legal hermeneutics. The third part of the book introduces variances or discrepancies. In Chapter 8, Julia Tanney offers her reading of the argumentative strategy contained in Sections 201 and 202 of Wittgenstein's *Philosophical Investigations* (1953) – the conclusion of the 'rule-following considerations' – which challenges a key hermeneutic assumption that making sense of a rule implies an interpretation. In Chapter 9, Pierre Legrand explores Jacques Derrida's protracted negotiation with Hans-Georg Gadamer's philosophical hermeneutics and assesses the significance for law of Derrida's qualified appreciation of hermeneutics. In Chapter 10, William Outhwaite discusses Jürgen Habermas's exchange with Gadamer at the end of the 1960s, before focusing more specifically on Habermas's engagement with law in *Between Facts and Norms* (1992) and with European issues in general. There ensues, in Chapter 11, Cosmin Cercel's exploration of the presence of law in the work of Giorgio Agamben, with a view to investigating the limits of legal hermeneutics. In the concluding chapter of the book, Ralf Poscher defends the hermeneutic character of legal construction.

As the range of topics illustrates, this collection of essays aims to generate a rewarding exchange between scholars from various disciplines in order to foreground the complex modalities under which understanding takes place. Specifically, it purports to afford lawyers the opportunity to engage more extensively and more critically with legal interpretation.

Bibliography

Aristotle (c. 350 BCE) *De interpretatione*, in *Categories and De interpretatione*, trans. J.L. Ackrill, Oxford: Oxford University Press, 1963.

Betti, E. (1955) *Teoria generale della interpretazione*, 2 vols, Milan: A. Giuffrè.

Bruns, G.L. (1992) *Hermeneutics: Ancient and Modern*, New Haven, CT: Yale University Press.

Chladenius, J.M. (1742) *Einleitung zur richtigen Auslegung vernünftiger Reden und Schriften*, Leipzig.

Davey, N. (2006) *Unquiet Understanding: Gadamer's Philosophical Hermeneutics*, Albany, NY: SUNY Press.

Dilthey, W. (1900) 'The Rise of Hermeneutics', trans. F.R. Jameson and R.A. Makkreel, in *Selected Works*, vol. IV, R.A. Makkreel and F. Rodi (eds), Princeton, NJ: Princeton University Press, 1996.

—— (1910) *The Formation of the Historical World in the Human Sciences*, in *Selected Works*, vol. III, R.A. Makkreel and F. Rodi (eds), Princeton, NJ: Princeton University Press, 2002.

Flacius Illyricus, M. (1567) *Clavis scripturæ sacræ*, Basel.

Gadamer, H.-G. (1986) *Truth and Method*, trans. J. Weinsheimer and D.G. Marshall, 2nd rev. Eng. edn, New York: Continuum, 2004.

—— (1993) *Gadamer in Conversation [With Carsten Dutt]*, R.E. Palmer (ed.), trans. R.E. Palmer, New Haven, CT: Yale University Press, 2001.

Grondin, J. (1991) *Introduction to Philosophical Hermeneutics*, trans. J. Weinsheimer, New Haven, CT: Yale University Press, 1994.

—— (1993) *L'Universalité de l'herméneutique*, Paris: Presses Universitaires de France.

—— (2008) *L'Herméneutique*, 2nd edn, Paris: Presses Universitaires de France.
Heidegger, M. (1923) *Ontology – The Hermeneutics of Facticity*, trans. J. van Buren, Bloomington, IN: Indiana University Press, 1999.
—— (1927) *Being and Time*, trans. J. Macquarrie and E. Robinson, Oxford: Blackwell, 1962.
Kaspers, J. (2014) *Philosophie – Hermeneutik – Jurisprudenz: Die Bedeutung der philosophischen Hermeneutik Hans-Georg Gadamers für die Rechtswissenschaften*, Berlin: Duncker & Humblot.
Keane, N. and Lawn, C. (eds.) (2016) *The Blackwell Companion to Hermeneutics*, Oxford: Wiley-Blackwell.
Krajewski, B. (ed.) (2004) *Gadamer's Repercussions*, Berkeley, CA: University of California Press.
Leyh, G. (ed.) (1992) *Legal Hermeneutics: History, Theory, and Practice*, Berkeley, CA: University of California Press.
Lieber, F. (1837) *Legal and Political Hermeneutics*, Boston, MA: Little & Brown.
Malpas, J. and Zabala, S. (eds) (2010) *Consequences of Hermeneutics*, Evanston, IL: Northwestern University Press.
Malpas, J. and Gander, H.H. (eds) (2014) *The Routledge Companion to Hermeneutics*, London: Routledge.
Meier, G.F. (1757) *Versuch einer allgemeinen Auslegekunst*, Halle.
Omaggio, V. and Carlizzi, G. (2010) *Ermeneutica e interpretazione giuridica*, Turin: G. Giappichelli.
Palmer, R.E. (1969) *Hermeneutics: Interpretation Theory in Schleiermacher, Dilthey, Heidegger, Gadamer*, Evanston, IL: Northwestern University Press.
Pöggeler, O. (1983) *Heidegger und die hermeneutische Philosophie*, Freiburg: K. Alber.
Schleiermacher, F.D.E. (1838) *Hermeneutics and Criticism*, A. Bowie (ed.), trans. A. Bowie, Cambridge: Cambridge University Press, 1998.
Senn, M. and Fritschi, B. (eds) (2009) *Rechtswissenschaft und Hermeneutik*, Stuttgart: F. Steiner.
Szondi, P. (1975) *Introduction to Literary Hermeneutics*, trans. M. Woodmansee, Cambridge: Cambridge University Press, 1995.
Warnke, G. (1987) *Gadamer: Hermeneutics, Tradition, and Reason*, Stanford, CA: Stanford University Press.
—— (ed.) (2016) *Inheriting Gadamer*, Edinburgh: Edinburgh University Press.
Zimmermann, J. (2015) *Hermeneutics*, Oxford: Oxford University Press.

Part I

A matrix

Chapter 1

Heidegger's hermeneutics[1]

Cristina Lafont

Among the many philosophical innovations that Martin Heidegger introduces in *Being and Time* (1927b), one of the most significant and rich in consequences is his claim that philosophy is hermeneutics. This claim does not refer merely to the kind of topics with which philosophy should be concerned (interpretation, the methodology of the human sciences, etc.), but aims at a radical paradigm shift within philosophy itself. Indeed, one of the main achievements of *Being and Time* is its articulation of the basic features of the philosophical paradigm of hermeneutics, which had a decisive influence on twentieth-century Continental philosophy (Gadamer 1967, 1983, 1986; Apel 1973; Habermas 1999; Ricœur 1969; etc.).

To bring about this paradigm shift, Heidegger generalizes hermeneutics from a traditional method for interpreting authoritative texts (mainly sacred or legal texts) to a way of understanding human beings themselves. As a consequence, the hermeneutic paradigm offers a radically new understanding of what is distinctive about human beings: to be human is not primarily to be a rational animal, but first and foremost to be a self-interpreting animal. It is precisely because human beings are nothing but interpretation all the way down that the activity of *interpreting a meaningful text* offers the most appropriate model for understanding any human experience whatsoever. This change of perspective amounts to a major break with traditional philosophy. For the latter has been mainly guided by a diametrically opposed attempt, namely to model all human experience on the basis of our *perception of physical objects*. It is for this reason that in *Being and Time* Heidegger articulates the new hermeneutic account of human experience through a detailed criticism of the traditional philosophical model, the subject–object model.

Although the shortcomings that Heidegger finds in the latter model are virtually innumerable, all of his criticisms are part of a single strategy, namely to show the overall superiority of the hermeneutic paradigm (and thus the need for a 'destruction' and new appropriation of the history of philosophy). In order to succeed with this ambitious goal he has to prove that the hermeneutic paradigm can give an appropriate account of all human experience, including the experience that underlies the subject–object model (namely perception and empirical knowledge of objects), whereas the reverse is not the case.[2]

The argumentative strategy that Heidegger develops in *Being and Time* in order to achieve this goal is based on two central objections to the subject–object model. First of all, Heidegger argues that by trying to model human experience on the basis of categories taken from a domain of objects radically different from human beings (i.e. physical objects), traditional philosophy provides an entirely distorted account of human identity. To show this, Heidegger articulates an alternative, hermeneutic model that makes it possible to understand human beings as essentially self-interpreting creatures. Once we understand that human beings are self-interpreting and thus self-misinterpreting beings, Heidegger's ambitious goal can be achieved. For he can then show both why philosophy can only be hermeneutics and how the errors of traditional philosophy are a direct consequence of the kind of beings that humans are. Second, Heidegger argues that by focusing on perception as the private experience of an isolated subject, the subject–object model incorporates a methodological individualism (even solipsism) that entirely distorts human experience with the world (giving rise to nothing but philosophical pseudo-problems such as the need to prove the existence of the external world). To defend this claim, Heidegger offers an alternative, hermeneutic account of our experience that makes it possible to understand human beings as inhabiting a symbolically structured world, in which everything they encounter is already understood as something or other. Once we understand the world in which human beings live as a holistically structured web of significance, Heidegger's overall goal can be achieved in this context as well. For he can show both that the model of understanding a meaningful text is indeed more appropriate for understanding our human experience in the world than the subject–object model, and that the account of perception, knowledge, truth, etc. that the hermeneutic model provides is superior to the traditional one.

In what follows, I will analyze the hermeneutic core of *Being and Time* in order to spell out the main features of this new philosophical paradigm. But before I do so, I will first situate the project of *Being and Time* in the philosophical context from which it emerged and which makes the sense and scope of Heidegger's hermeneutic transformation of philosophy understandable.

Historical background: philosophical continuities and discontinuities behind the project of *Being and Time*

From the point of view of the historical background out of which *Being and Time* grew, the most significant event was the development of the human sciences during the nineteenth century and the difficulties that this development brought to light. The question of how to obtain scientific knowledge of human realities such as history, culture and religion prompted philosophers of all kinds of persuasions to try to provide a philosophical foundation not only for the conditions of possibility of *explaining natural* processes, but also for the conditions of possibility of *understanding cultural* ones. Taking Immanuel Kant's critique of pure reason as a paradigmatic example of the first task, neo-Kantians of the Southwest School such as Wilhelm Windelband and Heinrich Rickert (who was Heidegger's teacher) were trying to extend transcendental philosophy in the direction of a *philosophy of value* that would be able to fulfil the second task. Within the Marburg School of neo-Kantianism, Ernst Cassirer's project of articulating a *critique of culture* was similarly motivated. Equally so, Edmund Husserl's project of developing a transcendental phenomenology that would provide a foundation for all regional ontologies, not just those that underlie the natural sciences, was an attempt to fulfil the same task. Within the tradition of the historical school, Wilhelm Dilthey's project of complementing Kant's work with a *critique of historical reason* had a similar inspiration.

However, all these attempts to complement Kant's work were confronted with an unprecedented difficulty, namely the need to reconcile the transcendental and the historical without sacrificing one to the other. From this point of view, as the young Heidegger argues, the main difficulty confronting the human sciences is not so much that they lack a scientific foundation, but rather that precisely in trying to apply scientific methodology they lose the possibility of accessing the very reality they aim to understand. Grasping the meaningfulness of human life's experience in its concrete facility requires a way to gain access to that reality as it is given to us prior to any scientific objectivities. Consequently, the problem of reconciling the transcendental and the historical can only be solved by breaking with the 'primacy of the theoretical' and thus with the key methodological assumption built on the basis of this priority, the subject–object model.

Keeping this background of philosophical issues in mind, we can now turn to the very dense Introduction of *Being and Time.* There, Heidegger accomplishes two important tasks. On the one hand, he makes explicit some of the methodological assumptions of his overall project and defends their plausibility by situating *Being and Time* in the context of other transcendental projects (the main references here are to Kant and Husserl). On the other hand, he also introduces the new conceptual framework that will make a hermeneutic transformation of transcendental philosophy possible.

Heidegger's way of situating his own philosophical project in the Introduction to *Being and Time* makes very clear that he shares the conception of philosophy common to the different versions of transcendental philosophy available at the time (phenomenology, neo-Kantianism, etc.). Philosophy is supposed to provide the foundation for the empirical sciences through an *a priori* investigation of their basic concepts, which makes accessible to the sciences their own objects of study in their essential constitution. Heidegger also agrees with his contemporaries on the need for extending Kant's transcendental project to provide a genealogy of the different possible ways of being (beyond the one of 'Nature'), but he thinks that this task cannot be properly accomplished without a prior clarification of the meaning of being in general. To the extent that this clarification would provide the *a priori* conditions not only for the possibility of the sciences but also for the possibility of the ontologies themselves, which are prior to them and provide their foundations, it constitutes philosophy's central task: articulating *a fundamental ontology*. Heidegger's short exposition of his specific project for accomplishing this task reveals a further commonality with transcendental philosophy. Heidegger accepts the key methodological assumption necessary for a transcendental strategy, namely the 'priority of Dasein over all other entities' (1927b: 13). As he argues, given that philosophy's central task is a clarification of the meaning of being and that Dasein is the only entity that has an understanding of being, Dasein provides 'the ontico-ontological condition for the possibility of any ontologies' (ibid.: 13). Thus fundamental ontology must take the form of an existential analytic of Dasein.

But just at this point the commonalities between Heidegger's project and those of traditional transcendental philosophy rapidly come to an end. For, as Heidegger explains in the following section of the Introduction, the existential analytic of Dasein focuses on the hermeneutics of a factical Dasein in its average everydayness. Thus, the project of providing a fundamental ontology through an existential analytic of Dasein is the attempt to follow a transcendental strategy without a transcendental subject. To be plausible at all, Heidegger's hermeneutic transformation of philosophy requires cashing out the empirical/transcendental distinction in different terms. This explains the second task that is accomplished in the Introduction, namely to set in motion a new framework of concepts that will make such transformation possible.

The new conceptual framework: the *ontological difference*

Although the term 'ontological difference' is not coined in *Being and Time*, the distinction between 'being' and 'entities' is introduced at the very beginning of the book. In §2 'being' is defined as 'that which determines entities as entities, that on the basis of which entities are already understood' (ibid.: 6) and 'entities' are defined as 'everything we talk about, everything we have in view, everything towards which we comport ourselves in any way', including 'what we are' and 'how we are' (ibid.: 6–7).

Taking the ontological difference as the key methodological distinction, Heidegger interprets what is distinctive about human beings (i.e. the priority of Dasein over all other entities) in an essentially different way than does traditional philosophy. In contradistinction to Kant, Heidegger's analysis rests not on *the fact of reason* but on a different fact, namely *the fact that human beings have a 'vague average understanding of being'* (ibid.: 5). This understanding is what allows Dasein to grasp the distinction between being and beings and thus to have an understanding of itself, the world, and everything that can show up within the world. Here, however, it is important to notice that Heidegger's full interpretation of the ontological difference involves much more than just ascribing to

Dasein the intuitive capacity for distinguishing between being and beings. It entails at least the following features:

1 Having an *implicit grasp* of the distinction between entities and their being, that is, between entities and how they are understood (ibid.: 6–7).
2 Understanding both as *irreducibly* distinct: 'the being of entities "is" not itself an entity' (ibid.: 6).
3 Understanding the *transcendental priority* of being over any entity: 'being can never be explained by entities but is already that which is "transcendental" for every entity' (ibid.: 208). Thus 'entities are in no way accessible without a prior understanding of their being' (1927–28: 38).
4 Understanding the transcendental priority in *hermeneutic* terms: 'there is being only in an understanding of being' (1927b: 212). Therefore, 'what determines entities as entities' is 'that on the basis of which entities are [. . .] understood' (ibid.: 6).
5 To recognize the *detranscendentalized* status of the understanding of being (as contingent, historically variable, plural, etc.): 'what determines entities as entities' is merely 'that on the basis of which entities are *always already* understood' (ibid., emphasis added). This follows from the fact that 'the meaning of being can never be contrasted with entities' (ibid.: 152).

The first feature of Heidegger's interpretation of the ontological difference seems clearly uncontroversial. At least in its most deflationary interpretation, it seems plausible to claim that we can intuitively distinguish between the entities we talk about and the way we understand them. However, the other features are hardly as uncontroversial. This becomes clear if we take into account the philosophical theses that lie behind each of them and, especially the philosophical positions that they are meant to rule out. Acceptance of the ontological difference entails, according to Heidegger, a strong anti-reductionist commitment: the meaningful and the factual are mutually irreducible. In virtue of this dualism, hermeneutic philosophy shares with transcendental philosophy its *anti-naturalism*. It also entails a decidedly anti-empiricist commitment: hermeneutic philosophy shares with transcendental philosophy its *opposition to any kind of metaphysical realism*. However, this opposition is based not on a transcendental but on a *hermeneutic idealism*, that is, on an idealism justified exclusively by hermeneutic reasons. Here lies Heidegger's hermeneutic transformation of transcendental philosophy.[3] In a nutshell, its main features can be explained as follows. On the basis of the ontological difference, the transcendental priority of being over entities is traced back to Dasein's fore-structure of understanding. As a consequence, Dasein's projections of the being of entities inherit the transcendental status that traditional philosophy ascribed to synthetic *a priori* knowledge: they are prior to all experience with entities (1), but determine all experience with those entities (2). However, the ascription of this status is not due to the alleged universal validity of such knowledge, but it is justified on merely hermeneutic grounds. As we shall see,

Heidegger defends assumption (1) on the basis of a hermeneutic constraint on communication, namely the assumption that *meaning determines reference*, and assumption (2) on the basis of a hermeneutic fact about interpretation, namely the *holistic* structure of understanding. As a result of this transformation, the opposition to metaphysical realism characteristic of hermeneutics involves, in contradistinction to traditional transcendental philosophy, a commitment to *conceptual pluralism* and a strong *incommensurability* thesis.

An important question in evaluating the strength and plausibility of the paradigm of philosophical hermeneutics inaugurated by Heidegger is certainly whether and to what extent Heidegger's interpretation of the ontological difference is a necessary element of hermeneutics or just a remnant of the transcendental paradigm that hermeneutic philosophy was meant to overcome. But before we focus on this problem, we need to analyze first the central steps of Heidegger's development of the paradigm of hermeneutics in *Being and Time*.

The hermeneutic notion of world

As already mentioned, the central feature of Heidegger's hermeneutic turn lies in his replacement of the subject–object model, that is, the model of an *observing* subject posed over against the world as the totality of entities, by the hermeneutic model of an *understanding* Dasein which finds itself always already *in* a symbolically structured *world*. The key for this transformation lies in the introduction of a new notion of world. After the hermeneutic turn, the world is no longer the totality of entities, but a totality of significance, a web of meanings that structures Dasein's understanding of itself and of everything that can show up within the world:

> [T]he world itself is not an entity within-the-world; and yet it is so determinative for such entities that only in so far as 'there is' a world can they be encountered and show themselves in their being as entities which have been discovered.
>
> (1927b: 72)

The importance of the new notion of world for understanding the paradigm shift from traditional to hermeneutic philosophy cannot be overestimated. For, as we will see, it is on its basis that the hermeneutic model that replaces the traditional subject–object model is built. But although Heidegger is very careful in his introduction of the new notion of world, many commentators of *Being and Time* seem to miss the crucial difference between the traditional and the hermeneutic notions. A common mistake that can be found in many commentaries is the interpretation of Heidegger's notion of world as referring to the totality of equipment with which Dasein is involved in its everyday dealings (i.e. what Heidegger calls 'the environment'). Under this interpretation, the difference between Heidegger's notion of world and the traditional one would be that whereas the latter is supposed to be the totality of occurrent entities as objectified by an observing subject, the former is the totality of available entities which are put to use by an acting Dasein. Thus, the new notion of world would serve the Heideggerian purpose of reversing the ontological priority traditionally ascribed to the occurrent vis-à-vis the available. However, this interpretation is untenable from an exegetical point of view, not just in view of Heidegger's extremely careful definition of his notion of world in §14, but at a much more crucial level, namely in view of the ontological difference. As Heidegger made clear in the quote mentioned before, 'the world is not itself an entity within-the-world'. Consequently, 'if we join [such entities] together, we still do not get anything like the "world" as their sum' (ibid.: 72). The world is a 'referential context of significance (*Verweisungszusammenhang der Bedeutsamkeit*)' (ibid.: 123), a system of meaningful relations toward which Dasein comports itself *understandingly* (ibid.: 86) and not a totality of entities of any kind, be it occurrent or available ones.

But, of course, exegetical considerations do not settle the crucial issue here, namely whether Heidegger's use of the term 'world' to refer to a totality of meaningful relations is plausible at all. At least, from the point of view of traditional philosophy, it is clearly unprecedented. Traditionally, the notion of world had been understood mainly in one of two ways: either as the totality of entities to which human beings also belong (empiricism) or as the totality of entities constituted by a transcendental, extraworldly subject (transcendental philosophy). However, as we pointed out at the beginning, with the development of the human sciences, philosophy saw itself confronted with objects of study such as history, culture and religion that did not fit well in that mold. Keeping this historical development in mind is very helpful for understanding the need for as well as the plausibility of Heidegger's notion of world. If one is not concerned with natural entities and our activities of coping with them, but with meaningful entities and our activities of making sense of them, it does seem plausible to think of entities such as cultures as totalities of significance (which enable human beings to understand themselves and everything around them as something or other). And it is in virtue of this quasi-transcendental function that in ordinary language we can refer to cultures as 'worlds' in expressions such as 'the world of the Renaissance man' or 'the medieval world'. Moreover, in light of this use of the term, the features that Heidegger ascribes to his notion of world seem plausible: cultures are the kind of things that humans can be said to be 'in' (or grow up 'into') in a non-spatial sense of the term; they are also the kind of things that can be understood or interpreted rather than perceived or manipulated, etc.

Assuming that Heidegger's notion of world is *prima facie* plausible, we now need to analyze the main features of the philosophical model that this notion makes possible to articulate and which should replace the subject–object model, namely Dasein's fundamental structure of *being-in-the-world*.

In §4, Heidegger distinguishes four possible senses of the term 'world': (a) 'World' in an ontical (extensional) sense means the totality of all occurrent entities – that is, the objective world; (b) 'world' in an ontological (intensional) sense means the being of a particular realm of entities – that is, the kind of being that all these entities have in common; Heidegger's examples are expressions such as 'the world of the mathematician'; (c) 'world' in an ontical but existentiell sense means specific social or cultural worlds, wherein a factical Dasein as such can be said to live – for example, 'the public world' or 'the world of the Renaissance man'; and (d) 'world' in the ontologico-existential technical sense means the *a priori* character of wordliness in general.

Heidegger indicates that in *Being and Time* he uses the term 'world' in the third signification. In order to show the specific features of his own concept of world, he contrasts it with the traditional notion of world as the totality of occurrent entities. First of all, he makes clear that, whereas the sense of being 'in' the world that corresponds to the traditional notion is the sense of *physical inclusion*, being 'in' a cultural world has instead the sense of *involvement*. *Being-in* is not a physical property but rather an *existentiale* of Dasein: it is the ability to understand and be involved with everything that shows up within the world, and thus to have a symbolic and not merely a causal relationship to it. Thus, in virtue of 'being-in-the-world' Dasein has the ability to take the internal perspective of a participant in a culture rather than the external perspective of an observer of the physical world. In fact, as mentioned before, one of the crucial aims of Heidegger's analysis of the structure of *Being-in-the-world* is precisely to show that the latter perspective, the subject–object model, is founded in the former.

But there is another aspect of Heidegger's concept of world that entails a deeper break with the traditional paradigm of mentalism. As Heidegger makes clear in the following chapter, the totality of significations that make up the world in which a factical Dasein grows up into is essentially *intersubjectively shared*: 'the world is always the one that I share with Others. The world of Dasein is a *with-world*' (1927b: 118, emphasis original). This is a phenomenological fact, however, that can hardly be accounted for within the constraints of the methodological individualism characteristic of the subject–object model. For the public world can be identified neither with the totality of objects nor with the private sphere of the mental acts of an isolated subject.[4] The specific relationship that Dasein has with others in virtue of sharing a public world cannot be modeled on the relationship of a subject either to itself or to objects different from itself. With the introduction of the hermeneutic concept of world, the resulting model reverses the order of explanation characteristic of the subject–object model. It is only to the extent that Dasein first learns to adopt the intersubjective perspective of a participant in its cultural world that it may later learn to adopt the subjective perspective of an (authentic) individual self. Heidegger explains: 'By "Others" we do not mean everyone else but me – those over against whom the "I" stands out. They are rather those from whom, for the most part, one does not distinguish oneself – those among whom one is too' (ibid.: 118). Consequently, 'the self of everyday Dasein is the one-self, which we distinguish from the *authentic self*. [. . .] As one-self, the particular Dasein has been dispersed into the "one", and *must first find Itself* (ibid.: 129, emphasis added).

Obviously, part of what it takes to grow up into a culture, that is, to become familiar with the whole of significations available within it, is first of all to learn the normative patterns of interpretation and conduct that such a culture prescribes. As Heidegger explains:

> We take pleasure and enjoy ourselves as one takes pleasure; we read, see, and judge about literature and art as one sees and judges; likewise we shrink back from the 'great mass' as one shrinks back. [. . .] The one, which is nothing definite, and which all are, though not as the sum, prescribes the kind of being of everyday-ness.
>
> (Ibid.: 126–7)

If cultural traditions thus precede individual subjects, who grow up into them, Heidegger seems right in rejecting the strategy of trying to explain the cultural world as a product of an (individual) subject, even a 'transcendental' one. Within the hermeneutic model, the world is not constituted by the subject but by 'the one'. Heidegger explains:

> If Dasein is familiar with itself as the one-self, this means at the same time that the 'one' itself prescribes that way of interpreting the world and being-in-the-world which lies closest. Dasein is for the sake of the 'one' in an everyday manner and *the 'one' itself articulates the referential context of significance.*
>
> (Ibid.: 129, emphasis added)

However, at this point an important question arises. For in the light of Heidegger's interpretation of the ontological difference, the world is a phenomenon that is hard to situate, given the rigid dichotomy established for methodological reasons between Dasein and all other entities. On the one hand, *Being-in-the-world* is a fundamental structure of Dasein, so 'the one' as an element of this structure is an *existentiale*, an ability of Dasein – the ability to take the community's perspective of the 'generalized other', in G.H. Mead's terms (1934: 154). But, on the other hand, the articulation of the world precedes each and every individual Dasein (Heidegger 1927b: 364). If it did not, if it were just the product of the meaning-conferring acts of an individual subject, the subject–object model would be re-established. But if 'the one' is prior to any individual Dasein and, obviously, is neither an occurrent entity nor a 'transcendental subject' (ibid.: 128–9), how is it constituted? Where is it situated? In his lectures of the summer semester of 1924, Heidegger gives a direct answer to this question:

> The *one* is the *genuine how of everydayness, of the average, concrete being-with-one-another.* Out of this 'one' grows the way in which man sees the world

> primarily and usually, how the world matters to man, how he addresses the world. The 'one' is the original how of the being of humans in everydayness and *the primordial bearer of the one is language*. The 'one' sustains itself, has its primordial dominance in language.
>
> (1924b: 64, emphasis original)

Along the same lines, Heidegger remarks in *Being and Time* that 'the "one" is constituted by the way things have been publicly interpreted, which expresses itself in idle talk' (1927b: 252).

This is another central feature of the hermeneutic notion of world: the world is always intersubjectively shared because it is *linguistically articulated*. It is by virtue of sharing a natural language that Dasein can share the *same* world with others. In this context, it is important to keep in mind one of the crucial differences between the traditional and the hermeneutic notions of world. Whereas the former is supposed to refer to a *single* objective world (to the extent that everything is supposed to be under the same causal laws), the latter admits of a plurality of worlds. Cultural worlds as totalities of significance are *plural*. This is why on the basis of this sense of the term Heidegger can plausibly refer to a factical Dasein '*in seiner jeweiligen Welt*', in its current world (ibid.: 145). This intrinsic plurality of worlds opens up an issue that had no equivalent in the framework of the traditional notion of world. In order to use the hermeneutic notion of world in a plausible way, one must first explain in virtue of what a particular Dasein can be said to share the *same* world with others. Heidegger addresses this issue explicitly in *The Concept of Time*:

> As this being-in-the-world, Dasein is, together with this, *being-with-one-another*, being with Others: having the same world there with Others [. . .]. Being with one another in the world [. . .] has a distinctive ontological determination. The fundamental way of the existence of world, namely, having world there with one another, is *speaking*. Fully considered, speaking is: oneself speaking out in speaking *with* another *about* something. [. . .] In speaking with one another [. . .] there lies the specific self-interpretation of the present, which maintains itself in this dialogue.
>
> (1924a: 113, emphasis original; see also 1927b: 167–8)

It is the phenomenon of a linguistically articulated world that definitively breaks with the functionality of the subject–object model. For it shows why the attempt to model the common perspective of subjects who share a public world on the isolated perspective of a subject perceiving a physical object must fail: from the private perceptions of isolated subjects there is no way to explain how these subjects could achieve a shared perspective *about the same objects*. The order of explanation is actually the reverse: the subject–object perspective is only possible as a result of success in achieving a shared subject–subject perspective.

As Heidegger explains in *Being and Time*, it is in virtue of sharing a language that speakers and hearers can talk about the same things even if those things are not accessible to all of them to the same extent, either because not all of them are in a position to simultaneously perceive them or because not all of them have the same level of understanding or expertise about those things:

> In the language which is spoken when one expresses oneself, there lies an average intelligibility; and in accordance with this intelligibility the discourse which is communicated can be understood to a considerable extent, even if the hearer does not bring himself into such a kind of being towards what the discourse is about as to have a primordial understanding of it. [. . .] We have *the same thing* in view, because it is in the *same* averageness that we have a common understanding of what is said.
>
> (1927b: 168, emphasis original)[5]

Now, if this claim is right, if subjects come to share a common world of objects only to the extent that they previously share a common understanding of those objects, the explanatory priority of perception that underlies the subject–object model can be shown to be just wrong. Heidegger explains:

> This way in which things have been interpreted in idle talk has already established itself in Dasein. [. . .] This everyday way in which things have been interpreted is one into which Dasein has grown in the first instance, with never a possibility of extrication. In it, from out of it, and against it, all genuine understanding, interpreting and communicating, all re-discovering and appropriating anew, are performed. *In no case is a Dasein, untouched and unseduced by this way in which things have been interpreted, set before the open country of a 'world-in-itself' so that it just beholds what it encounters.* The dominance of the public way in which things have been interpreted has already been decisive even for the possibilities of having a mood. [. . .] The 'one' prescribes one's affectivity, and determines what and how one 'sees'.
>
> (Ibid.: 169–70, emphasis added)

The priority of understanding over perception

It is in view of the linguistically articulated intelligibility that *Dasein* shares with others by sharing a natural language that Heidegger can justify the crucial hermeneutic claim of *Being and Time*, namely the *priority of understanding over perception*. As he expresses it, 'any mere prepredicative seeing [. . .] is, in itself, something which already understands and interprets' (ibid.: 149). If this claim is right, if every seeing something is already a seeing-as, the possibility of a neutral perception of merely occurrent objects that the subject–object model assumes can be unmasked as just a myth – the 'Myth of the Given', in Wilfrid Sellars's words

(1956). The goal of Heidegger's criticism of traditional philosophy is achieved: the mentalist paradigm collapses. Heidegger explains:

> By showing how all sight is grounded primarily in understanding [. . .] we have deprived pure intuition of its priority, which corresponds noetically to the priority of the occurrent in traditional ontology. 'Intuition' and 'thinking' are both derivatives of understanding, and already rather remote one.
>
> (1927b: 147)

Heidegger does seem right in claiming that establishing the priority of understanding over perception is all that is needed to motivate the radical shift from the traditional paradigm of mentalism to the hermeneutic paradigm. However, this cannot be achieved merely by pointing to the fact that subjects have a language at their disposal. This would not be news for traditional philosophy. As long as language is understood in the traditional sense, namely as a tool for expressing prelinguistic thoughts about objects that exist independently of language, it is not at all clear why it would be wrong to assume that subjects are set before the open country of a 'world-in-itself' so that they just behold what they encounter. Under the traditional conception of language as a bunch of names used to designate objects existing independently of language, subjects were supposed to do precisely that: to merely behold objects in themselves and use an arbitrary sign to name them. To be successful with his overall strategy, Heidegger first has to break with the traditional conception of language as a tool.

The way in which Heidegger tries to do that in his explicit discussion of language in §§33 to 35 can already be hinted at in the context of his crucial argument against the explanatory priority of perception, which takes place in §32. There, Heidegger questions the possibility of a neutral perception of 'objects in themselves' precisely by questioning the possibility of a neutral designation of such objects. His argument runs as follows:

> The circumspective question as to what this particular available thing may be, receives the circumspectively interpretative answer that it is for such and such a purpose. If we tell what it is for, we are not simply designating something; but that which is designated is understood *as* that *as* which we are to take the thing in question. [. . .] The 'as' makes up the structure of the explicitness of something that is understood. It constitutes the interpretation. In dealing with what is environmentally available by interpreting it circumspectively, we 'see' it as a table, a door, a carriage or a bridge. [. . .] Any mere pre-predicative seeing of the available is, in itself, something which already understands and interprets.
>
> (Ibid.: 149)

Here Heidegger questions the traditional view of designation as a neutral pointing at an object, but he does not offer a specific argument to support his own view of designation. There is, however, an argument to which Heidegger alludes repeatedly, although he never discusses it in detail (for a clear example of this line of argument, see 1931–32: 1–3). Perhaps the best way to express it would be with the help of W.V.O. Quine's maxim 'no entity without identity' (1969: 23). The idea behind it could be made explicit in the following way: communication requires speakers to identify which entities they want to talk about so that they can be distinguished from others. And this cannot be done unless the terms used to designate those entities provide an understanding of what distinguishes them from others – that is, unless they provide the resources to identify entities as *what* they are, that is, in their *being*. To the extent that it is meaningless to purport to refer to entities whose conditions of identity one cannot possibly indicate, our understanding of the being of entities must determine in advance which entities we are referring to – that is, *meaning must determine reference*. This constraint on communication explains why with the terms we use to designate entities 'we are not simply designating something; but that which is designated is understood *as* that *as* which we are to take the thing in question' (1927b: 149). And to the extent that the meaning of a designative term provides an understanding of the being of the entities it refers to, it determines at the same time *as what* these entities are accessible to us, it determines our experience with those entities. By designating entities as tables, doors, carriages or bridges, we are at the same time answering the ontological question of what can be in our world (namely tables, doors, carriages and bridges). As Heidegger explains in his *History of the Concept of Time*: 'It is not so much that we see the objects and things but rather that we first talk about them. To put it more precisely: we do not say what we see, but rather the reverse, we see what *one says* about things' (1925: 75). Thus Heidegger's claim that there can be no access to entities without a prior understanding of their being is justified by a hermeneutic constraint on intersubjective communication.

If this view is right, linguistic designation does involve much more than the use of a purely arbitrary sign to designate an object as the traditional conception of language assumes. If linguistic signs such as general names provide the individuating criteria of identity for the objects they refer to, without which we could not *identify* objects as something or other in the first place, then language can no longer be seen as merely a system of arbitrary signs. Its essential contribution lies in its *world-disclosing* function (Heidegger develops the view of language as world-disclosing in greater detail after the *Kehre*; see 1936: 33–48; 1959). Language makes it possible for Dasein to share the *same* world with others by articulating a common understanding of the being of entities that can show up in their world. Of course, this contribution is a function not of the arbitrariness of the signs that make up a specific empirical language and distinguish it from others (say English versus German or Swahili), but of the articulation of intelligibility that such a system of signs provides. In order to mark this distinction in *Being and Time*, Heidegger uses the term 'language' in an ontical (extensional) sense to refer to the different empirical languages that are the object of study in linguistics, and uses the term 'discourse' as an ontological term to refer to the 'articulation of intelligibility' that any language provides.[6]

The fore-structure of understanding

So far, we have focused on the central feature of Heidegger's hermeneutic model, namely the view of human beings as inhabiting a linguistically articulated world in which everything that might show up within the world is already understood as something or other. As already mentioned, this change of perspective makes it possible to claim that the hermeneutic model of understanding a meaningful text is the most appropriate one for giving an account of any human experience whatsoever. Now we need to know what the implications and consequences of adopting that model are.

If Heidegger is right and human experience does not arise primarily through perception (of entities) and its conditions, but through a prior understanding (of the being of entities) and their conditions, the existential analytic of Dasein must provide an analysis of the conditions of possibility of understanding. This is what Heidegger calls the fore-structure of understanding. Here again a crucial goal of the analysis is critical. For nothing would be achieved by arguing that understanding has explanatory priority over perception if understanding could in turn be explained on the basis of the model of a neutral perception, as traditional philosophy has always done. Thus, in the same way that Heidegger had first to show that there can be no neutral perception of something like a 'world-in-itself', he now has to show that there can be no neutral understanding of something like a 'literal meaning', no 'presuppositionless apprehending of something merely presented to us' (1927b: 150). It has to be shown that understanding is *always* interpretation or, as Heidegger puts it, that 'in interpretation, understanding does not become something different. It becomes itself' (ibid.: 148).

At this point in the argument Heidegger takes recourse to the hermeneutic model of textual interpretation in order to show that understanding is necessarily both projective and presuppositional. He does so by appealing to a well-known feature of the holistic activity of textual interpretation: the *circle of understanding*. In order to understand the meaning of a text, we need to understand the meaning of its parts. But we can only understand its parts by anticipating the meaning of the text as a whole. Thus, as Heidegger puts it, 'any interpretation which is to contribute understanding, must *already* have understood what is to be interpreted' (ibid.: 152, emphasis added). Without a *projection* of meaning, no activity of interpretation can get off the ground. But for this very same reason understanding is always *presuppositional*. There is no such thing as a presuppositionless grasping of a literal meaning (ibid.). Consequently, an analysis of the conditions of possibility of understanding must provide an answer to the question of where our anticipations or projections of meaning come from.

To answer this question, Heidegger distinguishes three elements of the fore-structure of understanding: *fore-having*, *fore-sight* and *fore-conception*. These are technical terms that Heidegger had introduced and defined in his lectures of summer semester of 1924 (1924b: 274–77), and which he describes only very briefly in *Being and Time* (1927b: 151). Taking both texts together, the sense of these terms can be explained briefly as follows. 'Fore-having' (*Vorhabe*) refers to the prior intelligibility with which we have understood in advance what we want to interpret, the particular way it is presented to us prior to our explicit interpretation. Heidegger's example in *Being and Time* is the way available entities are understood in terms of a totality of involvements prior to any activity of thematic interpretation. 'Fore-sight' (*Vorsicht*) refers to the specific perspective or point of view that guides the interpretation. Heidegger's examples in the lectures mentioned before are the specific understandings of being (occurrentness, availableness, etc.) that can guide a thematic interpretation. A clear example in *Being and Time* is Heidegger's analysis of three different perspectives from which it is possible to interpret human existence: in the everydayness, Dasein is understood from the perspective of the *available*, in the philosophical tradition Dasein is understood from the perspective of the *occurrent*, whereas in *Being and Time* Dasein is understood from the perspective of *existence* or care. Finally 'fore-conception' (*Vorgriff*) refers to the specific conceptuality, the particular vocabulary that is at the disposal of the interpretation. Here again the best examples in *Being and Time* are Heidegger's analyses of the matrix of concepts that articulate each specific understanding of being (e.g. his analysis of occurrentness as articulated through concepts such as substance, location, time, etc.).

According to this view, interpretation is always relative to a particular context, perspective and vocabulary (fore-having, fore-sight, fore-conception) that together constitute what Heidegger calls the 'hermeneutic situation' out of which interpretation evolves and which we cannot transcend at will. This projective view of interpretation presents a clear challenge to the traditional aspirations of absolute objectivity even within the narrow circle of the activity of interpreting a meaningful text. If interpretation is essentially contextual and perspectival, the hermeneutic ideal of getting the single right interpretation of what a text says, its 'literal meaning', makes no sense whatsoever. However, as decades of philosophical hermeneutics have made abundantly clear, recognizing that we are always interpreting out of a contingent, historical, hermeneutic situation may have constructive consequences in addition to the destructive ones. For it makes it possible for us to discover a different hermeneutic ideal that on reflection may be seen as *superior* to the traditional ideal. Precisely by discovering that interpretation entails a moment of application to our own hermeneutic situation, we finally realize what we wanted to know all along: the point of interpreting a text is to find out not so much what its author *literally said* at the time, but first and foremost what he may have to *say to us* now – that is, in our current situation. From this perspective, Heidegger's projective (and thus applicative) view of interpretation offers the basis for a positive contribution to the intricate issues that surround the activity of textual interpretation, as Hans-Georg Gadamer has convincingly shown in *Truth and Method* (1986).

However, these issues are by no means the target of Heidegger's analysis in *Being and Time*. As already mentioned, Heidegger's underlying strategy is to generalize the model of textual interpretation in order to provide a new account of human identity in terms of 'thrown projection', one that should be able to undermine the entirely distorted account of the self that results from the subject–object model. Following this strategy, Heidegger claims that the hermeneutic circle characteristic of the activity of textual interpretation is just a special case of what is in fact a much broader phenomenon, namely the necessarily circular structure of all human understanding: the 'circle of understanding [. . .] is the expression of the existential *fore-structure* of Dasein itself' (1927b: 153, emphasis original). It is Dasein itself who 'has, ontologically, a circular structure' (ibid.). These claims point to the task that will be accomplished in Division Two of *Being and Time*, namely to show that the circular structure of understanding derives from the temporality of Dasein.

I cannot discuss here all aspects of the genuinely fascinating account of human identity as 'thrown projection' that Heidegger develops on the basis of his projective view of interpretation throughout Division Two of *Being and Time*. Instead, I will focus only on the consequences of his view of interpretation for a specific element of his account of human experience, namely our knowledge of the empirical world. This issue is not only interesting in its own right, but it is crucial to evaluate the strength of the hermeneutic paradigm. For, as already mentioned, Heidegger's success in motivating the shift from traditional to hermeneutic philosophy depends on showing that the hermeneutic model can give a better account of the experience that underlies the subject–object model (namely perception and empirical knowledge of entities).

So far, it already seems clear that Heidegger's projective view of interpretation presents a direct challenge to any aspirations of absolute objectivity. If all human understanding is essentially contextual and perspectival, the ideal of an absolute objective truth is illusory not only with regard to textual interpretation but equally so with regard to our scientific understanding of the empirical world. However, this still leaves a further question open. Similar to what we saw with regard to textual interpretation, it remains to be seen whether by discovering the projective element of all understanding we can still make sense of our scientific activity without appealing to the traditional ideal of absolute objectivity.

Cognition as a mode of interpretation

The most challenging feature of Heidegger's application of his projective view of interpretation to cognition is the transformation of the traditional conception of *a priori* knowledge that follows from it. This transformation lies behind Heidegger's choice of the term '*fore-structure* of understanding' to explicitly mark the *presuppositional* character of all interpretation. As Heidegger announces in §32, the traditional conception of this phenomenon in terms of '*a priori* knowledge' is entirely unsatisfactory for it does not recognize its internal connection with the phenomenon of *projection*. However, he cannot offer his alternative explanation right away for this requires first developing his general conception of Dasein in terms of 'thrown projection'. Thus his explanation must wait until §69 of Division Two.

In this section, Heidegger shows how his projective conception of interpretation applies to the specific case of cognition by analyzing the historical transformation of science from the ancient conception of nature into modern natural science. In his opinion, the key to this transformation lies precisely in a change of 'projection' or, as it is called these days, in a paradigm shift. In an astonishing anticipation of Thomas Kuhn's conception of scientific revolutions (1962), Heidegger explains that this shift does not consist merely in the increasing emphasis on observation or experimentation, but in the projection of an entirely different understanding of the being of entities, a new world-disclosure brought about through the establishment and definition of new basic concepts by modern scientists such as Galileo and Newton. To the extent that these new concepts organize all possible experience in advance, the grounding postulates or axioms of these modern theories through which these concepts are defined are at the same time responsible for the constitution of objects. To this extent, they have the status of synthetic *a priori* knowledge in the traditional sense. However, and here lies the challenge to the traditional conception, this is a feature of any projection whatsoever. For it is just a consequence of a general constraint on meaningful concept use, namely that meaning must determine reference. As we already saw, in order to use concepts meaningfully the realm of objects to which these concepts apply must be determined in advance. And this determination requires establishing the criteria of identity of those objects *in advance* or, as Heidegger puts it, requires a prior projection of their being. Therefore, this is something that any projection of the being of entities does.

This hermeneutic discovery has very challenging consequences for the traditional conception of *a priori* knowledge. Whereas for Kant the special status of *a priori* knowledge was due to the (alleged) fact that no human experience would be possible without said knowledge, according to Heidegger the fact that scientific knowledge is based on an understanding of being as occurrentness (and its corresponding concepts such as motion, force, space and time), far from guaranteeing its absolute validity, as Kant thought, merely shows the particular fore-sight and fore-conception on which such knowledge is based. The historical and contingent nature of the prior projection that guides any understanding motivates Heidegger's transformation of the traditional into the hermeneutic conception of apriority or, as he calls it, the *perfect tense a priori* (i.e. the 'always already') that is anchored in the circle of understanding.

However, the insight into the contextual and relative character of all projections does not lead Heidegger to question their *absolute authority*, as would be expected. To the contrary, in light of his interpretation of the ontological difference, Heidegger accepts Kant's conception of the synthetic *a priori*, but generalizes it to cover any possible factual projection of the being of entities. As a consequence, such projections still have the normative status of synthetic *a priori* knowledge: they are prior to all experience with entities, and cannot be revised on the basis of the experience with those entities. However, this is the case only for those who happen to share such a historically contingent projection. Only the assumption of uniqueness implicit in the traditional ascription of universal validity to *a priori* knowledge is questioned in Heidegger's conception. This leads Heidegger to draw a very different consequence from Kant's transcendental idealism, namely *conceptual pluralism.*

As mentioned at the beginning, Heidegger's hermeneutic philosophy shares with transcendental philosophy its opposition to any kind of metaphysical realism. Throughout *Being and Time* Heidegger argues that it does not make sense to ask how and what entities are in themselves without a prior determination of which specific meaning of 'being in itself' – that is, what understanding of being – we have in mind. 'Real' or 'in itself' are specification-dependent terms. One example of this argument in *Being and Time* is Heidegger's claim that a prior understanding of being as availableness provides the basis on which available entities such as equipment 'can for the first time be discovered as they are "substantially" "in themselves"' (1927b: 88; for a more detailed explanation, see 1927a: 292–3).

In this context it is important to refer briefly to a possible misunderstanding of Heidegger's claim. Some commentators interpret it as part of an argument claiming to establish an absolute priority of the available over the occurrent. According to this interpretation, Heidegger's claim that 'available' is the way entities such as equipment are 'in themselves' would make him a metaphysical realist about the available, so to speak. In light of the ontological difference, though, it seems clear that Heidegger cannot possibly claim to have discovered the way things are 'in themselves' *independently of any prior understanding of being.* On the contrary, as the argumentative context makes clear, the sense of his claim is precisely to show that on the basis of our understanding of being as availableness we are perfectly able to discover available things as they are 'in themselves'. We can distinguish whether a piece of equipment, say a hammer, is a real hammer or not, whether it is a hammer 'in itself' or just a fake hammer, precisely because (and to the extent that) we understand in advance the criteria of appropriateness for that kind of available entity. Given that a hammer is for hammering, a hammer made out of dough, say, is not a 'real' hammer. Thus the point of his claim is to question the meaningfulness of the attempt to use terms such as 'real' or 'in itself' in an absolute sense, that is, independently of establishing in advance a criterion of identity or appropriateness that provides a determinate sense to them. For this very reason, Heidegger's claim that 'available' is the way of being of equipment in itself does not mean to exclude that these entities are also 'occurrent' – or, as he puts it, that we can discover 'something occurrent in what is available' (1927b: 158). Equally so, he never denies that human beings are also 'occurrent' entities. What he does mean to exclude is the *reductionist* view that would claim that such entities are 'really' occurrent entities, physical objects 'in themselves', and only available (or existent) in a 'subjective' sense. The scientific understanding of being (as occurrentness) is as contextual and perspectival as any understanding always is. Within the parameters of its own fore-having, fore-sight and fore-conception it is a perfectly acceptable kind of interpretation. What is unacceptable is its invasive attempt to monopolize the right to define reality in general and human reality in particular. It is in this sense that the projective view of interpretation leads to conceptual pluralism, that is, to the claim that there are many equally acceptable interpretations of reality.

From this perspective, Heidegger's projective view of interpretation definitively challenges one element of the traditional ideal of objectivity, namely the assumption that there is only one true description of the way the world is. However, the anti-reductionism entailed by this claim is not the only challenging consequence of Heidegger's approach. There is another consequence of the projective view of interpretation that challenges the ideal of objectivity even within the limits of the scientific knowledge of the empirical world, however narrowly conceived. It is the strong *incommensurability thesis* that Heidegger's conception of interpretation contains. This thesis challenges the most basic element of the ideal of scientific objectivity, namely the assumption that it is possible to compare and evaluate different scientific theories with regard to a single standard of objective truth.

Heidegger illustrates the impossibility of a comparison among different scientific projections by appealing to the holistic structure of understanding. Drawing on what these days is called confirmation holism (i.e. the underdetermination of theory choice by evidence) in *What Is a Thing?* (1935–36), he tries to make plausible the immunity from revision based on experience that he ascribes to the basic principles and axioms of scientific theories. Heidegger appeals to the example of different explanations for 'one and the same fact' within both the Aristotelian and Galilean paradigms, namely the fact that under normal conditions in the earth's field of gravitation, heavy bodies pass through a determinate distance faster than lighter bodies do. He comments:

> Both Galileo and his opponents saw the same 'fact'. But they made the same fact or the same happening visible to themselves in different ways, interpreted it in different ways. Indeed, what appeared to them in each case as the authentic *fact and truth* was something *different*.
>
> (Ibid.: 91, emphasis added)

From this incommensurability among different projections, Heidegger infers the impossibility of interpreting their historical change as a process of rational revision based on experience. As Heidegger claims in *Basic Questions of Philosophy*: 'it is simply pointless to *measure* the Aristotelian doctrine of motion against that of *Galileo* with respect to results, *judging* the former as backward and the latter as advanced. For *in each case, nature means something completely different*' (1937–38: 52–3, emphasis added).

Here Heidegger offers only the outline of an argument. A *factual* difference in meaning becomes a *normative* argument against the legitimacy of the comparison only under the assumption that meaning determines reference (and thus that a difference in meaning implies *ipso facto* a difference in reference). Given the assumption that what 'nature' in each case means determines that to which the respective theories refer, it follows that theories with entirely different conceptions of natural entities cannot be about the same entities. But only if they were would it make sense to think of one as a correction of the other. Consequently, a scientific projection cannot be disproved by a different one; at most, it can be put 'out of force' by a different stipulation of what and how things are. And conversely, from the point of view of an old projection, the new one cannot be seen as better or worse but simply as meaningless. In *What Is a Thing?* Heidegger explains this claim with the following remark:

> [Newton's First Law of Motion] was up until the 17th century not at all self-evident. During the preceding fifteen hundred years it was not only unknown; rather, nature and *entities in general* were *experienced* in a way with respect to which this law *would have been meaningless.*
>
> (1935–36: 78–9, emphasis added)

For this reason Heidegger claims in *Being and Time* that 'before Newton his laws were neither true nor false' (1927b: 227). From this view it follows that there is no absolute truth across incommensurable understandings of being (see Lafont 1994). They are unrevisable from within and inaccessible (meaningless) from without.

In view of these relativist consequences it seems doubtful that Heidegger's conception of interpretation can make sense of our scientific activity as giving us anything like *objective* knowledge of the empirical world. But precisely these consequences open up a further question, namely whether the assumption that meaning determines reference is the trivial constraint on concept use that Heidegger assumes it is. As we already saw, the hermeneutic idealism entailed by the ontological difference is supposed to follow from a seemingly trivial hermeneutic fact, namely that our understanding of what entities are determines what these entities are for us. However, this claim is not as trivial as it seems. For an essential component of our understanding of what entities are is precisely that they may be different from what and how we understand them as being. This fallibilist insight can be anchored in our practices of concept use without denying the interpretative dimension of these practices if it is possible to use designating expressions in a directly referential way – that is, if, contrary to Heidegger's assumption, the meaning of these expressions does not determine their reference.[7] This issue has been the focus of many contemporary debates in the philosophy of language that I cannot discuss here. But whatever the outcome of this debate may be, at the very least it should be clear that Heidegger's claim is far from being trivially correct. This opens up an important question for those interested in hermeneutics, namely to what extent the insights of Heidegger's hermeneutic turn can be defended without commitment to the hermeneutic idealism entailed by his peculiar interpretation of the ontological difference.

Endnotes

1 This chapter was originally published as C. Lafont, 'Hermeneutics', in H.L. Dreyfus and M.A. Wrathall (eds) *A Companion to Heidegger*, Oxford: Blackwell, 2005, pp. 265–84. The author and Wiley-Blackwell granted permission to reprint the text with minor editorial changes.

2 Contrary to what is often claimed, in *Being and Time* Heidegger does provide criteria to judge the validity of an interpretation. From the very beginning of the book, Heidegger uses the term 'primordial' (*ursprünglich*) to distinguish valid from invalid interpretations, but he only discusses the issue explicitly toward the end of Division Two. There he provides two further terms as *explanans* of the term 'primordial', namely 'authentically and wholly' (*eigentlich und ganz*) (1927b: 306). In the context of referring to the quality of specific interpretations, Heidegger disqualifies interpretations as 'inauthentic' (*uneigentlich*) by using terms such as 'unspecific', 'undifferentiated' or 'narrow'. Accordingly, an interpretation of some subject matter is valid if it can account for what is specific about its subject matter and can do so 'wholly' – that is, without leaving out any important, specific features of that subject matter. These two formal features, *completeness* and *specificity*, are the basis of Heidegger's claim of superiority for his own interpretation, the existential analytic of Dasein, vis-a-vis the traditional interpretation of human identity. I outline his argumentative strategy along these lines in what follows.

3 According to Heidegger, his claim that 'entities are in no way accessible without a prior understanding of their being' (1927–28: 38) is the appropriate way of expressing Kant's transcendental idealism in terms of the ontological difference. Paraphrasing Kant's highest principle of synthetic judgments, Heidegger's hermeneutic idealism could be expressed as follows: the conditions of possibility of understanding the being of entities are at the same time the conditions of possibility of the being of those entities.

4 As Heidegger argues, there is no route from the subjective meaning-conferring acts of an isolated subject to the constitution of a genuinely intersubjective, public world. See also Heidegger (1925: 339).

5 The possibility of understanding everything in advance of having direct experience of it, which is intrinsic to linguistic communication, generates a kind of communication that Heidegger designates with the negative term *Gerede*, idle talk. However, he also insists that the term should not be interpreted in a disparaging sense, for it points to a genuine phenomenon. Here the difficulty lies in the fact that Heidegger is using a single term to refer to both phenomena. On the one hand, as he defines the term, 'idle talk is the possibility of understanding everything without previously making the thing one's own' (1927b: 169). Here the term refers to a positive phenomenon, namely the fact that linguistic communication is possible despite the differences in experience and expertise among speakers – the 'division of linguistic labor', in Putnam's words (1975: 227–8). On the other hand, he uses the term also to refer to a specific kind of communication that this fact makes possible, namely

talking about things one does not really know, which is obviously a negative feature of communication that explains Heidegger's need to use a term with negative connotations.

6 There are further and more important methodological reasons for Heidegger's distinction between 'language' and 'discourse' in *Being and Time* that I cannot get into here. For a detailed account of the difficulties related to Heidegger's account of the distinction in *Being and Time*, see Lafont (1994).

7 For a more detailed analysis, see Lafont (1994).

Bibliography

Apel, K.-O. (1973) *Towards a Transformation of Philosophy*, trans. G. Adey and D. Frisby, London: Routledge, 1980.

Gadamer, H.-G. (1967) *Philosophical Hermeneutics*, D.E. Linge (ed.), trans. D.E. Linge, Berkeley, CA: University of California Press, 2008.

—— (1983) *Heidegger's Ways*, trans. J.W. Stanley, Albany, NY: State University of New York Press, 1994.

—— (1986) *Truth and Method*, trans. J. Weinsheimer and D.G. Marshall, 2nd rev. Eng. edn, New York: Continuum, 2004.

Habermas, J. (1999) 'Hermeneutic and Analytic Philosophy: Two Complementary Versions of the Linguistic Turn', in *Truth and Justification*, B. Fultner (ed.), trans. B. Fultner, Cambridge: Polity Press, 2003.

Heidegger, M. (1924a) *Der Begriff der Zeit*, in *Gesamtausgabe*, vol. LXIV, F.-W. von Herrmann (ed.), Frankfurt: V. Klostermann, 2004.

—— (1924b) *Grundbegriffe der aristotelischen Philosophie*, in *Gesamtausgabe*, vol. XVIII, M. Michalski (ed.), Frankfurt: V. Klostermann, 2002.

—— (1925) *Prolegomena zur Geschichte des Zeitbegriffs*, in *Gesamtausgabe*, vol. XX, P. Jaeger (ed.), Frankfurt: V. Klostermann, 1979.

—— (1927a) *Die Grundprobleme der Phänomenologie*, in *Gesamtausgabe*, vol. XXIV, F.-W. von Herrmann (ed.), Frankfurt: V. Klostermann, 1975.

—— (1927b) *Sein und Zeit*, Tübingen: M. Niemeyer, 2006.

—— (1927–28) *Phänomenologische Interpretation von Kants Kritik der reinen Vernunft*, in *Gesamtausgabe*, vol. XXV, I. Görland (ed.), Frankfurt: V. Klostermann, 1977.

—— (1931–32) *Vom Wesen der Wahrheit: Zu Platons Höhlengleichnis und Theätet*, in *Gesamtausgabe*, vol. XXXIV, H. Mörchen (ed.), Frankfurt: V. Klostermann, 1988.

—— (1935–36) *Die Frage nach dem Ding: Zu Kants Lehre von den transzendentalen Grundsätzen*, in *Gesamtausgabe*, vol. XLI, P. Jaeger (ed.), Frankfurt: V. Klostermann, 1984.

—— (1936) 'Hölderlin und das Wesen der Dichtung', in *Gesamtausgabe*, vol. IV, F.-W. von Herrmann (ed.), Frankfurt: V. Klostermann, 1981.

—— (1937–38) *Grundfragen der Philosophie: Ausgewählte 'Probleme' der 'Logik'*, in *Gesamtausgabe*, vol. XLV, F.-W. von Herrmann (ed.), 2nd edn, Frankfurt: V. Klostermann, 1992.

—— (1959) *Unterwegs zur Sprache*, in *Gesamtausgabe*, vol. XII, F.-W. von Herrmann (ed.), Frankfurt: V. Klostermann, 1985.

Kuhn, T.S. (1962) *The Structure of Scientific Revolutions*, Chicago, IL: University of Chicago Press.
Lafont, C. (1994) *Heidegger, Language, and World-Disclosure*, trans. G. Harman, Cambridge: Cambridge University Press, 2000.
Mead, G.H. (1934) *Mind, Self, and Society from the Perspective of a Social Behaviorist*, C.W. Morris (ed.), Chicago, IL: University of Chicago Press.
Putnam, H. (1975) 'The Meaning of "Meaning"', in *Mind, Language and Reality*, Cambridge: Cambridge University Press.
Quine, W.V.O. (1969) *Ontological Relativity and Other Essays*, New York: Columbia University Press.
Ricœur, P. (1969) *The Conflict of Interpretations: Essays in Hermeneutics*, D. Ihde (ed.), trans. W. Domingo and others, Evanston, IL: Northwestern University Press, 2004.
Sellars, W. (1956) *Empiricism and the Philosophy of Mind*, Cambridge, MA: Harvard University Press, 1997.

Chapter 2

Understanding the other

A Gadamerian view on conceptual schemes[1]

Charles Taylor

The great challenge of this century, both for politics and for social science, is that of understanding the other. The days are long gone when Europeans and other Westerners could consider their experience and culture as the norm toward which the whole of humanity was headed, so that the other could be understood as an earlier stage on the same road that they had trodden. Now we sense the full presumption involved in the idea that we already possess the key to understanding other cultures and times.

But the recovery of the necessary modesty here seems always to threaten to veer into relativism, or a questioning of the very ideal of truth in human affairs. The very ideas of objectivity that underpinned Western social science seemed hard to combine with that of fundamental conceptual differences between cultures, so that real cultural openness appeared to threaten the very norms of validity on which social science rested.

What does not often occur to those working in these fields is the thought that their whole model of science is wrong and inappropriate. Here Gadamer has made a tremendous contribution to twentieth-century thought. He has in fact proposed a new and different model, which is much more fruitful, and shows promise of carrying us beyond the dilemma of ethnocentrism and relativism.

In *Wahrheit und Methode* (1986a; 1986b), Gadamer shows how understanding a text or event that comes from our history has to be construed not on the model of the 'scientific' grasp of an object but rather on that of speech partners who come to an understanding (*Verständigung*). Following Gadamer's argument here, we come to see that this is probably true of human science as such. It is not simply knowledge of our own past that needs to be understood on the 'conversation' model, but knowledge of the other as such, including disciplines such as anthropology, where student and studied often belong to quite different civilizations.

This view has come to be widely accepted today, and it is one of the great contributions that Gadamer has made to the philosophy of this and succeeding centuries. I would like to lay out here why this is so.

First, I want to contrast the two kinds of operation: knowing an object and coming to an understanding with an interlocutor. Some differences are obvious.

The first is unilateral, the second bilateral. I know the rock, the solar system; I don't have to deal with its view of me or of my knowing activity. But beyond this, the goal is different. I conceive the goal of knowledge as attaining some finally adequate explanatory language, which can make sense of the object and will exclude all future surprises. However much this may elude us in practice, it is what we often seek in science: we look for the ultimate theory in microphysics, where we will finally have charted all the particles and forces, and we do not have to face future revisions.

Second, coming to an understanding can never have this finality. For one thing, we come to understandings with certain definite interlocutors. These will not necessarily serve when we come to deal with others. Understandings are party-dependent. And then, frequently more worrying, even our present partners may not remain the same. Their life situation or goals may change and the understanding may be put in question. True, we try to control for this by binding agreements and contracts, but this is precisely because we see that what constitutes perfect and unconstrained mutual understanding at one time may no longer hold good later.

Third, the unilateral nature of knowing emerges in the fact that my goal is to attain a full intellectual control over the object, such that it can no longer 'talk back' and surprise me. Now this may require that I make some quite considerable changes in my outlook. My whole conceptual scheme may be inadequate when I begin my inquiry. I may have to undergo the destruction and remaking of my framework of understanding to attain the knowledge that I seek. But all this serves the aim of full intellectual control. What does not alter in this process is my goal. I define my aims throughout in the same way.

By contrast, coming to an understanding may require that I give some ground in my objectives. The end of the operation is not control, or else I am engaging in a sham designed to manipulate my partner while pretending to negotiate. The end is being able in some way to function together with the partner, and this means listening as well as talking, and hence may require that I redefine what I am aiming at.

So there are three features of understandings – they are bilateral, they are party-dependent, they involve revising goals – that do not fit our classical model of knowing an object. To which our 'normal' philosophical reaction is: quite so. These are features unsuited to knowledge, real 'science'. The content of knowledge should not vary with the person who is seeking it; it can't be party-dependent. And the true seeker after knowledge never varies in her goal; there is no question of compromise here. Party dependence and altered goals are appropriate to understandings precisely because they represent something quite different from knowledge; deal cutting and learning the truth are quite distinct enterprises, and one should never mix the two on pain of degrading the scientific enterprise.

How does Gadamer answer these 'obvious' objections? His answer contains many rich and complex strands. I want to mention two here, leaving aside others that are equally, perhaps even more important (such as the whole issue of 'linguisticality', which is another of Gadamer's crucial contributions to the thought of our time).

The first is a negative point. Gadamer does not believe that the kind of knowledge that yields complete intellectual control over the object is attainable, even in principle, in human affairs. It may make sense to dream of this in particle physics, even to set this as one's goal, but not when it comes to understanding human beings.

He expresses this, for instance, in his discussion of experience. Following Hegel, he sees experience, in the full sense of the term, as '*Erfahrung der Nichtigkeit*' ('experience of negation') (Gadamer 1986a: 360; 1986b: 349). Experience is that wherein our previous sense of reality is undone, refuted, and shows itself as needing to be reconstituted. It occurs precisely in those moments where the object 'talks back'. The aim of science, following the model above, is thus to take us beyond experience. This latter is merely the path to science, whose successful completion would take it beyond this vulnerability to further such refutation.

> *Erfahrung selber kann nie Wissenschaft sein. Sie steht in einem unaufhebbaren Gegensatz zum Wissen und zu derjenigen Belehrung, die aus theoretischem oder technischem Allgemeinwissen fließt.*
>
> ([F]or experience itself can never be science. Experience stands in an ineluctable opposition to knowledge and to the kind of instruction that follows from general theoretical or technical knowledge.)
>
> (Gadamer 1986a: 361; 1986b: 349–50)

Now Gadamer sees it as part of the finitude of the human condition that this kind of transcending of experience is in principle impossible in human affairs. To explain fully why would involve talking a great deal about linguisticality, which I have no space for here. But perhaps the main point can be made tersely in terms of the place of culture in human life. Whatever we might identify as a fundamental common human nature, the possible object of an ultimate experience-transcending science is always and everywhere mediated in human life through culture, self-understanding, and language. These not only show an extraordinary variety in human history, but they are clearly fields of potentially endless innovation.

Here we see a big watershed in our intellectual world. There are those who hope to anchor an account of human nature below the level of culture, so that cultural variation, where it is not trivial and negligible, can be explained from this more basic account. Various modes of sociobiology and accounts of human motivation based on the (conjectured) conditions in which human beings evolved share this ambition. They have the necessary consequence that most cultural variation is placed in the first category and seen as merely epiphenomenal, a surface play of appearances. And then there are those who find this account of human life unconvincing, who see it as an evasion of the most important *explananda* in human life, which are to be found at this level of cultural difference.

Gadamer is one of the major theorists in the second camp, and hence he sees the model of science that I opposed above to understanding as inapplicable to human affairs.

This may help explain why he refuses this model, but not the adoption of his alternative based on interpersonal understanding. How does he justify party dependence, and what analogue can he find to revising goals?

The first can be explained partly from the fact of irreducible cultural variation. From this, we can see how the language we might devise to understand the people of one society and time would fail to carry over to another. Human science could never consist exclusively of species-wide laws. In that sense, it would always be at least in part 'idiographic' as against 'nomothetic'. But for Gadamer, party dependence is more radical than that. The terms of our best account will vary not only with the people studied but also with the students. Our account of the decline of the Roman Empire will not and cannot be the same as that put forward in eighteenth-century England, or those that will be offered in twenty-fifth-century China, or twenty-second-century Brazil.

It is this bit of Gadamer's argument that often strikes philosophers and social scientists as scandalous and 'relativist', abandoning all allegiance to truth. This interpretation is then supported by those among Gadamer's defenders who are in a 'postmodern' frame of mind.

But this grievously misunderstands the argument. Gadamer is anything but a 'relativist' in the usual sense of today's polemics. To see this, we have to bring out another way in which Gadamer breaks with the ordinary understanding of 'science'.

As we often have been led to understand it in the past, scientific explanation deploys a language that is entirely clear and explicit. It is grounded in no unthought-out presuppositions, which may make those who speak it incapable of framing certain questions and entertaining certain possibilities. This false view has been largely dispelled in our time by the work of such thinkers as Kuhn and Bachelard. We now understand that the practices of natural science have become universal in our world as the result of certain languages, with their associated practices and norms, having spread and being adopted by all societies in our time.

But what has been less remarked is that these languages became thus universally diffusable precisely because they were insulated from the languages of human understanding. The great achievement of the seventeenth-century scientific revolution was to develop a language for nature that was purged of human meanings. This was a revolution because the earlier scientific languages, largely influenced by Plato and Aristotle, were saturated with purpose and value terms. These could only have traveled along with a good part of the way of life of the civilizations that nourished them. But the new austere languages could be adopted elsewhere more easily.

We can see how different the situation is with the languages of 'social science'. These too have traveled, but very much as a result of the cultural influence of and cultural alignment of the 'West'. Moreover, they seem incapable of achieving the kind of universality we find with natural sciences. The study of human beings remains in a preparadigmatic condition, where a host of theories and approaches continue to compete, and there is no generally recognized 'normal' science.

This difference in the fate of the two kinds of 'science' is connected to the fact that the languages of human science always draw for their intelligibility on our ordinary understanding of what it is to be a human agent, live in society, have moral convictions, aspire to happiness, and so forth. No matter how much our ordinary everyday views on these issues may be questioned by a theory, we cannot but draw on certain basic features of our understanding of human life, those that seem so obvious and fundamental as not to need formulation. But it is precisely these that may make it difficult to understand people of another time or place.

Thus we can innocently speak of people in other ages holding opinions or subscribing to values without noticing that in our society there is a generalized understanding that everyone has, or ought to have, a personal opinion on certain subjects – say, politics or religion; or without being aware of how much the term 'value' carries with it the sense of something chosen. But these background understandings may be completely absent in other societies. We stumble into ethnocentrism, not in virtue so much of the theses that we formulate, but of the whole context of understanding that we unwittingly carry over unchallenged.

Now this is not a danger that we can conjure once and for all by adopting a certain attitude. That is because the context that will give its sense to any theoretical account of human life we are entertaining will be the whole, tacit, background understanding of what it is to be a human being. But this is so wide and deep that there can be no question of simply suspending it and operating outside of it. To suspend it altogether would be to understand nothing about human beings at all. Here is where the striking contrast with the languages of natural science emerges. There it was possible to develop languages for the objects of science that bracketed out human meanings and still think effectively – indeed, more effectively – about the target domain. But bracketing out human meanings from human science means understanding nothing at all; it would mean betting on a science that bypassed understanding altogether and tried to grasp its domain in neutral terms, in the language of neurophysiology, for instance.

If our own tacit sense of the human condition can block our understanding of others, and yet we cannot neutralize it at the outset, then how can we come to know others? Are we utterly imprisoned in our own unreflecting outlook? Gadamer thinks not. The road to understanding others passes through the patient identification and undoing of those facets of our implicit understanding that distort the reality of the other.

At a certain point, we may come to see that 'opinions' have a different place in our life-form than in theirs, and we will then be able to grasp the place of beliefs in their life; we will be ready to allow this to be in its difference, undistorted by the assimilation to 'opinions'.

This will happen when we allow ourselves to be challenged, interpellated by what is different in their lives, and this challenge will bring about two connected changes: we will see our peculiarity for the first time, as a formulated fact about us and not simply a taken-for-granted feature of the human condition as such; and at the same time we will perceive the corresponding feature of their life-form undistorted. These two changes are indissolubly linked; you cannot have one without the other.

Our understanding of them will now be improved through this correction of a previous distortion, but it is unlikely to be perfect. The possible ways in which our background could enframe them distortively cannot be enumerated. We may still have a long way to go, but we will have made a step toward a true understanding, and further progress along this road will consist of such painfully achieved, particular steps. There is no leap to a disengaged standpoint which can spare us this long march.

> *Wird ein Vorurteil fraglich [. . .], so heißt dies mithin nicht, daß es einfach beiseite gesetzt wird und der andere oder das Andere sich an seiner Stelle unmittelbar zur Geltung bringt. Das ist vielmehr die Naivität des historischen Objektivismus, ein solches Absehen von sich selbst anzunehmen. In Wahrheit wird das eigene Vorurteil dadurch recht eigentlich ins Spiel gebracht, daß es selber auf dem Spiele steht. Nur indem es sich ausspielt, vermag es den Wahrheitsanspruch des anderen überhaupt zu erfahren und ermöglicht ihm, daß er sich auch ausspielen kann.*
>
> (If a prejudice becomes questionable [. . .], this does not mean that it is simply set aside and the text or the other person accepted as valid in its place. Rather, historical objectivism shows its naivete in accepting this disregarding of ourselves as what actually happens. In fact our own prejudice is properly brought into play by being put at risk. Only by being given full play is it able to experience the other's claim to truth and make it possible for him to have full play himself.)
>
> (Gadamer 1986a: 304; 1986b: 298–9)

We can now see how our grasp of the other, construed on the model of coming to an understanding, is doubly party-dependent, varying not only with the object studied but also with the student: with the object studied, because our grasp will have to be true to them in their particular culture, language, way of being. But it will also vary with the student, because the particular language we hammer out in order to achieve our understanding of them will reflect our own march toward this goal; it will reflect the various distortions that we have had to climb out of, the kinds of questions and challenges that they in their difference pose to us. It will not be the same language in which members of that culture understand themselves; it will also be different from the way members of a distinct third culture will understand them, coming as they will to this goal through a quite different route, through the identification and overcoming of a rather different background understanding.

That is why the historiography of the Roman Empire, carried out in twenty-fifth-century China or twenty-second-century Brazil, is bound to be different from ours. They will have to overcome different blocks to understanding; they will find the people of that time puzzling in ways which we do not; they will need to make them comprehensible through a different set of terms.

The coming-to-an-understanding model fits here, with its corollary of party dependence, because the language of an adequate science of the Ys for the Xs reflects both Xs and Ys. It is not, as with the knowledge-of-object model, a simple function of the object, the scientific theory that is perfectly adequate to this reality. It is a language that bridges those of both knower and known. That is why Gadamer speaks of it as a 'fusion of horizons'. The 'horizons' here are at first distinct; they are the way that each has of understanding the human condition in their nonidentity. The 'fusion' comes about when one (or both) undergo a shift; the horizon is extended so as to make room for the object that before did not fit within it.

For instance, we become aware that there are different ways of believing things, one of which is holding them as a 'personal opinion'. This was all that we allowed for before, but now we have space for other ways and can therefore accommodate the beliefs of a quite different culture. Our horizon is extended to take in this possibility, which was beyond its limit before.

But this is better seen as a fusion rather than just as an extension of horizons, because at the same time we are introducing a language to talk about their beliefs that represents an extension in relation to their language. Presumably, they had no idea of what we speak of as 'personal opinions', at least in such areas as religion, for instance. They would have had to see these as rejection, rebellion, and heresy. So the new language used here, which places 'opinions' alongside other modes of believing as possible alternative ways of holding things true, opens a broader horizon, extending beyond both the original ones and in a sense combining them.

Here we see the full force of the Gadamerian image of the 'conversation'. The kind of operation described here can be carried out unilaterally and must be when one is trying to write the history of the Roman Empire, for instance. But it borrows its force from comparison with another predicament, in which live interlocutors strive to come to an understanding, to overcome the obstacles to mutual comprehension, to find a language in which both can agree to talk undistortively of each. The hermeneutic understanding of tradition limps after this paradigm operation; we have to maintain a kind of openness to the text, allow ourselves to be interpellated by it, take seriously the way its formulations differ from ours; all things which a live interlocutor in a situation of equal power would force us to do.

Horizons are thus often initially distinct. They divide us, but they are not unmovable; they can be changed, extended. I want to discuss this notion of horizon next, but first I must say a word about why this picture of a language for science that varies with both knower and known is quite different from the common idea of 'relativism' and has a clear place for the concepts of correctness and truth.

Relativism is usually the notion that affirmations can be judged valid not unconditionally but only from different points of view or perspectives. Proposition p could be true from perspective A, false from perspective B, indeterminate from C, and so forth, but there would be no such thing as its being true or false unconditionally.

It does not seem to me that Gadamer is into this position at all. If the historiography of the Roman Empire in twenty-fifth-century China is different from our own, this will not be because what we can identify as the same propositions will have different truth values. The difference will be rather that different questions will be asked, different issues raised, different features will stand out as remarkable, and so forth.

Moreover, within each of these enterprises of studying Rome from these different vantage points, there will be such a thing as better or worse historiography. Some accounts will be more ethnocentric and distortive than others; still others will be more superficial. Accounts can be ranked for accuracy, comprehensiveness, nondistortion, and so forth. Some will be more right than others, will approach closer to the truth.

But beyond this, we can also see a possible ranking between accounts from different starting points. Let us say that twenty-fifth-century Chinese historians take account of the work of Gibbon, Symes, Jones, Peter Brown, and so forth. They will be trying not just to fuse horizons with the Romans but also with us as we try to do the same thing. The fusion will not only be bipolar but triangular, or if we see Gibbon as a distinct standpoint, quadrangular.

We can see now that there is another virtue here of accounts. They can be more or less comprehensive in a new sense, not depending on how much detail and coverage they offer of the object studied, but rather on their taking in and making mutually comprehensible a wider band of perspectives. The more comprehensive account in this sense fuses more horizons.

The ideal of the most comprehensive account possible ought in a sense to take the place of the old goal of a point-of-view-less nomothetical science that grasps all humanity under one set of explanatory laws. Instead we substitute the ideal of languages that allow for the maximum mutual comprehension between different languages and cultures across history. Of course, this is a goal that can in the nature of things never be integrally realized. Even if, *per impossibile*, we might have achieved an understanding to which all cultures to date might sign on, this could not possibly pre-empt future cultural change, which would require the process of fusion to start over again.

But it is nevertheless an important ideal both epistemically and humanly: epistemically, because the more comprehensive account would tell more about human beings and their possibilities; humanly, because the language would allow more human beings to understand each other and to come to undistorted understandings.

For human affairs, the model of scientific theory that is adequate to an object is replaced by that of understanding, seen as a fusion of horizons. '*Verstehen [ist] immer der Vorgang der Verschmelzung [. . .] vermeintlich für sich seiender Horizonte*' ('*[U]nderstanding is always the fusion of these horizons supposedly existing by themselves*') (Gadamer 1986a: 311; 1986b: 305, emphasis original).

Gadamer's concept of 'horizon' has an inner complexity that is essential to it. On one hand, horizons can be identified and distinguished; it is through such distinctions that we can come to grasp what is distorting understanding and impeding communication. But on the other hand, horizons evolve, change. There is no such thing as a fixed horizon. '*Der Horizont ist vielmehr etwas, in das wir hineinwandern und das mit uns mitwandert. Dem Beweglichen verschieben sich die Horizonte*' ('The horizon is, rather, something into which we move and that moves with us. Horizons change for a person who is moving') (Gadamer 1986a: 309; 1986b: 303). A horizon with unchanging contours is an abstraction. Horizons identified by the agents whose worlds they circumscribe are always in movement. The horizons of A and B may thus be distinct at time t and their mutual understanding imperfect. But A and B by living together may come to have a single common horizon at $t + n$.

In this way 'horizon' functions somewhat like 'language'. One can talk about the 'language of modern liberalism', or the 'language of nationalism', and point out the things they cannot comprehend. But these are abstractions, freeze frames of a continuing film. If we talk about the language of Americans or Frenchmen, we can no longer draw their limits *a priori*, for the language is identified by the agents who can evolve.

This way of understanding difference and its overcoming through the complex concept of a horizon is to be contrasted with two others. On one hand, we have the classic model that comes from the epistemological tradition, whereby our grasp of the world is mediated by the inner representations we make of it, or the conceptual grid through which we take it in. This way of construing knowledge easily generates the conjecture that there may be unbridgeable differences. What if our inner representations diverge, even as we stand before the same external objects? What if our conceptual grids are differently constructed, through which all the information we receive is filtered? How will we ever be able to convince each other, even understand each other? Any consideration that one may adduce in argument will already be represented or enframed by the other in a systematically different way. All reasoning stops at the borders of conceptual schemes, which pose insurmountable limits to our understanding.

In reaction to this, there is the attempt to establish the possibility of universal communication through an outright rejection of the idea of a conceptual scheme, as famously proposed by Donald Davidson (1974). Davidson means his argument to be taken as a repudiation of the whole representational epistemology. 'In giving up the dualism of scheme and world, we do not give up the world, but re-establish unmediated touch with the familiar objects whose antics make our sentences and opinions true or false' (ibid.: 198).

As a rejection of the old epistemology (or at least attempted rejection; I am not sure that Davidson shakes off the shackles of the representational view), this is welcome. And Davidson's argument against the idea that we could be imprisoned in utterly incongruent schemes, invoking the 'principle of charity', is obviously a powerful one. Davidson's principle of charity requires that I, the observer/ theorist, must make sense of him, the subject studied, in the sense of finding most of what he does, thinks, and says intelligible; else I cannot be treating him as a rational agent and there is nothing to understand, in the relevant sense, at all.

What this argument shows is that total unintelligibility of another culture is not an option. To experience another group as unintelligible over some range of their practices, we have to find them quite understandable over other (very substantial) ranges. We have to be able to understand them as framing intentions, carrying out actions, trying to communicate orders, truths, and so forth. If we imagine even this away, then we no longer have the basis that allows us to recognize them as agents. But then there's nothing left to be puzzled about. Concerning nonagents, there is no question about what they are up to and hence no possibility of being baffled on this score.

The problem with this argument is that it is in a sense too powerful. It slays the terrifying mythical beast of total and irremediable incomprehensibility. But what we suffer from in our encounters between peoples are the jackals and vultures of partial and (we hope) surmountable noncommunication.

In this real-life situation, Davidson's theory is less useful. Mainly because it seems to discredit the idea of 'conceptual schemes' altogether – this in spite of the fact that the argument only rules out our meeting a totally unintelligible one. But in dealing with the real, partial barriers to understanding, we need to be able to identify what is blocking us. And for this we need some way of picking out the systematic differences in construal between two different cultures, without either reifying them or branding them as ineradicable. This is what Gadamer does with his image of the horizon. Horizons can be different, but at the same time they can travel, change, extend – as you climb a mountain, for instance. It is what Davidson's position as yet lacks.

Without this, Davidson's principle of charity is vulnerable to being abused to ethnocentric ends. The principle tells me to make the best sense of the other's words and deeds as I can. In translating his words into my language, I should render him so that as much as possible he speaks the truth, makes valid inferences, and so forth. But the issue is to know what counts as 'my language' here. It can mean the language I speak at the moment of encounter, or it can mean the extended language, the one that emerges from my attempts to understand him, to fuse horizons with him. If we take it in the first way, it is almost certain that I will ethnocentrically distort him.

The problem is that the standing ethnocentric temptation is to make too quick sense of the stranger – that is, sense in one's own terms. The lesser breeds are without the law because they have nothing we recognize as law. The step to branding them as lawless and outlaw is as easy as it is invalid and fateful. So the conquistadores had an easy way of understanding the strange and disturbing practices of the Aztecs, including human sacrifice. While we worship God, these people worship the Devil.

Of course, this totally violates Davidson's intent. But the problem is that we need to understand how we move from our language at the time of encounter, which can only distort those we encounter, to a richer language that has place for them, from making the 'best sense' in our initial terms, which will usually be an alien imposition, to making the best sense within a fused horizon. I cannot see how we can conceive of or carry out this process without allowing into our ontology something like alternative horizons or conceptual schemes. This I think marks the superiority of Gadamer's view over Davidson's.

Davidson's argument is nonetheless very valuable in pointing out the dangers, even the paradoxes involved in using any such terms. We can see this when we ask the question, what does the concept 'scheme' contrast with? The term 'content' is certainly bad, as though there were stuff already lying there, to be framed in different schemes. There is certainly a deep problem here.

It belongs to the very idea of a scheme, in the sense one is tempted to use it in intercultural studies, that it indicates some systematic way in which people are interpreting or understanding their world. Different schemes are incombinable such ways of understanding the same things.

But what things? How can you point to the things in question? If you use the language of the target society to get at them, then all distinction between scheme and content disappears. But what else can you use? Well, let us say our language, that of the observer/scientists, about this target area. But then we still will not have got at the 'content' we share in common, which would have to be somehow identifiable independently of both schemes.

The point is well taken and needs to be kept in mind in order to avoid certain easy pitfalls, such as thinking that one has a neutral, universal categorization of the structures or functions of all societies – for example, 'political system', 'family', 'religion', and so forth – which provide the ultimately correct description for what all the different fumbling, cultural languages are aiming at, the noumena to their phenomenal tongues. But the notion of two schemes, one target area, remains valid and indeed indispensable.

Let's go back to the case of the conquistadores and the Aztecs. We might say that one thing the conquistadores had right was that they recognized that ripping out of hearts in some way corresponded in Spanish society to the Catholic Church and the Mass, and that sort of thing. That is, the right insight, yielding a good starting point for an eventual fusion of horizons, involves identifying what something in the puzzling life of an alien people can usefully be contrasted with in ours. In Gadamerian terms, what we are doing is identifying that facet of our lives which their strange customs interpellate, challenge, offer a notional alternative to.

An example will show what is at stake here. A few years ago a wildly reductivistic American social scientist produced a theory of Aztec sacrifice in which it was explained 'materialistically' in terms of their need for protein. On this view the right point of comparison in Spanish society would be their slaughterhouses rather than their churches. Needless to say, from such a starting point, one gets nowhere.

The fruitful supposition is that what went on atop those pyramids reflected a very different construal of an X, which overlaps with what Christian faith and practice is a construal of in Spain. This is where thinking and inquiry can usefully start. It has one powerful – and in principle challengeable – presupposition: that we share the same humanness and that therefore we can ultimately find our feet in Aztec sacrifice, because it's a way of dealing with a human condition we share. Once this is accepted, then the notion of two schemes, same X, becomes inescapable. Only we have to be careful what we put in the place of the 'X'.

In a general proposition, we might say that what we put in place of the X is dimension, or aspect of the human condition. In the particular case, it is much more dangerous to specify. 'Religion' would be an obvious candidate word. But the danger is precisely that we happily take on board everything this word means in our world and slide back toward the ethnocentric reading of the conquistadores. So we perhaps retreat to something vaguer, like 'numinous', but even this carries its dangers.

The point is to beware of labels here. This is the lesson to be learned from attacks on the scheme-content distinction. But that the Mass and Aztec sacrifice belong to rival construals of a dimension of the human condition for which we have no stable, culture-transcendent name, is a thought we cannot let go of, unless we want to relegate these people to the kind of unintelligibility that members of a different species would have for us. If rejecting the distinction means letting this go, it is hardly an innocent step.

The conception of horizons and their fusion shows how the 'science' we have of other times and people is, like the understandings we come to, party-dependent. It will differ both with the object and the subject of knowledge.

But how about the analogue to the other property of understandings I mentioned above, that they may involve changing our goals? The analogous point here is that in coming to see the other correctly, we inescapably alter our understanding of ourselves. Taking in the other will involve an identity shift in us. That is why it is so often resisted and rejected. We have a deep identity investment in the distorted images we cherish of others.

That this change must occur falls out from the account of the fusion of horizons. To recur to our example: we come to see that attributing 'opinions' to them is distortive. But we only ever did so originally, because it seemed to go without saying that this is what it meant to have beliefs in certain areas. To get over the distortion, we had to see that there were other possibilities, that our way of being isn't the only or 'natural' one, but that it represents one among other possible forms. We can no longer relate to our way of doing or construing things 'naively', as just too obvious to mention.

If understanding the other is to be construed as fusion of horizons and not as possessing a science of the object, then the slogan might be: no understanding the other without a changed understanding of self.

The kind of understanding that ruling groups have of the ruled, that conquerors have of the conquered – most notably in recent centuries in the far-flung European empires – has usually been based on a quiet confidence that the terms they need are already in their vocabulary. Much of the 'social science' of the last century is in this sense just another avatar of an ancient human failing. And indeed, the satisfactions of ruling, beyond the booty, the unequal exchange, the exploitation of labor, very much includes the reaffirmation of one's identity that comes from being able to live this fiction without meeting brutal refutation. Real understanding always has an identity cost – something the ruled have often painfully experienced. It is a feature of tomorrow's world that this cost will now be less unequally distributed.

The cost appears as such from the standpoint of the antecedent identity, of course. It may be judged a gain once one has gone through the change. We are also enriched by knowing what other human possibilities there are in our world. It cannot be denied, however, that the path to acknowledging this is frequently painful.

The crucial moment is the one where we allow ourselves to be interpellated by the other; where the difference escapes from its categorization as an error, a fault, or a lesser, undeveloped version of what we are, and challenges us to see it as a viable human alternative. This unavoidably calls our own self-understanding into question. This is the stance Gadamer calls 'openness'. As against the way I stand to what I see as an object of science, where I try '*[mich] selber aus der Beziehung zum anderen herauszureflektieren und dadurch von ihm unerreichbar zu werden*' ('reflecting [myself] out of [my] relation to the other and so becoming unreachable by him') (Gadamer 1986a: 366; 1986b: 354), '*Offenheit für den anderen schließt [. . .] die Anerkennung ein, daß ich in mir etwas gegen mich gelten lassen muss, auch wenn es keinen anderen gäbe, der es gegen mich geltend machte*' ('Openness to the other [. . .] involves recognizing that I myself must accept some things that are against me, even though no one else forces me to do so') (Gadamer 1986a: 367; 1986b: 355).

Gadamer's argument in *Wahrheit und Methode* deals with our understanding of our own tradition, the history of our civilization, and the texts and works which belong to this. This means that what we study will be in one way or another internal to our identity. Even where we define ourselves against certain features of the past, as the modern Enlightenment does against the 'Middle Ages', this remains within our identity as the negative pole, that which we have overcome or escaped. We are part of the *Wirkungsgeschichte* of this past and as such it has a claim on us.

My point in this essay has been that Gadamer's account of the challenge of the other and the fusion of horizons applies also to our attempts to understand quite alien societies and epochs. The claim here comes not from their place within our identity, but precisely from their challenge to it. They present us different and often disconcerting ways of being human. The challenge is to be able to acknowledge the humanity of their way, while still being able to live ours. That this may be difficult to achieve, that it will almost certainly involve a change in our self-understanding and hence in our way, has emerged from the above discussion.

Endnote

1 This chapter was originally published as C. Taylor, 'Understanding the Other: A Gadamerian View on Conceptual Schemes', in J. Malpas, U. Arnswald and J. Kertscher (eds) *Gadamer's Century: Essays in Honor of Hans-Georg Gadamer*, Cambridge, MA: MIT Press, 2002, pp. 279–97. The author and MIT Press granted permission to reprint the text with minor editorial changes.

Bibliography

Davidson, D. (1974) 'On the Very Idea of a Conceptual Scheme', in *Inquiries into Truth and Interpretation*, 2nd edn, Oxford: Oxford University Press, 2001.

Gadamer, H.-G. (1986a) *Wahrheit und Methode*, 5th edn, Tübingen: Mohr Siebeck.

—— (1986b) *Truth and Method*, trans. J. Weinsheimer and D.G. Marshall, 2nd rev. Eng. edn, New York: Continuum, 2004.

Chapter 3

Gadamer's interest for legal hermeneutics

Jean Grondin

> *Die juristische Hermeneutik vermag das wirkliche Verfahren der Geisteswissenschaften an sich selbst zu erinnern.*
>
> Hans-Georg Gadamer (1986a: 333)

> Legal hermeneutics is capable of reminding the humanities of what they are actually doing.
>
> Hans-Georg Gadamer (1986b: 324, translation modified)

Hermeneutics, as is well known, has a fondness for double meanings. My title is no exception. It wants to be understood in two ways that command the division of this chapter in two parts, of very unequal length. The title means, first, that I will focus on Gadamer's *own* interest for legal hermeneutics – that is, the reasons why he was attracted by the paradigmatic nature of legal hermeneutics and what he has to say about it. Second, the title means that Gadamer might present an interest for legal hermeneutics itself: what is it that jurists could learn from Gadamer? Naturally, it is up to them to determine what they can garner from Gadamer, if anything. This is why this second part will be much shorter than the first: I am not a legal scholar, but at best something like a Gadamer specialist.

1. Gadamer's own interest for legal hermeneutics

Why and how did Gadamer become interested in legal hermeneutics? The question has to be raised because Gadamer had no meaningful upbringing or training in legal hermeneutics. His education was in philosophy and Greek philology, both domains for which legal hermeneutics is a rather distant preoccupation. His main mentors, teachers such as Paul Natorp, Nicolai Hartmann, Martin Heidegger or Paul Friedländer, were by no means legal scholars. When Gadamer lists the many disciplines of the humanities he studied at the university, he never names law or jurisprudence.[1] Gadamer also wrote very little on the topic of legal hermeneutics *per se*. A glance at the table of contents of his ten-volume *Complete Works* edition, published between 1985 and 1995, reveals that there is hardly a single piece that is entirely devoted to the issue of legal hermeneutics. Gadamer was not a legal scholar and never claimed to be. However, he took a pronounced interest in the subject matter, which can be seen in the fact that he devoted a key chapter of his 1960 masterpiece, *Truth and Method*, to 'The Exemplary Significance of Legal Hermeneutics' (1986a: 330–46; 1986b: 321–36).

Though most important, this chapter is in some ways surprising. This is the case not only because Gadamer had never written meaningfully on legal matters before *Truth and Method*, but also given the fact that his interest in legal hermeneutics only seems to emerge forcefully at a relatively late stage in what is by all accounts a substantial book: indeed, the reference to law does not appear until page 330 of the German edition (1986a) and not until page 321 in the English translation (1986b). All the same, the book is ripe with allusions to legal hermeneutics well before this chapter, which have yet to be studied systematically. For example, Gadamer mentions legal hermeneutics within the very first paragraph of the book,[2] then in the chapters on judgment and taste,[3] and finally as he discusses what is for him the key issue of legitimate prejudices.[4] Furthermore, the crucial chapter on law, which incidentally addresses theological hermeneutics in addition to legal hermeneutics, aims to show the 'exemplary' nature of legal practice for the hermeneutics that he develops throughout his entire book. In this chapter, Gadamer does not discuss specific judicial decisions, nor legal theory as such, but claims to approach legal hermeneutics as an *illustration* of hermeneutics writ large – for instance, as regards the application of meaning, of tradition and of binding texts in a fair way to our present and pressing concerns. In this respect, one could argue that Gadamer defends a very original thesis because the main hermeneutics specialists before him – say, philosophers such as Friedrich Schleiermacher, Wilhelm Dilthey or Heidegger – displayed little interest in the field of law.

There are always exceptions. Thus, it must be observed that the important Italian hermeneutics scholar, Emilio Betti (1890–1968), was a trained jurist and a legal historian who published a very ambitious theory of hermeneutics under the title *Teoria generale della interpretazione* (1955). It is an impressive, voluminous work, which, since it was written in Italian, was probably not widely read. However, Gadamer alludes to Betti and to some of his distinctions in the first edition of *Truth and Method*, and indeed in all the publications where he addresses legal hermeneutics. Betti was clearly a central source of inspiration in prompting Gadamer's interest in legal hermeneutics, even though Betti himself did not regard legal hermeneutics as an exemplary discipline for *all* hermeneutics. For Betti, the task of hermeneutics was to provide a methodology for the understanding of meaning. He finds his model for this cognitive task in philological and historical hermeneutics where the interpreter's goal is to ascertain the meaning that is expressed in 'objectivations' or expressions (Grondin 1990).[5] In Betti's eyes, legal hermeneutics also pursues this goal when it strives to understand legal norms, but it can assume an additional task: its endeavour becomes normative when a judge has to *apply* a law to a particular case. Application of the law by the judge confers to the law a concrete dimension and integrates it within the life of a community.[6] Betti thus distinguished the primary cognitive or recognitive task of interpretation from that of application, which would only take place in 'normative' types of interpretation such as judicial and theological interpretation (1954b: 67).[7] Betti's focus on the task of application in law (not to mention theology) may well have caught Gadamer's attention and alerted him to the exemplary status of legal hermeneutics as a whole.

What if, Gadamer asked, application was not an *additional* task that legal hermeneutics would take on, but constituted the heart and soul of every interpretation? Application is here the magic word. It has a distinct meaning for a judge who has to apply a law or judicial guidelines to a given case, but it came to acquire for Gadamer a far-reaching, indeed universal dimension for all hermeneutics: his basic thesis is that there is an element of application in *every* form of understanding, when I understand a text, an event, an artwork, a historical source or when I apply a law. Each time I do this, I apply the meaning I understand, in some way, to the situation I find myself in. It is not the only form of application that is in play in this process according to Gadamer: in every event of understanding it is also 'effective history' (*Wirkungsgeschichte*) which comes to be applied to my situation. This is another grand thesis of Gadamer: the interpreter is not the sole master of 'what happens' in the process of interpretation (Gadamer is fond of this idea of 'what happens' in interpretation, beyond our knowing and doing); history and the views of one's time are also at work, and much more so, Gadamer seems to contend, than the interpreter's own conscious reasoning and doing in the case of the judge. According to Gadamer, we are never fully aware of the application to our situation and of effective history because this twofold application happens to a large extent behind our backs. But of that, of this happening of application and tradition beyond our awareness, we can become aware. This consciousness of effective history and thus of the limits of our knowledge is much more important in understanding, one gets the feeling, than the conscious following of a methodology where the subject would control all the steps.

The great irony in this, *if* Betti was the decisive influence on Gadamer (which I think he was because most of the examples and distinctions Gadamer discusses come from Betti), is that the Italian jurist himself was most allergic to this view of hermeneutics that 'celebrated' the element of application in *every* understanding effort. He equaled this with the worst form of subjectivism and would be followed by many critics of Gadamer, starting with E.D. Hirsch and up to Hans Krämer (2007). For Betti, the *whole point* of hermeneutics, as the methodology of interpretation, was precisely to *offset* the subjective involvement of the interpreter, and its situation, in the act of understanding. Hermeneutics provided for him the rigorous methodology and 'canons' which would hold this subjectivism in check and would thus enable the humanities to be regarded as respectable sciences. Without such a methodology or hermeneutics, the humanities would not be able to escape the accusation of relativism.

Betti could not know Gadamer's hermeneutics when he published his general theory of hermeneutics in 1955, but he was familiar with what he called the 'heretic' hermeneutic doctrine ('*Irrlehre*') (Betti 1954b: 37) of authors such as Heidegger and Rudolf Bultmann who seemed to extol the 'pre-understanding' of the interpreter, and view it as a condition for interpretation. In 1954, Betti published a piece in the *Festschrift* for Ernst Rabel under the title 'Contribution to a general doctrine of interpretation' (1954a), where he summed up his view of hermeneutics, which he would present more thoroughly in Italian in his *Teoria generale* (1955) and in which he already condemned the 'perverted' doctrines of Heidegger and Bultmann.[8] I believe it is this piece that probably nourished Gadamer's interest in legal hermeneutics (and more so than the Italian summa of 1955) because all the examples of Gadamer and the (often unreferenced) quotations from Betti one finds in *Truth and Method* are to be found in it.

Unlike Betti – totally unlike Betti – Gadamer was attracted and influenced by the doctrines of Heidegger and Bultmann, especially their idea that the interpreting subject had a say and a stake in the interpretative effort. Instead of seeking to neutralize it, as Betti advocated, hermeneutics should seek to defend the legitimacy of this implication, or application as Gadamer liked to call it, without opening the door to the perils of relativism. When *Truth and Method* came out in 1960, Betti was one of the first to react to it and to denounce its anti-methodologism and subjectivism, evident in his eyes in Gadamer's contention that one's prejudices could be *conditions* of understanding. Betti would do this in a pamphlet published in German in 1962, where he again summed up his views on methodological hermeneutics and took Gadamer to task (1962a).[9]

The views of Gadamer and Betti, on the methodological vocation of hermeneutics and the import of application in understanding, are far apart, if not diametrically opposed. Nonetheless, they had a fascinating debate and some correspondence with one another which Betti quoted in his pamphlet of 1962 (ibid.: 51)[10] and which led Gadamer to write anew on legal hermeneutics, namely in the long piece 'Hermeneutics and Historicism' (1965a, 1965b). This text was added as an appendix to later editions of *Truth and Method*, and also in the afterword to the third edition of the volume in 1972. It is also significant of Gadamer's respect for Betti's works – of which he would say they had high merits, but were disoriented by an emotional polemics (1986a: 264 n. 172; 1986b: 266 n. 172)[11] – that he saw to it that his *Teoria generale* (1955a, 1955b) was published in a slightly abridged version in German, by his own publisher, Siebeck, in 1967. Moreover, Gadamer was certainly instrumental in having Betti's pamphlet of 1954 re-edited for the same publisher in 1988 to which he contributed an afterword in the form of a text, 'Betti and the Idealistic Heritage', that he had previously released (1978).

We shall return to Betti, but let us focus on the motives of Gadamer's interest in the exemplary character of legal hermeneutics. It is true that Gadamer was not and never claimed to be a legal scholar, but this only serves to underscore that one does not have to be a specialist of a given subject to have something interesting to say about it. I will refrain from discussing the mischievous idea of whether the reverse also holds: namely that one can be a specialist of an issue without having anything meaningful to say about it. I will concentrate on three aspects of this interest Gadamer takes in legal hermeneutics, before I broach the issue of the interest of Gadamer's perspective for legal scholars.

1.1. Legal hermeneutics as exemplary of the application involved in all understanding

The first point naturally has to deal with the paramount issue of application. Gadamer views it as nothing less than *the* 'fundamental hermeneutical problem'. The chapter on legal hermeneutics in *Truth and Method* is indeed to be found in a section titled 'The recovery (*Wiedergewinnung*) of the fundamental hermeneutical problem' (1986a: 312; 1986b: 306). It obviously presupposes that this problem was 'lost' at some point. It was lost or forgotten when hermeneutics took on a purely 'methodological' or 'epistemological' function. For Gadamer, this happened in the work of Schleiermacher and Dilthey, but it could be argued that this methodological function appeared much earlier, indeed in the work of the creator of the notion of hermeneutics, Johann C. Dannhauer, whose seminal work was entitled *Hermeneutica sacra sive methodus exponendarum sacrarum literarum* (1654). Gadamer's contention is that hermeneutics' 'methodological turn' was inspired in the nineteenth century by the model of objectivity provided by the very successful exact sciences: valid knowledge seems to depend in them on the exclusion of the point of view of the knower or interpreter. This would guarantee objective, independently verifiable results in the exact sciences. The traditional 'problem' with the humanities was – and still is in the eyes of many, if not most – that their 'results' always seem to be tinged by the views and ideology of the interpreter. How this 'bad' subjective input could be avoided or put in check became, according to Gadamer, the main obsession of the methodological hermeneutics of the nineteenth and twentieth centuries. It is true that it helped hermeneutics gain a certain visibility and currency: its methodological guidelines, which promised to cancel out the implication of the interpreter, could finally make it possible for the humanities to be regarded as sciences.

Gadamer opposes here two views: first, the idea that hermeneutics would have to be or to provide a methodology of this nature; second, the notion that the implication of the observer is always a bad thing. Why is it that we study the humanities? Is it not because we are interested in them, because they have something to say to us and they respond to our questions? For Gadamer, it would be ridiculous to claim that the 'results' of the humanities are totally independent of the interpreter (or their time). Why would one interpret and read texts if one was not interested by them? Hermeneutics could thus be something other than a methodology for Gadamer (and in this redefinition of hermeneutics, he was quite successful): instead of focusing solely on the methods that would guarantee subject-free objectivity, hermeneutics could strive to justify the extent to which this implication of the interpreter is indispensable in the humanities. It is here that Gadamer discerns the 'fundamental hermeneutical problem', which would have been lost in the heyday of methodological hermeneutics in the nineteenth and twentieth centuries. Legal hermeneutics was of crucial help in this rediscovery of the 'fundamental hermeneutical problem', that of application.

In the decisive chapter on legal hermeneutics of *Truth and Method*, Gadamer takes up Betti's distinction of three types of interpretation: cognitive, normative and reproductive. The cognitive (or recognitive) and basic task, whose aim is the epistemological determination of meaning, would be evidenced by philology and history according to Betti. The normative task, that of application, would serve an *additional* goal, that of deciding a particular case and providing guidelines for action. This additional task would take place in the fields of law and theology, and only in them because of their practical vocation. The main illustrations of this type of interpretation that are discussed here, by Betti as well as by Gadamer, are the judge who has to apply a law to a given case and the priest or preacher who applies a given text of Scripture to the situation of a given congregation. The third task of interpretation, the reproductive, concerns for the most part the situation where an interpreter has to 'interpret' a text, or a partition, for a specific public. It is evidenced by the activity of the translator (also called an interpreter in English) and by all the performing arts, especially theatrical and musical interpretation.[12]

We will not discuss here in any depth the issue of the performing arts, which would be important in their own right because Gadamer also views them, in the first part of *Truth and Method*, as exemplary for his understanding of interpretation as a 'playing out' of meaning by an interpreter (Grondin 2007). For Gadamer's chapter on legal hermeneutics, the decisive distinction (which will, however, not turn out to be one for him!) is that between the cognitive and normative tasks, or that between understanding and application. It is a distinction Betti introduced in order to point out the difference there is between the hermeneutic situation of the judge and that of the law historian, a difference he was most familiar with since it corresponded to his own discipline. The tasks of the two are fundamentally different, Betti argued. The purpose of the law historian is merely contemplative or theoretical: he wants to reconstruct ('*nachkonstruieren*') the coherent meaning of a given legal expression or law, just as the philologist or the historian do with their texts and documents (Betti 1954b: 44). The jurist or judge (both are often confounded by Betti and Gadamer) does this also, but takes on a subsequent task: the law is not just a text from the past that must be understood; it must also be applied to a present case, for which it was perhaps not foreseen, and by being so applied it can affect, through its actual force and validity ('*aktuelle Kraft und Geltung*'), the social life of the present (ibid.: 44). In Betti's somewhat heavy-handed terminology: in the contemplative-cognitive type of interpretation, the subject must get closer to its object ('*das Subjekt and das Objekt heranbringen*'), and in the normative-applicative type, it is the object (i.e. the law or legal guideline) that must be brought closer to the subject ('*das Objekt an das Subjekt anzunähern*') in order to take part in its actual life (ibid.: 45).

This distinction between the law historian and the judge will also be crucial to Gadamer's discussion of legal hermeneutics in *Truth and Method*. But instead of separating the cognitive and applicative tasks, as Betti did, he will conflate them. Gadamer is, of course, aware of the different positions of the judge and the law historian. Their activities also have different consequences: the judge determines the law and can send people to prison, whereas the historian's function is more theoretical. Nonetheless, Gadamer argues and underlines, the difference between the dogmatic-normative interest (of the judge) and the historical interest is not unequivocal (1986a: 331; 1986b: 322). Gadamer shows this by concentrating on the task of the historian. Is it true that the only task here is theoretical and contemplative? How can the historian understand a law without taking into account the fact that it was meant to be applied to given situations? She cannot study a law or a legal context without applying, in her own reflection, this law to a situation. She too must therefore perform an act of application, just as the judge does[13] (without the immediate practical consequences perhaps, but this is secondary for Gadamer). This application takes on at least three forms for the historian (as it does with the judge following Gadamer):

1 On a general and obvious level, the historian cannot understand a law without understanding its possible field of application in the past: the law was instituted to deal with specific situations and be applied to them.
2 The historian who reflects on a law of the past is also aware of the historical transformations to which the law and legal contexts have been subjected; in this her reflection parallels that of the judge who must take into consideration this historical change when applying a law to a different and new context; both the historian and the judge perform a historical reflection which has implications for the understanding and application of the law.
3 The historian cannot understand a law without her own juridical expectations and her sense of what is right, even if she studies legal contexts that are different from her own. Let us say, for instance, she studies a legal disposition according to which it was permissible in ancient times to allow newborns suffering from a major physical or intellectual defect to starve to death. This will be repellent to anyone today, but the historian will always understand this measure of the past out of her expectation of what is right and of what made it right or 'sensible' in the past. We always understand matters of right or wrong, good or evil, by investing ourselves in them.

In the distinction between the law historian and the judge, it is the paradigmatic situation of the judge that Gadamer wishes to highlight because the task of the judge is not a merely theoretical or 'epistemological' one, but a practical one. The judge has to decide and solve a case with real-life consequences; he is not studying the law for its own sake or for the purpose of assuring the 'objectivity' of the legal system. His function is one of service ('*Dienstform*'); it is subjected to the case at hand and the concrete justice to be served. Following Max Scheler,

Gadamer distinguishes hermeneutic 'knowledge' – that is, application as a form of service to the thing (the law, the case) – from any kind of 'knowledge as domination' ('*Herrschaftswissen*') (1986a: 316; 1986b: 310), which would be characteristic of natural sciences (and would imply an objectifying distance toward the matter to be studied).

This is the first reason why legal hermeneutics, as performed by the judge with a view to application, is exemplary for Gadamer's hermeneutics: it is never performed for the pure sake of knowledge; it is there to serve a practical task with real-life implications. And it can only do this by being applied, and by being applied differently, to specific cases. The legal decision is thus rooted in a practical context to which it must do justice, with fairness. Out of this task of practical application follow other exemplary qualities of legal hermeneutics for the larger purpose of a hermeneutics of the human sciences:

1.2. Legal hermeneutics as exemplary of effective history ('Wirkungsgeschichte')

The second exemplary nature of legal hermeneutics and application for Gadamer lies in the fact that it provides an illustration of the type of *historical* understanding that is characteristic of the humanities and, more generally, of human understanding. It is, of course, Gadamer's contention that all understanding is characterized by its historical nature. However, one has to understand precisely how this is the case for Gadamer because it is also his stated aim throughout *Truth and Method* to *overcome* the problem of historicism. Historicism is the view that all knowledge is historically determined and that there is consequently no valid knowledge that could claim to stand above history. The resulting problem is naturally that of relativism: how can there be true or valid knowledge if everything is framed by its historical context? It is this aporia of historicism that Gadamer wishes to overcome. His view of historicity can thus not be reduced to the commonplace notion that all human understanding, and that of the humanities, is 'historically determined'. If Gadamer would only utter this, he would probably be a pure historicist and relativist. More pointedly said, he would not overcome historicism; he would reassert it, which does not seem to be his stated aim. His overriding and much more nuanced view is indeed that the undeniable historical nature of human understanding does not condemn one to the consequence of relativism. He says this for at least three reasons: because it is simply not true that all is relative in the field of human knowledge, because our own historicity (i.e. our historical concerns) constitutes the driving force of our understanding and because history does provide us with guidelines and signposts that can help us attain valid understanding.

The example of legal hermeneutics enables him to make these very important points and thus to overcome the fatal flaw of historicism. The historical character of legal reasoning is obvious: it has to deal with a present case, rooted in a given situation, and its judicial guidelines come from the past and need to be adapted or integrated to the present (as we have seen when we stressed the notion of application). What fascinates Gadamer here is that the legal situation accomplishes a fusion of horizons, which is in principle felicitous, between the past and the present. As he writes in *Truth in Method*: 'Legal hermeneutics serves to remind us what the real procedure of the human sciences is. Here we have the model for the relationship between past and present that we are seeking' (1986a: 333; 1986b: 324). Legal hermeneutics, especially as it is accomplished from the position of a judge (but, as we have seen, for Gadamer the situation of the legal historian is not fundamentally different), provides a prime illustration of the productive interplay of past and present which constitutes effective history or *Wirkungsgeschichte*. A legal decision in the present, with real-life consequences, is always the effect of a law from the past and its own jurisprudence – that is, the productive ways in which it has been applied in the past:

1 First, it demonstrates the productivity of the past in the present: a law from the past is not a dead or unchangeable letter, but something that reaches into the present, impregnates it and has to be applied to it.
2 Second, the legal decision (or reflection) of today is not one that has to 'transport itself' ('*sich versetzen*') in the context of the past in order to understand the law, say, as it was framed by its authors (which is, I believe, the view of intentionalism or originalism in legal theories; see Poscher 2015; Zimmermann 2015: 98–115). No, in the real reasoning of the judge, the focus has to be on the present – that is, the practical task of a precise case that requires a legal decision. The past is thus always interpreted in the light of the present and for the present.
3 Third, this concern for the present is itself only possible thanks to the productive work of history – that is, to the jurisprudence that is the history of the ways, prudent and less than prudent, in which the law has been applied to various cases in the past. In most instances to be decided by a judge, the relevant law has already been applied – albeit differently – by past judges. Any serious judgment will take into consideration these earlier decisions and the variety (perhaps the incommensurability) of contexts to which the law was applied in order to determine how it can come to bear on the present case. The decision of the judge concerning the case at hand will itself have a productive influence on the future. It will, in turn, become a precedent (or, as the French language has it, it will 'make jurisprudence', *faire jurisprudence*). Juris*prudence* is a very apt term for Gadamer because it alludes to the 'prudence' displayed through the work of history and of the decisions that have been brought to the fore. The application of the law is not a matter of science or pure method, whereby the particular case would have automatically to be subsumed under the universal rule (as Hans Kelsen famously held), *nor* is it a matter of arbitrary whim. Rather, it is the result of the prudence manifested throughout history and up to the present. If 'imprudent' verdicts

have sometimes been issued, history can revise them for being unwise, which is why we have appellate courts.

This productive interaction between the past, the history of its transmission and the present that is constitutive of legal reasoning is a model that Gadamer wants to recognize in *all* the humanities. In them too, a given present strives to understand the past. But it does not do this by disregarding the present or by transporting itself ('*sich versetzen*') in the past (which is not possible according to Gadamer) over and beyond the ways in which it has been understood and 'applied', until our day. No, the understanding of the past in the humanities is an understanding in the present, for the present, and which is only possible because this present understanding rests on the work of history, on historical jurisprudence as it were. In this, legal hermeneutics is most exemplary for Gadamer.

1.3. Legal hermeneutics as exemplary for the fairness and truth one can expect in the field of interpretation

It is also exemplary in a third, very important and often overlooked sense. The fertile import of the present and of effective history in legal decisions does not mean that legal reasoning is an arbitrary affair. One customarily opposes 'intentionalism' (the fidelity to the intention of the framers of the law or the constitution) to subjectivism in the application of the law. This is a fatal dichotomy for Gadamer, which is attributable to the false aporia of historicism: either we apply the law according to the original intent of the framers or else 'anything goes'. This fear of arbitrariness disregards the fact that legal decision and reasoning has by definition to be wise and prudent. Any legal decision – it is trivial to say this – has to be governed by what is right, fair and just. In Latin, French and German, the field of law is called *ius*, *le droit*, *das Recht*. It is not called 'the violence of the judge' or 'the realm of pure subjectivism'. What is important in law is that it be done right in that it does justice to its cases. It is this regulative view for what is right that determines how the law and the jurisprudence have to be applied in a precise case. The concern of the judge can never only be to apply the law blindly or mechanically; it must take into consideration the requirements and particularities – for instance, the attenuating circumstances of any given case. Not to do so would amount to a grave injustice, regarding the particular case and the law itself that wants to be applied wisely and differently to the cases to which it pertains.[14] This necessarily different and therefore fair application of the law is expressed in the famous saying of Cicero: '*Summum ius summa iniuria*' (*De officiis*: 1.10.33) – that is, supreme justice can equal supreme injury, or the law that is applied blindly can cause the greatest injustice.

This is why there are unavoidable 'variations' in the field of law: a case can be decided in such a way by one judge, in a different way by another. According to Gadamer, those fluctuations are not arbitrary, at least in principle (there are certainly ideological biases in the field of law, as in all human affairs); they are required by the law itself which wants to be applied prudently, 'jurisprudently', in order to do justice. One can say that legal hermeneutics is governed by two poles, or requirements to which it must do justice: (1) it has to be faithful to the law from the past and its jurisprudence (this requirement is that of the fidelity to the law and its spirit); and (2) it has to be equally faithful to the present, the present case that requires justice. Both demands are fused with one another in legal understanding and application. In this fusion of horizons, legal hermeneutics appears exemplary for all types of hermeneutics and human understanding.

1.4. Conclusion

In our analysis of the exemplary nature of legal hermeneutics, we saw how Gadamer is and is not a historicist. He appears to be a historicist when he claims that our knowledge is determined by history. But he is not – and I believe this is unfortunately the most disregarded contribution of his philosophy, which is often viewed (and at times dismissed) as purely historicist – when he argues that this historicity does not condemn us to relativism (following what he terms the aporia of historicism). On the contrary, as legal hermeneutics illustrates, history and effective history provide us with proven guidelines, wisdom and prudence that can be viewed as binding sources of truth in the decisions that have to be rendered today. The historicity of legal reasoning does not entail that all is relative in the field of law. Actually, the opposite is true and constantly demonstrated by the wisdom of jurisprudence to the extent that it is the concrete illustration of the productive interplay between the past, the history of its transmission and the present.

Judicial reasoning is in sum exemplary for hermeneutics (1) because it diligently performs a task of application, required by a present case with real-life implications; (2) because it exemplifies the productive work of history; and (3) because it shows that this historical and jurisprudential application is by no means arbitrary, but fully defensible in the name of justice.

2. The possible interest of Gadamer's approach for jurists

As indicated, this part will be short since it is up to jurists to decide this matter, prudently and wisely. I would just like to give my modest take on this possible interest in a few short theses:

1 The most obvious contribution of Gadamer resides in the fact that his hermeneutics offers a satisfying account of the truth experience in the humanities (and hence in legal practice) that eschews both the temptation of a methodology modeled on exact science, for which truth has to be independent from the observer and its context, and the excesses of the anti-methodologism of deconstruction (which has been very influential in legal

circles) with its ideas that 'everything is equivocal' and that 'the law is on the whole arbitrary'. Both models fail to do justice to the argumentative structure of legal reasoning and its claim to fairness. On the one hand, legal practice and scholarship do not have to adopt the widespread model of objectivity that wishes to do away with the situatedness and prejudiced nature of understanding. In his famous analysis of the prejudices of understanding, Gadamer called attention to the unacknowledged prejudice against prejudices in this prevailing understanding of objectivity. On the other hand, the obvious limits of the scientist model do not have to lead to the suicidal relativism of deconstruction and its *de facto* abandonment of the idea of truth and reason. There are other modes of knowledge than the one promoted by exact science. Legal reasoning was for Gadamer a welcome example of this other form of knowledge, and Gadamer's hermeneutics can in return provide jurists with a philosophical reflection that accounts for the truth claim of legal hermeneutics and the humanities as a whole.

2 Nonetheless, it is important to stress that all the points of Gadamer's (certainly incomplete) analysis of legal hermeneutics merit consideration and supplementation on the part of jurists. We signaled three pivotal aspects: the importance devoted to the notion of application as the crux of judicial hermeneutics, the positive assessment of the 'work of history' ('*Wirkungsgeschichte*') and the fecundity of jurisprudence as well as the guiding ideal of fairness in law which enable us to state that the variations of legal verdicts are not to be confused with any kind of relativism in the bad sense of the word. Jurists will also have to ponder Gadamer's view that there is no fundamental difference between the judge, the law historian and the law scholar reflecting on his or her discipline. There are, of course, differences, and Gadamer points them out, but for him the unitary focus is more precious for the task of hermeneutics. Jurists will also have to determine whether or not there are some idealizations in Gadamer's analysis that do not correspond to what happens in practice. Gadamer always insists on the notion that hermeneutic theory has to be based in practice (he says so in the third sentence of *Truth and Method* and mentions legal hermeneutics as a prime example of this). This is why 'method' is for him not all that essential, unless one understands method in its original Greek sense of '*met-hodos*' – that is, as the way with something and thus as a walking with one's subject matter.

3 More specifically, I think jurists can learn from Gadamer that the opposition between intentionalism and pure subjectivism is a false opposition that does not do justice to the reality and requirements of legal reasoning. The intention of the framers of legal texts is a legitimate focus of inquiry, but it can only be determined from the backdrop of history and with an eye to the current situation, its language and pressing issues.

4 Finally, I would like to emphasize that jurists can also learn that it is not only them who can learn from different approaches in the humanities or philosophy. As Gadamer argued, it is also the humanities that have much to

gain from legal hermeneutics: the humanities might thus overcome their own historicism. In helping them to achieve this, legal theory could claim or reclaim its rightful status as an indispensable interlocutor in the ongoing debate about the significance of the humanities. This is the great promise of this volume.

Endnotes

1 In his autobiography, Gadamer explains that in his first semesters in Breslau (1918–19) he studied German literature, roman languages, philosophy, history, art history, music theory and even Sanskrit and islamology (1977:10). In Marburg (1919–29), he would focus on philosophy and ancient philology, but he will also name the great teachers he had in literature (Ernst Robert Curtius, Max Kommerell, who was also a friend) and art history (Richard Hamann). He was also close to Friedrich Wolters, from the George-Kreis, who was an historian of economics (ibid.: 16). His most influential teachers were in philosophy and ancient philology: Hönigswald, Natorp, Hartmann, Heidegger and Friedländer. None of them, it is safe to say, had a great interest in law (with the possible exception of Hönigswald whose neo-Kantian epistemology was interested in the issue of the validity, *Geltung*, of law).

2 Gadamer alludes to legal (and theological) hermeneutics in the first sentences of *Truth and Method* (1986a: 1; 1986b: xx) to underscore the point, actually the very first point of the book, namely that the 'fundamental hermeneutical problem' does not only concern the methodology of the *Geisteswissenschaften* or humanities, but also the practical activity of those who, like the judge or the priest (Gadamer likes to discuss the two activities at the same time), deal with, and practice, interpretation all the time. We shall return to this point below.

3 See the development on the activity of the judge in the chapter on taste in Gadamer (1986a: 44; 1986b: 34): 'Our knowledge of law and morality too is always supplemented by the individual case, even productively determined by it. The judge not only applies the law in concreto, but contributes through his very judgment to developing the law ("judge-made law"). Like law, morality is constantly developed through the fecundity of the individual case'.

4 'In German legal terminology a "prejudice" is a provisional legal verdict before the final verdict is reached' (Gadamer 1986a: 275; 1986b: 273).

5 For the distinction between the cognitive and normative tasks of interpretation, see Betti (1954b: 64).

6 On this twofold task of *Konkretisierung* and *Integration*, which go beyond the task of a contemplative knowledge of meaning, see Betti (1954b: 57): 'The juridical interpretation, far removed from being a merely contemplative consideration of the rules of law, viewed in the abstract and the general, goes further and accomplishes a concrete realization and integration of the guideline of behaviour to be interpreted' ('*Die juristische Auslegung also, weit davon entfernt, sich in einer bloß kontemplativen Betrachtung der Rechtsnormen, abstrakt und allgemein genommen, zu erschöpfen, greift hier weiter und bewirkt damit eine Konkretisierung und Integration der auszulegenden Richtlinie des Verhaltens*').

7 Betti thus saw the proximity of judicial and theological hermeneutics. To those two forms of normative hermeneutics, he added the 'psychotypical interpretation', which would deal with psychological life situation and moral or value issues (Betti 1954b: 68). He is thinking here of the interpretation that is carried out by those who are persons of authority in the field of education.
8 For the criticisms of Heidegger and Bultmann, see Betti (1954b: 13, 37, 40).
9 For the criticism of Gadamer in this booklet, see Betti (1962a: 38–52; 1962b).
10 On this correspondence, see Avenarius (2013: 70).
11 See also Gadamer's comments to Franz Wieacker about Betti, quoted in Avenarius (2013: 79n).
12 On these types of interpretation, see Betti (1954b: 64–5).
13 'Must he [the legal historian] not then *do exactly the same thing* as the judge does – i.e., distinguish between the original meaning of the text and the legal meaning which he as someone who lives in the present automatically assumes? The hermeneutic situation of both the historian and the jurist seems to me *to be the same* in that, when faced with any text, we have an immediate expectation of meaning. There can be no such thing as a direct access to the historical object that would objectively reveal its historical value. The historian has to undertake *the same reflection as the jurist*' (Gadamer 1986a: 332–3; Gadamer 1986b: 323, emphasis added).
14 'The judge who adapts the transmitted law to the needs of the present is undoubtedly seeking to perform a practical task, but his interpretation of the law is by no means for that reason an arbitrary revision' (Gadamer 1986a: 333; Gadamer 1986b: 324).

Bibliography

Avenarius, M. (2013) 'Universelle Hermeneutik und Praxis des Rechtshistorikers und Juristen: Die Entwicklung ihres Verhältnisses im Lichte der Diskussion zwischen Gadamer und Wieacker', in S. Meder and others (eds) *Juristische Hermeneutik zwischen Vergangenheit und Zukunft*, Baden-Baden: Nomos.

Betti, E. (1954a) 'Zur Grundlegung einer allgemeinen Auslegungslehre', in W. Kunkel and H.J. Wolff (eds) *Festschrift für Ernst Rabel*, vol. II, Tübingen: Mohr Siebeck.

—— (1954b) *Zur Grundlegung einer allgemeinen Auslegungslehre*, Tübingen: Mohr Siebeck, 1988.

—— (1955a) *Teoria generale della interpretazione*, 2 vols, Milan: Giuffrè.

—— (1955b) *Allgemeine Auslegungslehre als Methodik der Geisteswissenschaften*, Tübingen: Mohr Siebeck, 1967.

—— (1962a) *Die Hermeneutik als allgemeine Methodik der Geisteswissenschaften*, Tübingen: Mohr Siebeck.

—— (1962b) 'Hermeneutics as the General Methodology of the *Geisteswissenschaften*', trans. J. Bleicher, in J. Bleicher (ed.) *Contemporary Hermeneutics: Hermeneutics as Method, Philosophy and Critique*, London: Routledge, 1980.

Dannhauer, C.F. (1654) *Hermeneutica sacra sive methodus exponendarum sacrarum literarum*, Augsburg.

Gadamer, H.-G. (1965a) 'Hermeneutik und Historismus', in *Gesammelte Werke*, vol. II, Tübingen: Mohr Siebeck, 1993.

—— (1965b) 'Hermeneutics and Historicism', in *Truth and Method*, trans. J. Weinsheimer and D.G. Marshall, 3rd edn, New York: Continuum, 2004.
—— (1977) *Philosophische Lehrjahre*, Frankfurt: V. Klostermann.
—— (1978) 'Emilio Betti und das idealistische Erbe', in E. Betti, *Zur Grundlegung einer allgemeinen Auslegungslehre*, Tübingen: Mohr Siebeck, 1954, repr. 1988.
—— (1986a) *Wahrheit und Methode*, 5th edn, Tübingen: Mohr Siebeck.
—— (1986b) *Truth and Method*, trans. J. Weinsheimer and D.G. Marshall, 3rd edn, New York: Continuum, 2004.
Grondin, J. (1990) 'L'herméneutique comme science rigoureuse selon Emilio Betti (1890–1968)', *Archives de philosophie*, 53: 177–98.
—— (2007) 'L'art comme présentation chez Gadamer. Portée et limites d'un concept', *Études Germaniques*, 246: 337–49.
Krämer, H. (2007) *Kritik der Hermeneutik: Interpretationsphilosophie und Realismus*, Munich: C.H. Beck.
Poscher, R. (2015) 'Hermeneutics, Jurisprudence and Law', in J. Malpas and H.-H. Gander (eds) *The Routledge Companion to Hermeneutics*, London: Routledge.
Zimmermann, J. (2015) *Hermeneutics: A Very Short Introduction*, Oxford: Oxford University Press.

Chapter 4

The interpretation of foreign law

How germane is Gadamer?

Simone Glanert

Globalization processes attest to foreign law's increasing relevance. Consider how the US Supreme Court, one of the most influential interpreters in the legal world, has been referring to foreign law in high-profile decisions regarding the meaning of the US Constitution.[1] Also, in cases involving immigrants German judges make foreign law a component part of their legal reasoning as they assess whether a defendant's cultural background should impact a decision on guilt or civil responsibility.[2] Meanwhile, New York University has established the Hauser Global Law School, Georgetown the Center for Transnational Legal Studies, Harvard the Institute for Global Law and Policy, and King's College London the Dickson Poon Transnational Law Institute. Law reviews such as the *Columbia Journal of Transnational Law*, the *Indiana Journal of Global Legal Studies* and *Transnational Legal Theory* have emerged, not to mention an immense proliferation of exchange programmes, summer schools, curricula, courses, symposia, colloquia, books, dissertations and blogs. This massive paraphernalia of collective intellectual effort corroborates the fact that in a globalizing world incessantly featuring legal settings informed by multiculturalism and plurilingualism, intercultural legal understanding must now be deemed well-nigh inevitable. Arguably, the intensified interaction between foreign and local legal knowledges makes particular interpretive demands on lawyers. It must follow that legal initiatives aiming for intercultural understanding ought to assume a sensible and sensitive theoretical framework – theory being understood here as being practically oriented – that is, as being destined to be applied.

In this respect, Hans-Georg Gadamer's philosophical hermeneutics solicits special attention. Gadamer had a profound impact on literary and social theory by underwriting the 'interpretive turn'. At least as importantly for lawyers, he devotes aspects of his *Truth and Method*, his masterpiece originally published in 1960 and last revised in 1986, to law. The specific question I want to address is as follows: to what extent can Gadamer's work on interpretation assist ascription of legal meaning – understanding – across cultural lines?

With a view to a critical appreciation of the relevance of Gadamer's model to the interpretation of foreign law, I operate as follows. First, I briefly discuss Gadamer's approach to legal hermeneutics as I apprehend it. Interestingly, Gadamer regards legal hermeneutics as exemplary for understanding in general. Although I agree in principle with Gadamer regarding the hermeneutic typicality of law in certain respects, his analysis of legal hermeneutics strikes me as too narrow. Second, I inquire whether philosophical hermeneutics can account for intercultural understanding with specific reference to law. Reactions regarding the applicability of Gadamer's interpretive insights to understanding across cultures diverge widely. I address this controversy as I proceed and conclude that it would be unduly optimistic to derive from philosophical hermeneutics, at least as currently articulated, a framework that could be mobilized to account for intercultural understanding.

I. Legal hermeneutics: how typical?

In the second part of his *Truth and Method* (Gadamer 1986b: 321–36), Gadamer includes fifteen pages on legal hermeneutics. Although the book addresses the understanding of texts in general and does not specifically discuss the interpretation of law at any length, Gadamer regards legal hermeneutics as 'exemplary' since, according to him, it illustrates the habitual hermeneutic situation (ibid.: 321). He thus writes that '*[i]n reality [. . .], legal hermeneutics is no special case but is, on the contrary, capable of restoring the hermeneutical problem to its full breadth*' (ibid.: 325, emphasis original).

Overall, Gadamer's philosophical project aims to explore and explain the modalities under which understanding occurs. In *Truth and Method*, Gadamer expresses his position pointedly: '[Hermeneutics'] work is not to develop a procedure of understanding, but to clarify the conditions in which understanding takes place' (ibid.: 295). In Gadamer's view, the hermeneutic situation is fundamentally constituted by the interpreter's set of 'prejudices' ('*Vorurteile*'). Prejudices, which Gadamer largely understands in a positive way, refer to knowledge transmitted either consciously or unconsciously to the interpreter through the tradition to which she inevitably belongs. According to Gadamer, 'the prejudices of the individual, far more than his judgments, constitute the historical reality of his being' (ibid.: 278, emphasis omitted).

In Gadamer's (Hegelian) language, the interpreter's set of prejudices delineate the cultural, not least historical, 'horizon' within which she can make sense of the world. For Gadamer, the term 'horizon' refers to 'the range of vision that includes everything that can be seen from a particular vantage point' (ibid.: 301). Now, understanding, as Gadamer envisages the term, always involves the encounter of two or more horizons. When, in the context of a conversation, two horizons meet one another – for example, when a reader's horizon encounters the horizon of a text – a much larger horizon is formed. Gadamer calls this important moment, when understanding effectively happens, the 'fusion of horizons': '*[U]nderstanding is always the fusion of these horizons supposedly existing by themselves*' (ibid.: 305, emphasis original). The metaphor of the 'fusion of horizons' allows Gadamer to emphasize the dialogical or conversational character of understanding.[3] According to him:

> [O]ne intends to *understand the text itself*. But this means that the interpreter's own thoughts too have gone into re-awakening the text's meaning. In this the interpreter's own horizon is decisive [. . .]. [. . .] We can now see that this ['fusion of horizons'] is what takes place in conversation, in which something is expressed that is not only mine or my author's, but common.
>
> (Ibid.: 390, emphasis original)

To return to law, the key reason why Gadamer regards legal hermeneutics as 'exemplary' is because it readily demonstrates how ***application*** constitutes an integral part of all understanding, an important aspect of Gadamer's appreciation of understanding. For him, 'application is an element of understanding itself' (ibid.: xxix), 'an integral element of all understanding' (ibid.: 307). In *Truth and Method*, in order to delineate the scope of application, Gadamer compares and contrasts the interpretive tasks of the judge with those of the legal historian. The task of the judge is thus 'to concretize the law in each specific case – i.e., it is a work of application' (ibid.: 325, emphasis omitted). Taking the broad hermeneutic view, Gadamer claims:

> [W]e have [here] the model for the relationship between past and present that we are seeking. The judge who adapts the transmitted law to the needs of the present is undoubtedly seeking to perform a practical task, but his interpretation of the law is by no means merely for that reason an arbitrary revision. Here again, to understand and to interpret means to discover and recognize a valid meaning. The judge seeks to be in accord with the 'legal idea' in mediating it with the present.
>
> (Ibid.: 324)

Accordingly, historical understanding means 'that the tradition reaching us speaks into the present and must be understood in this mediation – indeed, *as* this mediation' (ibid.: 325, emphasis original). Although I think Gadamer makes an important point about legal interpretation, which is that the judge applies the pre-existing law – the past – to the matter at hand – the present – he does not account for the complexity of legal hermeneutics.

First, Gadamer inscribes problematic restrictions. At least according to the English version of his book, Gadamer addresses only those cases 'in which legal texts are interpreted legally, in court' (ibid.: 322). I mention the English version because the words 'in court' are not in the German original (Gadamer 1986a: 330), as the French translation of *Wahrheit und Methode* confirms (Gadamer 1986c: 347). Be that translative issue as it may, while judges have the authority to pronounce on the meaning of legislative documents, the fact is that legal interpretation takes place every time a legal agent – not necessarily an official – needs to ascribe meaning to a law text. This situation includes, among others, the application of immigration law by administrative bodies, the interpretation of contracts by lawyers and the study of foreign law by legally trained comparatists undertaking research abroad. Any delimitation of legal hermeneutics to the case of judges would therefore be untenable. There is also another issue arising from Gadamer's treatment of the legal as he confines the scope of his analysis to statutes – what his English translators call 'legal texts'. Here, the German term '*Gesetzestext*' validates the justness of the English wording (Gadamer 1986a: 330) as does the French translation, '*texte législatif*' (Gadamer 1986c: 347). The circumvention to statutes is immediately objectionable from the standpoint of the common-law world where judges regularly engage in the interpretation of judicial precedents deemed normatively authoritative. Indeed, a leading theoretician of the common law expressly connects hermeneutics and the doctrine of precedent in a substantial book chapter he entitles 'Hermeneutics: Precedent and Interpretation' (Goodrich 1986: 126–67). Obviously, this commentator is unwilling to withstand Gadamer's curtailment.

Second, Gadamer seems to suggest that the meaning of the law can somehow be confidently identified before it can be applied to the case at hand. In *Truth and Method*, he writes:

> [I]n a state governed by law, there is legal certainty – i.e., it is in principle possible to know *what the exact situation is.* Every lawyer and every counsel is able, in principle, to give *correct advice* [and] can accurately predict the judge's decision on the basis of the existing laws.
>
> (Gadamer 1986b: 326, emphasis added)

Further, Gadamer states that 'it is always possible to grasp the existing legal order *as such*' (ibid., emphasis added).[4] If I may be allowed to react somewhat bluntly, these assertions misrepresent the law which is inherently, structurally, ambiguous or equivocal – and which can only be so given how it consists of words. There is therefore simply no law 'out there', a stabilized and fixed object that would be readily available to the legal interpreter, that would signify identically to all legal interpreters interchangeably, awaiting to be grasped 'as is'. There is no law to be seized correctly, exactly, because words, no matter how precise, simply do not carry a correct or exact, an 'obligatory' meaning. As my law students well know, the sign that reads 'No vehicles in the park' is open to a seemingly infinite range of interpretations, not all of them unreasonable.

Third, Gadamer's work suggests that legal agents, such as judges and lawyers, find themselves in a subordinated role vis-à-vis the legislator who would occupy an elevated, somewhat God-like position. In Gadamer's view:

> We have the ability to open ourselves to the superior claim the text makes and to respond to what it has to tell us. [. . .] Of this, [. . .] legal hermeneutics and theological hermeneutics are the true model. To interpret the law's will or the promises of God is clearly not a form of domination but of *service*.
>
> (Ibid.: 310, emphasis added)

As he links law and theology, Gadamer projects an image of law and legal interpretation that is at once unduly transcendental and too harmonious or consensual. Contrary to what Gadamer seems to suggest, law features important tensions, indeed recurrent antagonisms. Arguably, the abiding task of judges is therefore not to serve the legislator, but actively to arbitrate disputes and assertively allocate entitlements. To these ends, judges are prepared to deploy audacious readings of the law which may go so far as to intervene *contra legem*. Meanwhile, the work of lawyers is to offer an interpretation of the law that will serve not the legislator but the best interests of their clients – hence the usual clash of conflicting interpretations surrounding the same legislative text. Consider a typical lawsuit involving a contractual dispute between a distributor and a retailer. As any seasoned law practitioner can confirm, the parties will very soon be talking past one another, each litigant holding fast to a particular interpretation of the contract favouring his interest and not even being prepared to allow that the other side's opposite interpretation might have something to commend itself. Here, as in every single legal dispute, the language of conversation, dialogue or 'fusion of horizons' fails to capture the profoundly adversarial character of the legal dynamics at issue – an anthropologist studying the language of the law talks of 'dueling' (Mertz 2007: 5) – which the negotiatory dimension that can occasionally emerge in the law does not come close to supplanting. Let me be clear: litigants do not aim to understand each other through some display of goodwill, but they seek to win – and winning is something that is not done consensually but takes place at the expense of someone else, who loses.

Crucially – and, on reflection, unsurprisingly – Gadamer's understanding of legal hermeneutics appears to be informed by a specifically German approach to law. In Germany perhaps more than anywhere else, jurists believe in legal texts having one correct or exact meaning, in that meaning existing as such. For German jurists, law is emphatically a science, and it is therefore to be approached scientifically or, to use a favourite local term, dogmatically – that is, neutrally, objectively. In the same way in which they assume that the biologist in her laboratory has the molecules before her, there, that these exist as such, that there is one correct or exact meaning to the assemblage of two molecules of hydrogen and one molecule of oxygen, that her experiment can therefore be replicated irrespective of her and that her experimental work is in the disinterested service of science or knowledge, that it exists not to 'fabricate' the world but to reveal it, German jurists – and Gadamer – take the view that judges and lawyers exist to service the law, to apply it, to replicate these applications and certainly not to construct or edify it. Although this position is shared to varying degrees in other countries having strong historical links with Roman law (for instance, Article 5 of the French *Code civil* expressly prohibits any judicial law-making), it cannot account for the common-law tradition where, ever since the twelfth century, judges have been unabashed and legitimate law-makers.[5] And common-law judges have been active law-makers who moreover, through the publication of concurring or dissenting opinions, have consistently expressed public disagreement over the meaning of legal texts, whether statutes or prior judgments, which have never been assumed to carry but one exact or correct meaning and to exist as such.[6] Now, it is a noteworthy feature of common-law adjudication that dissenting opinions can, in later decisions, be incorporated into majority views, a fact which shows that in the common-law world disagreements or misunderstandings, themselves based on the intrinsic polysemy of legal texts, are an important vector of legal development. In other words, discord is seen to harbour potential merit.

To return to Gadamer, it is not only his understanding of the law that appears to be bounded by local knowledge but key aspects of his philosophical hermeneutics also. For example, his idea of the 'fusion of horizons' applies to the overcoming of the distance between historical epochs *within one and the same tradition*. It is 'the historical "worlds" that succeed one another in the course of history' that are emphatically Gadamer's focus (1986b: 444). And he regards understanding across different historical epochs as being possible because ultimately the past and the present belong to one and the same tradition, which constitutes the 'great horizon' within which reconciliation may take place (ibid.: 303). This framework prompts me to revert to the intercultural issue I raised at the beginning of my argument.

If I find myself ranging across legal cultures – that is, across legal traditions, laws and languages – are Gadamer's hermeneutic insights useful to me? Can I derive assistance from Gadamer's philosophical hermeneutics as I embark on the transnational journeys that legal globalization has made seemingly uncircumventable? Are Gadamer's *Truth and Method* and the later writings (Gadamer 2007) a helpful supplement to the toolbox that I take along as I make my way abroad to undertake research in foreign law? Can the Gadamerian 'fusion of horizons' help me to make sense of what happens as I proceed, as a German lawyer, to consider Canadian or Chinese law? I suggest that Gadamer's model is marred by key epistemological inflexions that disqualify within an intercultural situation.

II. Legal understanding: how limited?

In Gadamer's work, language is paramount. Indeed, for Gadamer 'language is the universal medium in which understanding occurs' (1986b: 390, emphasis omitted). And '[t]he fusion of horizons that takes place in understanding is actually the achievement of language' (ibid.: 370, emphasis omitted). The fact that different people speak different languages, an empirical fact that Gadamer obviously appreciates, is not an obstacle to understanding. Gadamer thus asserts that while '[i]t is true that those who are brought up in a particular linguistic and cultural tradition see the world in a different way from those who belong to other traditions[,] [. . .] every such world is of itself always open to every possible insight and hence to every expansion of its own world picture, and is accordingly available to others' (ibid.: 444). To be sure, Gadamer is aware 'how very hard it is to read a text out loud in a foreign tongue [. . .] in such a way that one can make good sense of it[,] [. . .] that what is meant really comes across' (Gadamer 1978: 255). Yet he maintains:

> [I]t is possible for one to find [the word that can reach another person]; [that] one can even learn the language of the other person[;] [that] [o]ne can cross over into the language of the other in order to reach the other.
>
> (Gadamer 1990: 106)

Because 'each worldview can be extended into every other' (Gadamer 1986b: 445), it follows that as regards intercultural understanding no one must ever contend with finiteness, that one must 'never have a truly closed horizon' (ibid.: 303). In the end, intercultural understanding for Gadamer is but a variation on the general theme of understanding. In other words, translation is another case of interpretation. In Gadamer's own terms, '[t]he translator's task of re-creation differs only in degree, not in kind, from the general hermeneutical task that any text presents' (ibid.: 389). Observe that an important aspect of Gadamer's thinking has to do with the fact that for him, different traditions are but so many 'linguistically constituted experience[s] of world' (ibid.: 454). This view means that, according to Gadamer, each 'linguistically mediated experience' (ibid.: 546) is ultimately, and can only be, an experience of the one world there is, what he calls 'the world-in-itself' (ibid.: 444). In Gadamer's terms, '[i]n every worldview the existence of the world-in-itself is intended' (ibid.). And 'in linguistic communication, "world" is disclosed' (Gadamer 1986b: 443). Gadamer's use of the singular – the one and only world there is – is most deliberate.

These passages from Gadamer's work prompt me to react in two ways. First, I find that Gadamer's emphasis on the central role of language in the process of understanding is of the utmost importance for judges, lawyers and other legal agents. Law's stock in trade consists of words, indeed of a particular type of words – that is, normative words or words having a concrete impact on individuals' daily lives and on the workings of society generally. All individuals who operate in the law consistently address words as they seek to interpret law texts and then to communicate their interpretations to judges, clients or whoever else. Second, and contrary to the view that the universality of language makes cultural alterity accessible and intercultural understanding feasible – for example, Lawrence Schmidt, a prominent exponent of Gadamer's philosophy holds that 'justified critique in intercultural conversations is possible within Gadamer's philosophical hermeneutics' (Schmidt 2014: 226) – I regard Gadamer and his partisans as underestimating the way in which language deeply, and indeed insolubly, problematizes intercultural communication.

Suitably, Peter Goodrich reminds one that '[h]ermeneutics was never an innocent discipline' (1986: 134). In a paper published in 1995, Marina Vitkin thus challenges Gadamer's *commitments*, discerningly so in my view. Specifically, she argues that 'Gadamer's framework does not have inner resources to defend its fundamental "prejudice" of the one world against the challenge of incommensurablity' (Vitkin 1995: 66). No matter how earnestly Gadamer *states* that language features a universal dimension allowing for the 'fusion of horizons' in intercultural understanding and irrespective of how steadfastly he *asserts* that different languages are but linguistic versions of one and the same world, it remains, in Vitkin's critique, that there is 'nothing in Gadamer's conception [that] can guarantee the sameness of objects, of the world, across traditional boundaries' (ibid.). To state is not to prove, and to assert is not to demonstrate. To refer, as Gadamer does, to 'the superior universality with which reason rises above the limitations of any given language' is to enunciate a (transcendental) proposition that remains wholly unestablished (Gadamer 1986b: 403). And for Vitkin, Gadamer's stance cannot be redeemed as pertaining to simple wishful thinking or even as being tainted by 'mere theoretical imperfection' (Vitkin 1995: 74). Indeed, Vitkin condemns Gadamer for 'the violence involved in "fusing" the unfusable' (ibid.: 73). In particular, she stigmatizes the passage where Gadamer, discussing translation, refers to the hermeneutic predicament as involving 'alienness and its *conquest*' (Gadamer 1986b: 389, emphasis added) – the German word is '*Überwindung*' (Gadamer 1986a: 391) – the idea being 'to make one's own what the text says' (Gadamer 1986b: 390). It is this strategy of interpretive arraignment of alterity and of legitimation of the self that, along with Vitkin, I find incompatible with the ethical comportment based on recognition and respect that ought to inform intercultural research in general and inquiries into foreign law in particular.

Consider translation, a key feature of Gadamer's argument in favour of the universality of language and thus in support of intercultural understanding – for example, he writes that '[t]he translation process fundamentally contains the whole secret of how human beings come to an understanding of the world and communicate with each other' and claims that translation produces 'an indissoluble unity' (ibid.: 552). My illustration is the opening sentence of Albert Camus's novel *L'Étranger*, first published with Gallimard in 1942 and ever since one of the most celebrated and most widely read novels in the French language (Camus 1942). I argue that these few words offer a striking example of how incommensurability challenges translatability even in the most basic linguistic situations – the kind of difficulty that prompts Vitkin to chastize Gadamer, aptly in my view, for his universalizing prejudice, for his 'presumption that all horizons reveal the same world', that 'each is [. . .] an "aspect" of the thing itself' (Gadamer 1986b: 468), a postulate she calls 'illegitimate' (Vitkin 1995: 68).

Camus's original French text starts with the sentence, '*Aujourd'hui, maman est morte*' (Camus 1942: 9). Frankly, it is hard to imagine a plainer, more straightforward opening for a novel in the French language. Yet, over the past seventy years or so, these four words have given rise to many interpretations which collectively point to the insuperable difficulty the English language faces as it attempts to account justly for the French, not least for the term '*maman*', presumably one of the most elementary words in the French language.

In 1946, translating for Knopf, Stuart Gilbert wrote, 'Mother died today' (Camus 1946: 4). This translation that injected a certain formality in the main character's exclamation which will be unrecognizable to a French readership but nonetheless remained unchallenged in print for many years, even finding itself confirmed in 1982 in Joseph Laredo's revised translation for Hamish Hamilton (Camus 1982).[7] In her June 2014 *New York Review of Books* article on *L'Étranger*'s English career, Claire Messud in fact opines that such formality could even be construed as 'heartlessness' (Messud 2014). Then, in 1989, Random House issued a Matthew Ward translation, generally regarded as an 'Americanized' version of *L'Étranger* (Camus 1989: vi). Ward concluded that the intimacy informing the French 'maman' could not be rendered in English (ibid.: vii) and chose to keep the original French thus writing, 'Maman died today' (ibid.: 3). Ward did not even see fit to italicize 'maman'. In this case, the difficulty, of course, is that the preservation of the French term leaves the Anglophone reader puzzled as to what feelings it conveys.

Now, Sandra Smith in her new 2012 translation for Penguin has chosen to solve the conundrum by writing, 'My mother died today' (Camus 2012: 3). In an interview with *The Guardian* released on 28 November 2013, Smith indicates that, for her, '["My mother"] implie[s] the closeness of "maman" you get in the French' (Smith 2013). But then, revealing a pragmatic touch, she adds:

> Afterwards [in the novel], I used 'mama', partly because it sounds like 'maman' and partly because I was aware that a British audience would probably prefer 'Mum' and an American reader 'Mom' so I needed something that worked on both sides of the Atlantic.
>
> (Ibid.)

Meanwhile, author, literary critic and Camus translator Ryan Bloom targeted the various translative efforts purporting to account for the first sentence of Camus's novel in a short article in *The New Yorker* dated 11 May 2012 (Bloom 2012). Bloom's conclusion is crisp: 'The sentence, the one we have yet to see correctly rendered in an English translation of "L'Étranger", should read: "Today, Maman died"' (ibid.). (Note how Bloom capitalizes 'Maman', possibly adding a measure of deference that is missing from Camus's French.[8]) Interestingly, Smith, the 2012 translator, offers a reaction to this very suggestion in her *Guardian* interview of the following year: 'In French, the emphasis often comes at the end of the sentence while in English it is at the beginning. I felt that "Today my mother died" sounded awkward and did not give the proper stress' (Smith 2013).

The summons to Gadamer – in effect, the point of Vitkin's remonstrance – is to explain how something like a 'fusion of horizons' can materialize across languages if five Camus translators (I include Bloom) are unable over a seventy-year period to agree on the passage into English of the simple French sentence '*Aujourd'hui, maman est morte*'. How can Gadamer contend, as he does, that understanding, even across traditions, cultures or languages is 'in a fundamentally universal way what *always* happens' (Gadamer 1986b: 513, emphasis original)? And how can he maintain, as he does, that 'each worldview [. . .] can understand and comprehend, from within itself, the "view" of the world presented in another language' (ibid.: 445)? The fact of the matter is that there is no object '*maman*', no self-same '*maman*', no '*maman*' as such that unites the original Camus text and its various interpreters. Or, if you will, unlike what Gadamer holds, there is no 'common subject matter [that] binds the two partners, the text and the interpreter, to each other' (ibid.: 389).[9] Ultimately, '*maman*' keeps its secret encrypted, beyond the reach of the various English translations. In other words, '*maman*' is *unwitnessable* in English.

At best, we have what Vitkin calls 'the appearance of understanding', a 'redescribing [of] genuine alienness in familiar and domestic terms', in effect an 'inevitabl[e] distorti[on]' (Vitkin 1995: 57). The 'communion' that Gadamer posits (1986b: 371) simply fails to emerge. There is no 'encounter in a common world of understanding' (ibid.: 386). And there is certainly no such (transcendental) thing as 'the miracle of understanding' (ibid.: 337). When Gadamer defends the view that 'men's coming to a linguistic understanding with one another through the logos reveals the existent itself' (ibid.: 442), it remains, to use a familiar US sports metaphor, that one cannot even get to first base: there is no 'linguistic understanding' in the first place. Literally, the English translators are unable to engage in dialogue – that is, they are unable to pass through (*dia*) the French wording (*logos*). The intercultural situation registers an interruption, and no matter how many translators try their hand at the French text it proves impossible to cancel the interruption: '*maman*' stubbornly remains in its singularity.

Here, I am minded to quote Jacques Derrida:

> No matter how correct and legitimate they are, and no matter what *right* one grants them, [translations] are all maladjusted, as if unjust in the deviation that affects them: within themselves, of course, since their meaning remains necessarily equivocal, and in their relation amongst themselves and thus in their multiplicity, finally or primarily in their irreducible inadequacy to the other language [. . .]. The excellence of translation cannot help it.
>
> (1993: 43)

What Gadamer styles 'the unity of meaning in a text or a conversation [that] rests upon the being-together of people with each other' is nowhere to be seen . . . on the horizon (Gadamer 1994: 395). The fact is that the semantic range of '*maman*' in English is contested and remains uncertain, no English word being determinative of its meaning. What Gadamer acclaims as 'the event of agreement in understanding' (he also talks of 'the communicative event') simply does not come to pass (1984: 21, 35). It cannot be acceptable that Gadamer, since he reckons that 'a peaceful separation of the two sides really will not do in philosophy' (1994: 376) – to transpose a formulation he uses in another context – should attempt to force the square peg of commensurability into the round hole of untranslatability. Although my Camus example, concerned as it is with primordial language, makes this objection particularly meaningful, my illustration represents a typical rather than an exceptional case.

While I dispute Gadamer's exalted sense of understanding – at any rate as it purports to operate interculturally – I find it possible to identify passages supporting my anti-Gadamerian stance in Gadamer's own work. For example, it is Gadamer himself who writes that 'we understand in a *different* way, *if we understand at all*' (1986b: 296, emphasis original). Now, an analyst could readily argue that this observation insightfully accounts for the discrepancies among Camus's Anglophone translators. Indeed, to the extent that any one of them understood Camus in the first place – and one must remain in the realm of indeterminacy in this regard – what understanding was had differed – and had to differ – from Camus's own and from those that other translators brought to bear on the French text since everyone was operating from a singular interpretive vantage point. Elsewhere, it is also Gadamer himself who refers to the way in which 'self-knowledge [. . .] both prescribes and limits every possibility for understanding any tradition whatsoever in its historical alterity' (ibid.: 301). Again, this intuition helpfully describes what is taking place as Gilbert, Laredo, Ward, Smith and Bloom approach *L'Étranger*. Each translator is intervening against the background of his 'self-knowledge', and it is each translator's very 'self-knowledge' that prompts each translation to underscore selected accents, to constitute a preferred text. And it is that pre-existing disposition that will at once inform the translator's intervention and frame it, thus accounting for what Derrida styles its intrinsically 'maladjusted' condition. Although Gadamer's disciples and partisans will presumably seek to reconcile such passages with Gadamer's philosophical hermeneutics as a whole, I find it remarkable how these two quotations strike a much more nuanced chord regarding understanding than the somewhat lofty pronouncements about 'communion' and 'miracle'.

Now, lawyers must not assume that legal language would somehow be immune from the impassability that I have just described. To recall that the English 'estoppel' cannot be rendered in French or that the Spanish '*amparo*' cannot be translated into German without either loss of meaning or semantic accretion (I am reminded of Ortega y Gasset's 'deficiencies' and 'exuberances') seems to me to be stating the obvious (Ortega y Gasset 1946: 493). More interesting perhaps – and arguably even more disturbing from a Gadamerian standpoint – is the fact that terms *within the same language* also hinder intercultural understanding across space. For instance, the word 'privacy', which is part both of the US and UK legal landscapes, shows well the absence of Gadamer's 'communion'.

The idea of a right to privacy, which refers to the law governing the treatment of personal information (the law which, for example, prohibits one from using a person's name for trade or advertising purposes without consent), was first addressed within a legal context in the United States as Louis Brandeis (later a Supreme Court justice) and another young lawyer, Samuel D. Warren, published an article on point in the 1890 edition of the *Harvard Law Review*. 'The Right to Privacy' argues that both the constitution and the common law allow for the formulation of a general 'right to privacy' (Brandeis and Warren 1890). Later, in 1960, William Prosser, a prominent US torts lawyer, articulated specific principles to govern privacy law (Prosser 1960). Nowadays, the law of privacy represents an important facet of US tort law (Epstein and Sharkey 2012).

By contrast, in English law there is no freestanding right of privacy. Thus, the House of Lords (now the Supreme Court of the United Kingdom) refuses to recognize a tort of privacy, a stance it made clear in *Wainwright v Home Office* (2003). Rather, English law requires the claimant to refer either to a recognized tort such as 'breach of confidence' (as in *Douglas v Hello! Ltd* [2007]) or to a specific legal text such as the *Data Protection Act 1998* or the *Human Rights Act 1998* (as in *Campbell v MGN Ltd.* [2004]).[10] Indeed, it is argued that there will never be a tort of privacy as a matter of English common law (Wacks 2006).

Within a legal context, then, the word 'privacy' carries a substantially different meaning for a US lawyer and for her English counterpart, especially if one allows, as one must, that the legal treatment of privacy connects with the social expectations informing the idea of control over one's personal information which itself is linked to deep-rooted local understandings of the values of dignity and autonomy, to 'the social norms by which we live', to 'the way of life that happens to constitute us' (Post 1989: 970, 1010). After all, in the words of James Whitman, '[t]he law will not work *as law* unless it seems to people to embody the basic commitments of their society' (Whitman 2004: 1220, emphasis original). Still according to Whitman, '[t]here is no such thing as privacy *as such*' (ibid:. 1221, emphasis original). Rather, 'the norms of "civility", far from being universal, vary dramatically from community to community' (ibid.: 1168). If, to write like Walter Benjamin, the 'way of meaning' ('*die Arten des Meinens*') as regards 'privacy' is not the same in the United States and in England, in addition, *pace* Benjamin, 'what is meant' ('*das Gemeinte*') is not the same either (Benjamin 1923: 257). It cannot be surprising therefore that the comparatist, as she purports to ascribe meaning to privacy law in the United States and in England, faces 'different ultimate understandings of what counts as a just society' (Whitman 2004: 1163). Again, if I may be allowed to rehearse the point, Gadamer's 'communion' remains a figment of his imagination, the more thoughtful argument being the late Robert Cover's: '[U]nification of meaning [. . .] exists only for an instant, and that instant is itself imaginary' (Cover 1983: 15). As Goodrich indicates, the predicament of philosophical hermeneutics as it faces the matter of intercultural understanding is very much a structural issue: 'Hermeneutics, because it is concerned primarily with passing on or teaching a tradition, is not really equipped to examine [. . .] the construction and communication of legal meanings and messages to different audiences' (Goodrich 1986: 165).

Although Gadamer argues that language is 'the medium of understanding' (1986b: 386), it appears that language is at the same time an *obstacle* to understanding, in particular in the intercultural context I have been discussing. In other words, 'the medium of understanding' is in effect a medium of *misunderstanding*, the relation a *disrelation*. It appears that Humboldt, the pre-eminent nineteenth-century linguist, was highly perspicuous when he wrote that because '[n]obody means by a word precisely and exactly what his neighbour does' – a 'difference, be it ever so small, [that] vibrates, like a ripple in water, throughout the entire language' – in effect 'all understanding is always at the same time a not-understanding, all concurrence in thought and feeling at the same time a divergence' (Humboldt 1836: 63). Although Gadamer heaps praise on Humboldt in his *Truth and Method* on more than one occasion (1986b: 415, 437–8, 440), he does not discuss this specific enunciation of his, with which he would no doubt disagree.

III. Legal Gadamer: how pertinent?

If one considers philosophical hermeneutics at a certain level of generality, one can derive from this mode of philosophical inquiry and engagement some helpful advice for legal agents (understood in the broadest sense) acting as readers, writers and thinkers. Primarily, perhaps, Gadamer reminds one that all modes of understanding are inevitably linguistic and calls attention to the historical continuity of language, that is, to the role of tradition – evidently significant arguments for judges, lawyers and legal scholars, law being at once an eminently linguistical (Mertz 2007: 12) and a strongly traditionary discipline (Krygier 1986; Goodrich 1986: 140–1). But Gadamer also invites attentiveness to the textually and historically situated character of interpretation. Specifically, he teaches that no interpreter can stand outside a given horizon – no one can jettison one's social and political situation or other worldly embeddedness – and that prejudice is the condition of judgment. Although judgment therefore depends upon patterns not necessarily available to consciousness, critical philosophical hermeneutics encourages self-reflection with a view to coming to terms with one's prejudices as much as is feasible. Self-introspection notwithstanding, however, one must forego the idea of interpretive impartiality or objectivity.

As he defends the symbiosis between knower and known – say, between an interpreter and a text – neither being isolated and both existing as historical entities located within the tradition's purview, Gadamer objects to the post-Cartesian search for a scientific method that would ensure unassailably certain knowledge. Rather, there takes place a dialogical encounter between interpreter and text, as two constitutive components of the tradition, that takes the form of a linguistic interaction. And that meeting is thoroughly informed by the dynamic of question and answer as sense-disclosing strategy. Other summaries of Gadamer's work would possibly frame his hermeneutics differently, but I do not think I am doing him an injustice in enunciating his philosophical project as I do, especially in view of the fact that I am deliberately leaving the more contentious aspects of his model to one side (for example, Gadamer retains the idea of 'truth'). In sum, philosophical hermeneutics offers a rich reservoir of insights for lawyers who constantly deal with words and are incessantly pressed to engage in interpretation. To be more specific, the primordial hermeneutic insight that the other may be correct – '[t]o understand someone else is to see the justice, the truth, of their position' (Gadamer 1992: 152) – is no doubt relevant for lawyers. Again, though, in as much as it runs contrary to the adversarial streak informing the law – in law, '[o]ne does not really listen to the other; rather, one employs whatever means one can muster to defeat the other' (Schmidt 2014: 222) – it remains unclear to what extent this lesson can be embraced except in strictly theoretical fashion. As I indicated, in law more than in many other fields 'one of the conversation partners [. . .] presumes to already know the truth of the subject matter'; now '[a] case of failing to meet the prerequisites for a hermeneutic conversation is to aim only to win the argument' (ibid.).

But there is at least one more lesson to be had from philosophical hermeneutics, which I actually consider crucial for law. This other teaching arises, so to speak, counterfactually – that is, from what I regard as Gadamer's failure to convince. To be sure, Schmidt, who, as I mentioned, is prepared to argue the significance of Gadamer's work as regards intercultural understanding, holds that an intercultural situation is, if you will, optimally hermeneutic, that it is particularly 'advantageous' from a hermeneutic standpoint because it involves 'a greater distance, a greater otherness, between the interpreter and the text or other person' (ibid.: 215). It follows, according to Schmidt, that the interpreter is invited to review more of her prejudices and to interrogate those more fundamentally than would be the case if she had stayed within the tradition. Schmidt argues that '[t]he greater distance increases the chances of a true experience where one learns that what one thought was the case is not the case. Reading a text from a contemporary, like-minded author in one's own tradition is less likely to challenge any prejudgments in the reader; the horizons of meaning are too similar' (ibid.). By contrast, '[t]ravelling in another country, one is confronted with difference, and this often allows one to become aware of one's own customary behaviours and prejudgments, which may then be questioned' (ibid.: 216).

In my opinion, though, Gadamer, very much despite himself, ultimately teaches lawyers that intercultural understanding is beyond reach, no matter how earnestly it would be wanted. Now, I do not pronounce on whether intercultural understanding is in fact desirable or not. My deflationary claim is descriptive rather than prescriptive: I argue that intercultural understanding cannot be achieved, and I maintain that Gadamer's argument in effect confirms this impediment. At best, what goes under the designation 'intercultural understanding' will feature not a 'fusion of horizons' but an approximation thereof (Vasilache 2003: 62), which means that it will in effect amount to a *misunderstanding*. If one (desperately) wishes to retain something of the Gadamerian idea of 'universality', one can perhaps argue the universal character of the *possibility* of understanding arising from the ontological nature of language or more assuredly the *impossibility* of understanding entirely and authentically (ibid.: 114). Contrary to his stated intention, then, Gadamer in the end would reveal a 'paradox' that would be inherent to intercultural understanding: only 'the impossibility of universality is universal' (ibid.).

To conclude anecdotally, I find it interesting to recall that Gadamer himself experienced the limits of intercultural understanding late in his life. I am thinking of the famous discussion with Jacques Derrida that took place at the Goethe-Institute in Paris in April 1981.

> In the Gadamer–Derrida debates in April of 1981, we have an encounter that is usually seen as a kind of family squabble between the intellectual children of Heidegger, a dialogue (or in Gadamer's opinion, a lack of dialogue) between hermeneutics and deconstruction. It was also an encounter between generations, between languages, and between nations which, less than forty years earlier, had been at war.
>
> (Janz 2015: 479)

What took place in 1981 in Paris was undoubtedly a meeting of two great minds arising in an intercultural setting. Whether there happened a 'fusion of horizons' between the German and the French philosophers is very much a different story.

Endnotes

1 For example, *Atkins v Virginia*, 536 U.S. 304 (2002); *Lawrence v Texas*, 539 U.S. 558 (2004); *Roper v Simmons*, 543 U.S. 551 (2005).
2 For example, BGH, 28 January 2004, 2 StR 452/03.
3 Dialogue and conversation both translate the German '*Gespräch*', Gadamer's term.
4 In this instance, the English text appears to be fair to the German original which features terms such as '*Rechtssicherheit*' ('legal certainty') and '*Rechtsordnung als solche*' ('legal order as such') (Gadamer 1986a: 335).
5 Interestingly, Gadamer observes that 'the concrete passing of judgment in a legal question is no theoretical statement but an instance of "doing things with words"' (1978: 256). Given his overall appreciation of the law, I assume he means these words in a restrictive sense.
6 In this regard, it is important to observe that Ronald Dworkin's 'right-answer' thesis is concerned in important respects with the objectivity of moral determination.
7 This translation was subsequently acquired by Penguin in 1983.
8 Ward also writes 'Maman' but since this word opens the sentence one cannot know whether he had in mind 'maman' or 'Maman'.
9 Such enunciations are particularly difficult to credit as they come from someone who acknowledges how '[t]he requirement that a translation be faithful cannot remove the fundamental gulf between the two languages' (Gadamer 1986b: 387).
10 *Wainwright v Home Office*, [2004] 2 A.C. 406 (H.L.); *Douglas v Hello! Ltd*, [2008] 1 A.C. 1 (H.L.); *Campbell v MGN Ltd*, [2004] 2 A.C. 457 (H.L.).

Bibliography

Benjamin, W. (1923) 'The Task of the Translator', trans. H. Zohn, in *Walter Benjamin [:] Selected Writings*, M. Bullock and M.W. Jennings (eds), vol. I, Cambridge, MA: Harvard University Press, 1996.

Bloom, R. (2012) 'Lost in Translation: What the First Line of "The Stranger" Should Be', *The New Yorker*, 11 May. Online. Available at www.newyorker.com/books/page-turner/lost-in-translation-what-the-first-line-of-the-stranger-should-be (accessed 30 June 2016).

Brandeis, L.D. and Warren, S.D. (1890) 'The Right to Privacy', *Harvard Law Review*, 4: 193–220.

Camus, A. (1942) *L'Étranger*, Paris: Gallimard.

—— (1946) *The Stranger*, trans. S. Gilbert, New York: Knopf.

—— (1982) *The Outsider*, trans. J. Laredo, London: Hamish Hamilton.

—— (1989) *The Stranger*, trans. M. Ward, New York: Random House.

—— (2012) *The Outsider*, trans. S. Smith, London: Penguin.

Cover, R.M. (1983) '*Nomos* and Narrative', *Harvard Law Review*, 97: 4–68.

Derrida, J. (1993) *Spectres de Marx*, Paris: Galilée.

Epstein, R.A. and Sharkey, C.M. (2012) *Cases and Materials on Torts*, 10th edn, New York: Wolters Kluwer.

Gadamer, H.-G. (1978) 'Hermeneutics as a Theoretical and Practical Task', trans. F.G. Lawrence, in *The Gadamer Reader: A Bouquet of the Later Writings*, R.E. Palmer (ed.), Evanston, IL: Northwestern University Press, 2007.

—— (1984) 'Text and Interpretation', trans. D.J. Schmidt and R. Palmer, in D.P. Michelfelder and R.E. Palmer (eds) *Dialogue and Deconstruction: The Gadamer–Derrida Encounter*, Albany, NY: SUNY Press, 1990.

—— (1986a) *Wahrheit und Methode*, 5th edn, Tübingen: Mohr Siebeck.

—— (1986b) *Truth and Method*, trans. J. Weinsheimer and D.G. Marshall, 2nd rev. Eng. edn, New York: Continuum, 2004.

—— (1986c) *Vérité et méthode*, trans. P. Fruchon, J. Grondin and G. Merlio, 2nd Fr. edn, Paris: Éditions du Seuil, 1996.

—— (1990) '*Destruktion* and Deconstruction', trans. G. Waite and R. Palmer, in D.P. Michelfelder and R.E. Palmer (eds) *Dialogue and Deconstruction: The Gadamer–Derrida Encounter*, Albany, NY: SUNY Press, 1990.

—— (1992) 'Interview: The 1920s, the 1930s, and the Present: National Socialism, German History, and German Culture', in D. Misgeld and G. Nicholson (eds) *Hans Georg Gadamer on Education, History, and Poetry*, trans. L. Schmidt and M. Reuss, Albany, NY: SUNY Press.

—— (1994) 'Hermeneutics Tracking the Trace (On Derrida)', trans. R.E. Palmer, in *The Gadamer Reader: A Bouquet of the Later Writings*, R.E. Palmer (ed.), Evanston, IL: Northwestern University Press, 2007.

—— (2007) *The Gadamer Reader: A Bouquet of the Later Writings*, R.E. Palmer (ed.), Evanston, IL: Northwestern University Press.

Goodrich, P. (1986) *Reading the Law*, Oxford: Blackwell.

Humboldt, W. von (1836) *On Language: On the Diversity of Human Language Construction and its Influence on the Mental Development of the Human Species*, trans. P. Heath, Cambridge: Cambridge University Press, 1988.

Janz, B. (2015) 'Hermeneutics and Intercultural Understanding', in J. Malpas and H.-H. Gander (eds) *The Routledge Companion to Hermeneutics*, London: Routledge.

Krygier, M. (1986) 'Law as Tradition', *Law and Philosophy*, 5: 237–62.

Mertz, E. (2007) *The Language of Law School*, Oxford: Oxford University Press.

Messud, C. (2014) 'A New "L'Étranger"', *The New York Review of Books*, 5 June. Online. Available at www.nybooks.com/articles/archives/2014/jun/05/camus-new-letranger (accessed on 30 June 2016).

Ortega y Gasset, J. (1946) 'La reviviscencia de los cuadros', in *Obras completas*, 2nd edn, vol. VIII, Madrid: Alianza Editorial, 1994.

Post, R.C. (1989) 'The Social Foundations of Privacy: Community and Self in the Common Law Tort', *California Law Review*, 77: 957–1010.

Prosser, W. (1960) 'Privacy', *California Law Review*, 48: 383–423.

Schmidt, L.K. (2014) 'Intercultural Understanding in Philosophical Hermeneutics', in M. Xie (ed.) *The Agon of Interpretations: Towards a Critical Intercultural Hermeneutics*, Toronto: University of Toronto Press.

Smith, Sandra (2013) 'On Translating Camus' [an interview with Sam Jordison and various Internet users], *The Guardian*, 28 November. Online. Available at www.theguardian.com/books/booksblog/2013/nov/28/translating-camus-the-outsider-sandra-smith (accessed on 30 June 2016).

Vasilache, A. (2003) *Interkulturelles Verstehen nach Gadamer und Foucault*, Frankfurt: Campus Verlag.

Vitkin, M. (1995) 'The "Fusion of Horizons" on Knowledge and Alterity: Is Inter-Traditional Understanding Attainable Through Situated Transcendence?', *Philosophy and Social Criticism*, 21: 57–76.

Wacks, R. (2006) 'Why There Will Never Be an English Common Law Privacy Tort', in M. Richardson and A. Kenyon (eds) *New Directions in Privacy Law*, Cambridge: Cambridge University Press.

Whitman, J.Q. (2004) 'The Two Western Cultures of Privacy: Dignity Versus Liberty', *Yale Law Journal*, 113: 1151–221.

Part II

Concurrences

Chapter 5

Ricœur's legal hermeneutics

Mapping the non-place of critique

Fabien Girard

Hans-Georg Gadamer's philosophical hermeneutics (1986) heralds a rehabilitation of tradition, a notion which has made it possible to confer new meaning to various devalued concepts in modern philosophy such as authority and prejudice. Gadamer thus speaks of positive prejudices (ibid.: 295–8). He has in mind prejudgments that are authoritative – that constitute 'binding precedents' (Grondin 1993: 176) – inasmuch as these anterior understandings construct and shape tradition: they speak to everyone within a given community. For example, judges applying the law (not unlike other jurists) are pre-oriented to follow the beliefs prevailing within the legal community to which they belong. Ultimately, then, judicial decisions materialize as 'the historically proven *topoi* of a received ethos' (Habermas 1992: 207). It remains the case, though, that this pre-understanding ought not to be allowed to prevail over the ethics that must regulate hermeneutic activities. Indeed, what is uttered must be challenged, and what is implicit and hiding in silence within what is said must be disclosed. It follows that understanding, which inevitably takes place in language, cannot eschew dialogue. Now, such dialogue is infinite. As far as law is concerned, this dialogical dynamic must entail a constant questioning of legal traditions and texts.

Within modern pluralistic societies, however, Jürgen Habermas is concerned that dialogue may not prove adequate to guard against ideologies and to protect from the appearance of consensus: the kind of pseudo-consensus that would have been achieved through coercion (1992: 200). Importantly, Paul Ricœur offers a response, which specifically answers Habermas's warning. Ricœur's rejoinder appears in the seminal scholarly writings he has dedicated to the hermeneutics of the text rather than in the writings he has expressly devoted to law. Aspects of Ricœur's retort can be discerned in his famous essays on ideology, especially 'Hermeneutics and the Critique of Ideology' (1973) and 'Science and Ideology' (1974). But Ricœur's stance is more readily visible in his reaction to Gadamer's hermeneutics and to what he regards as the main aporia tainting Gadamer's philosophical endeavour (1975b: 68–71).

The impasse at issue is itself derived from an earlier perplexity lying at the core of Martin Heidegger's philosophy of being: the impossible shift from ontology to epistemology. According to Ricœur, Gadamer succeeded in circumventing

Heidegger's limitation by drawing upon the 'scandal constituted, at the level of modern consciousness, by the sort of *alienating distanciation* (*Verfremdung*) that seems to him to be the presupposition of [. . .] [the human] sciences' (1975b: 68, emphasis original). Indeed, in Gadamer's view, the methodology deployed by the humanities inevitably implies 'a distancing, which in turn expresses the destruction of the primordial relation of belonging (*Zugehörigkeit*)', in the absence of which there is no possible relation to the historical (ibid.). Gadamer's whole approach in the hermeneutic field has effectively been shaped and framed by his attempt to demonstrate this primordial relation of belonging in the three spheres where the hermeneutic experience obtains: the aesthetic, the historical and the linguistic.

If, however, as Ricœur indicates, understanding in all fields depends on the relation of belonging and on the struggle against estrangement and alienating distanciation, it remains to be seen to what extent a critical instance can be grounded '*into a consciousness of belonging that is expressly defined by the rejection of distanciation*' (ibid.: 70, emphasis original). All of Ricœur's undertakings lie in this proposition: *a critical instance is possible if and only if the historical consciousness* ('the principle of history of effect' or '*Wirkungsgeschichte*') (Gadamer 1986: 299) *is not confined to repudiating this distanciation, but applies itself to assuming it* (Ricœur 1975b: 70).

It would be an exaggeration to contend that Gadamer's thought does not include some elements of distanciation. Ricœur notices these in many parts of Gadamer's work, such as in the 'principle of history of effect' (Gadamer 1986: 299) and in the concept of the 'fusion of horizons' (ibid.: 305). Not coincidentally, however, it is mainly in the concept of '*Sprachlichkeit*' (Weinsheimer and Marshall 2004: xvii), or the 'linguistic element' of language (Grondin 2003: 127), and in the idea of the *dialogue that we are* that Ricœur sees the figure of the word of the text unfolding (1975b: 70–1). Through the interpretation of the signs, texts and works in which our cultural heritage is embedded, we are experiencing, developing and expanding our belonging to tradition. Also, lingual experience operates its mediating function 'only because the interlocutors fade away in the face of the things said that, as it were, direct the dialogues' (ibid.: 71). It is thus the '*matter of the text*' that enables us 'to communicate at a distance', the '*matter of the text*' that 'belongs neither to its author nor to its reader' (ibid., emphasis original). This 'matter of the text', what Ricœur calls the 'world of the text' (1983: 10), and the distanciation that the notion entails, is maintained throughout Ricœur's endeavour, forms the backbone of his work and informs his later writings, namely those on translation (2004) and, above all, on legal hermeneutics (1995b; 1995d; 1996).

All the secondary concepts come to graft themselves on 'the world of the text' which forms the nerve centre of his philosophy: *sense* and *reference*, *event* and *meaning*, *explanation* and *understanding*, *interpretation* and *argumentation*, to which may be added the pair '*self*' and '*foreign*' (or the '*other*'). But before we are able to move towards these *ancillary* concepts – and principally those that might be of interest in the understanding of Ricœur's writings on legal hermeneutics – it appears necessary to dwell upon this first moment that Ricœur calls '*critical instance*' (1975b: 70, emphasis original), the very moment of the advent of the 'world of the text' and the breakthrough of distanciation (1). Strong emphasis will then be placed on what can be seen as the genuine formalization of the 'critical moment', which is grounded on the dialectic explanation/understanding (2). The last section will focus on Ricœur's efforts to transpose 'critical instance' to the legal field, thereby bringing life to a new dialectic between interpretation and argumentation (3).

1. The advent of the critical instance: the world of the text and distanciation

We need first to note, in a summary fashion, the eminent position held by text in Ricœur's theory of interpretation. In this respect, special attention is to be paid to one of his greatest hermeneutic works, 'The Hermeneutical Function of Distanciation' (1975a: 72–85), in which he contends *ab initio* that 'the text is much more than a particular case of intersubjective communication: it is the paradigm of distanciation in communication' (ibid.: 72); a proposition which reflects what he says a little later about the 'world of the work' ('*monde de l'œuvre*') where he locates the 'center of gravity of the hermeneutical question' (ibid.: 73). The importance of the text is to be gauged against the productive function of distanciation that it fulfils – a function which helps overcome the alternative between the 'methodological' stance (at the expense of the 'ontological density of the reality we study') and the attitude of 'truth' (to the detriment of the 'objectivity of the human sciences') (ibid.: 72).

It would be a mistake, though, to equate text with writing. The sought distanciation does not stem from writing, but is rooted in a deep dialectic which characterizes every form of discourse, including oral discourse, and in which must be searched the 'roots of all subsequent dialectic' (ibid.: 73): the dialectic of *event* and *meaning*. If we say that the discourse is an *event*, it is because, unlike language (the speech or the mere 'sign') – which is virtual and outside the world, without a subject and closed on itself (language refers only to others signs within a system) – discourse is realized 'temporally and in the present'; it 'refers back to its speaker by means of a complex set of indicators' (thereby we can say it is 'self-referential'); finally, it opens up a world by *saying something about something* (ibid.: 74). Furthermore, the messages embedded in discourse are exchanged, thereby assuming an interlocutor to whom the discourse is addressed and supposing a temporal dimension – the *dialogue* (ibid.: 75).

But far from being only an event, *the setting into motion of our linguistic competence*, discourse is called upon to surpass itself through the process of understanding, and it is not the event, the fleeting advent of discourse, that we want to grasp, but its long-lasting meaning. Even so, it remains crucial to clarify in what way the discourse as meaning has linked its fate with the phenomenon of fixation: writing does not fix the event of speaking, but the intentional exteriorization (intentionality) of language, the noema of the saying, its meaning (Ricœur 1975a: 76, 78; Ricœur 1976e: 27). As Ricœur states, '[o]nly when the *sagen* – the "saying" – has become *Aus-sage*, e-nunciation, only then, is discourse accomplished as discourse in the full expression of its nuclear dialectic' (1976e: 27, emphasis original). This gives us a hint of what is added to discourse when it passes from speaking to writing: fixation deeply impacts the schema of communication, chiefly on the 'factors' of communicative discourse identified by Roman Jakobson (1960), as a set of relationships between message and medium, message and speaker, message and hearer, message and code, and message and reference (Ricœur 1976e: 26).

Three relationships deserve special consideration. First, in the relationship between *message* and *speaker*, writing gives the text autonomy with respect to the authorial intention. Henceforth, textual meaning ('*signification verbale*') and psychological meaning 'have different destinies' (Ricœur 1975a: 80; see also Ricœur 1976e: 29). Likewise, while unfolding a new 'world', the text may sever the bonds that hold it to the sociological and psychological conditions of its production – psychological and sociological decontextualization and recontextualization are thus made possible (Ricœur 1975a: 80). More precisely, the end of the dialogical relation at the core of orality enables the deployment of what Ricœur calls the 'semantic autonomy of the text' (1976e: 29). Second, the transformation implied by writing impinges upon the relation between *message* and *hearer*, now *reader* since written discourse is able to generate its own audience, a virtually infinite readership (Ricœur 1975a: 80). This is the point at which consequences of the semantic autonomy of the text become noticeable: due to the *distanciation* the dialogue breaks down, and a work of *appropriation* – that is, a work of *interpretation* – becomes necessary: 'Hermeneutics begins where dialogue ends' (Ricœur 1976e: 32).

Fundamental to Ricœur's account of the dialectic distanciation/appropriation is the fact that, along with the autonomy of the text, *distanciation* cannot be seen at all as the result of methodology and 'hence something superfluous and parasitical' (Ricœur 1975a: 80). Rather, Ricœur declares, that it is the very condition of interpretation: '*Verfremdung* is not only what understanding must overcome but also what conditions it' (ibid.: 81, emphasis original).

At this point, there appears the third transformation, which impacts upon the pair message/reference. This enables Ricœur to introduce his basic hermeneutic concept of 'the world of the text' built upon Gottlob Frege's distinction between *sense* and *reference* (1892). This is precisely in that respect that the main discrepancy between Ricœur's and Gadamer's thoughts may be noticed. Along the lines of Plato (Grondin 1993: 257–61), Gadamer argues that language cannot be confined to a monologue (Gadamer 1986: 356–63, 393–5). Indeed, '[a] pronouncement [. . .] necessarily contains unstated presuppositions that it has neither the time, nor the patience, nor the capacity to spell out (or recall), but to which we must force ourselves to listen if we wish to understand what seeks to express itself' (Grondin 2003: 130). Whilst belonging to the realm of dialogue, language can only be understood as the reply to a question. Accordingly, all writing is to be seen as a kind of estrangement (Gadamer 1986: 394–5).

For this kind of pre-critical approach to language, Ricœur substitutes an iconic understanding of writing: the inscription of a thought is emphatically not to be conceived as supplying an image of reality without relief or contrast (along the lines of Plato's *eikon*, his rhetorical term for copies and imitations), but rather, bearing in mind Dagognet's insights on writing and iconography (1973), as a sort of 'iconic augmentation' of reality (Ricœur 1976e: 40). As for painting, whose strategy is to 'resist the entropic tendency of ordinary vision' (ibid.: 40), '[w]riting, in the limited sense of the word, is a particular case of iconicity' (ibid.: 42). The text (writing) creates a genuine distanciation and an objectification that passes through the structures of the work (of discourse). The breadth of the transformation must not be overlooked. When the discourse is oral, there is not much difficulty to gain access to reference, insofar as the discourse has retained its ostensive function. Writing, however, and most of all the structure of the work, distorts reference 'to the point of rendering it entirely problematic' (Ricœur 1975a: 82). The abolition of a first-order reference – abolition almost perfectly achieved by some kinds of fictions and poetry – frees a second-order reference, '*which reaches the world not only at the level of manipulable objects but at the level that Husserl designated by the expression* Lebenswelt *[life-world] and Heidegger by the expression* being-in-the-world' (ibid.: 82, emphasis added). What is thus to be interpreted in a text is 'a *proposed world* that I could inhabit and wherein I could project one of my ownmost possibilities' (ibid.: 83, emphasis original). In no way is the subject of interpretation another person – his/her inner state of mind when he/she brought his/her work into being – but a *pro-ject*, a new way to inhabit the world. Regarding legal interpretation, this means that:

> As one would say in the terms of a nonintentional theory of the literary text, the meaning of a law, if it has one, is to be sought in the text and its intertextual connections, and not in the will of a legislator, juridically symmetrical with the intention attributed to the author of a literary text.
>
> (Ricœur 1995b: 112)

Let us not forget the basic idea. In any event, there is no room for comprehension/understanding in the absence of two forms of distanciation: distanciation as the result of writing and distanciation generated by the objective structures of the work, that can never be overcome since they constitute the very condition of understanding. As Ricœur convincingly contends throughout his writings on translation, the *other* (the *foreign*, the *stranger*) lies at the core of any instance of understanding even as the process entails a labour of mourning in the sense of the Freudian notion of 'working through' or '*Durcharbeitung*' (Kearney 2006: xv; Ricœur 1999: 23): understanding renounces first and foremost the possibility of really making 'one's own' what was 'alien'. However, this does not mean that all effort is unavailing. On the contrary, the awareness of the *constitutive nature* of estrangement is a productive factor, 'the dynamic counterpart of our need, our interest, and our effort to overcome cultural estrangement' (Ricœur 1976e: 43). The parallel with Ricœur's notion of 'linguistic hospitality' is enlightening. Against the background of Émile Benveniste's book, *Le Vocabulaire des institutions indo-européennes* (1969: 87–101), which underlines *hospitality*'s complex etymology and shows how the term ranges from *hospes* (to host) to *hostis* (hostility), one may highlight, as Ricœur indeed does to a certain extent (1999: 24–9; 2001b), *translation* and *understanding*'s complex trajectories.[1] In effect, these processes operate at once through the ongoing dialogue between self and stranger (Kearney 2006: xvii) and via the *dialectic between distanciation and appropriation* (Steiner 1998: 314–5). However, the emphasis put on strangeness – even 'dialogue' incorporates this idea, since *dia-legein* means 'welcoming the difference' (Kearney 2006: xv) – leaves an indelible mark of foreignness (*overexposure*), which paradoxically requires a last moment of distanciation.

Here lies the last hermeneutics movement identified by Ricœur: the subjectivity of the reader can come to itself only insofar as his/her subjectivity is 'placed in suspense, unrealized, potentialized', just as the world of the text 'is real insofar as it is imaginary' (Ricœur 1975a: 85). The metamorphosis of the ego thus implies a moment of distanciation up to and including in the relation of 'self to itself' (ibid.; see also 1976a: 94–5). This last moment of distanciation allows, from Ricœur's viewpoint, *the advent of a real critical instance and the response to the claim for internal critique.* As Ricœur argues in 'The Hermeneutical Function of Distanciation': 'The critique of ideology is the necessary detour that self-understanding must take if the latter is to be formed by the matter of the text and not by the prejudices of the reader' (1975a: 85). The concept of distanciation, understood as a condition of understanding, and above all analyzed as an inseparable part of the advent of a critical instance, leads to the couple explanation/understanding. Placed in a dialectical relationship, these two concepts ensure the formalization of critical instance.

2. The formalization of the critical moment: the dialectic explanation/understanding

As Ricœur recalls, it is to German Romanticism (Romanticist Hermeneutics), and especially to Dilthey, that we must attribute the clear distinction, replicated on the ontological plane (separating *Nature* and *Spirit*), between explanation (pertaining to the natural sciences – *Naturwissenschaften*) and understanding (belonging to the human sciences – *Geisteswissenschaften*) (1976b: 73). Contrariwise, he contends, explanation and understanding should be articulated dialectically and arranged symmetrically with respect to the dialectic of *event* and *meaning* (ibid.: 73, 79; Zaccaria 2003: 539–40). Understanding would thus correspond to the event (the 'intentional unity of discourse') and explanation to verbal and textual autonomy – that is, the objective meaning of discourse, the structure of the text (Ricœur 1976b: 71–2). As to interpretation, it would be the result, or more specifically the dynamic, encapsulating the whole dialectical process (ibid.: 74).

It remains to elucidate the working of the sophisticated dialectical relationship. The first stage takes the form of a 'guess', a kind of supposition that is followed by a validation process. This 'guess' is *the original act of understanding*, if only because, owing to the rupture with the mental meaning, the unfolding of the semantic autonomy, '[t]he text is mute' (ibid.: 75). In this confrontation between text and reader, the former is in some way silenced while the latter must speak for both of them. Indeed, within a completely de-psychologized and genuinely semantic space, the *intention of the author is out of reach* (ibid.: 76).

This guess and the subject thereof are clearly visible through three main phases that mark this initial approach to the text. The first consists of construing the text as a 'whole' – that is, a 'work' whose creating process is not linear but cumulative (ibid.). As a kind of multi-scalar ensemble generating intricate plays of resonance, the work displays a sort of original plurivocity far more complex than the polysemy of words and the ambiguity of sentences. Such plurivocity can be overcome only by resorting to the type of judgment that Immanuel Kant has theorized in the *Critique of Judgment*: the whole must be derived from the parts and the parts from the whole (ibid.: 77; see also 1971: 154).

Moreover, being the result of *technê*, which only generates individuals (whereas *epistêmê*, according to Aristotle's classification, grasps species), the 'work of discourse' requires a specific type of judgment that Ricœur (1976b: 77) is tempted, once again, to relate to the Kantian judgment of taste (which is equally about individuals). The individualization of the text is still a guess and it seems very much like the judgment that Luigi Pareyson placed at the centre of his theory of interpretation and whose aim was to 'grasp the reality of a form through the fortunate correspondence between one of its aspects and the subjective perspective from which it is being considered' (Pareyson 1961: 226; Ricœur 1976b: 77–8).

Finally, the text and the work of discourse open up new propositions of world. Whilst abolishing the ostensive character of reference, the text frees itself from the reality referred to by (oral) discourse. Affected by this, the referential function of the text yet offers a new world unfolded by the secondary meaning. Thus marked by plurivocity, it lends itself to several readings, but it is nevertheless still 'ruled by the prescriptions of meaning belonging to the margins of potential meaning surrounding the semantic nucleus of the work' (Ricœur 1976b: 78). It remains that these prescriptions provided for by the text need to be 'guessed' before they can regulate the activity of interpretation (ibid.).

If there is no method to lead this 'guess', procedures exist for validation through which 'we test our guesses' (ibid.). The articulation of the first dialectical movement between *erklären* and *verstehen* that draws upon these procedures for validation is one of these procedures. Expressly relying on E.D. Hirsch's works (1967: 63), Ricœur describes the pre-explanatory phase as being built upon a logic of probability and one that never leads to empirical verification (1976b: 99, n. 2). The aim is only to show that 'an interpretation is more probable in the light of what we know' (ibid.: 78). Interestingly, in Ricœur's view, the validation process pertains to an argumentative discipline that is comparable to the juridical procedures used in legal interpretation (ibid.).

The second interpretive phase ranges from explanation to understanding, while focusing on another polarity in the structure of discourse: meaning and reference. Reference is the *full exteriorization of the discourse, in that sense that meaning is not only the ideal object intended (the noema), but also the 'actual reality aimed at by the utterance'* (ibid.: 80, emphasis added). As the text no longer refers to a situation commonly shared by the writer and the reader because of the semantic autonomy, language thus gives itself a world that is merely designated. Thus a 'complete abstraction of the surrounding reality becomes possible' (ibid.). The suspension of the ostensive reference sets up a first stance exploiting the text in its closed, worldless dimension. This suspension allows for a real explanatory attitude, which was praised by the structural schools of the literary criticism, and which relies on the structural method reordered for semiology (ibid.: 80–1).

Regardless of the practicability of the transposition, which Ricœur doubts, an explicative phase is required in order to compensate a 'highlighting' ('*Überhellung*') (Gadamer 1986: 388) produced by the initial impetus of the guess. This remains an intermediate step falling between a 'naive' or 'surface' interpretation (Ricœur 1976b: 87) and a new form of interpretation that unfolds, the 'deep' interpretation. Here lies a second interpretative stance, this time completely dependent upon the *pro-ject* or *power-to-be* ('*pouvoir-être*') (Ricœur 1975a: 83). There is a sort of distanciation underpinning any work of discourse, the property of which is to open up a new world that the subject cannot grasp except by a movement of appropriation. Appropriation is made possible through the 'foreignness' brought about by the second-rank reference; it is always a 'critical moment' of 'unrealisation' or 'potentialisation' for the subjectivity of the reader – a moment of disappropriation (ibid.: 85).

The formalization of the 'critical instance' is achieved through the dialectic explanation/understanding that calls for two 'levels' of scrutiny. The first introduces a procedure for validation of the initial guesses made on the basis of an early overall grasp of the text as a singular work. The second stems from the structure of the text and operates by retrieving *possible worlds* from its codified nucleus. Reading is then led or guided by protocols, akin to grammar codes, to the narrative systems set out by the structural analysis (Ricœur 1977: 125–6; Zaccaria 2003: 540; Cananzi 2008: 82–3). Finally, an ultimate *critical* phase is implied by, and included in, the hermeneutic movement of appropriation. This is the moment where the subject/reader, exposed to the world-proposition revealed by the reference of the text, is placed in suspense before coming back to the road of self-comprehension. It remains to be seen to what extent this model has been transposed to legal interpretation.

3. The transposition of the 'critical instance' in the legal field: the dialectic interpretation/argumentation

Ricœur's approach to legal interpretation is entirely driven by his works on the hermeneutics of text, and it is revealed through three works that he specifically devoted to legal hermeneutics (1995d; 1995b; 1996). All of these three works are placed under the aegis of the dialectic explanation/understanding (Ricœur 1995b: 110; Zaccaria 1998: 133–4; Zaccaria 2003: 546). The dialectic is central to the concept of legal interpretation which as a process is the result of the opposing discoveries between the spontaneity of understanding and the constraints and rules presiding over explanation. This polarity adopts different forms in the legal field: explanation becomes argumentation, and interpretation (previously an all-encompassing concept designating a kind of intermediary dynamic) takes the place of understanding (Ricœur 1995b: 110). The dialectical play here is essential. It features a confrontation of inventiveness or creativeness on the one hand, and constraints and the *reign of norms* on the other – in sum, the direct opposition between interpretation and argumentation. In Ricœur's view (1995d: 181), the two sides of this dialectical tension are alternately praised in Dworkin's theory (1985) and in the works of theoreticians of legal argumentation such as Robert Alexy (1978) and Manuel Atienza (2006).

As Ricœur himself indicates, the model of 'interpretation' is thus to be found in Dworkin. Interpretation is, however, far from being of primary concern to Dworkin's theory of law. All his efforts are focused on the refutation of H.L.A. Hart's *No Right Answer* thesis, and all his energy is devoted to working out a theory that would adequately explain the situation of the judge (Dworkin 1985: 119–20) when confronted with a so-called *hard case* (Ricœur 1995d: 181–2). But theory of interpretation is soon encountered on this route to analytical positivism as Dworkin was not indifferent to the law and literature movement.[2] He found in the typologies and techniques of literary critics, especially within the model of the literary text and the sub-model of the narrative text, all the tools necessary to tackle the *No Right Answer* issue (Ricœur 1995b: 112). For Ricœur (1995d: 182), this encounter with the general theory of the literary text is of paramount importance since it is through the sub-model of the narrative text that Dworkin can introduce the idea that every interpretation appeals to some concepts of rightness or fittingness, of 'adjustment between the proposed interpretation of a difficult passage and the overall interpretation of the work' (1995b: 113; see also 1995d: 182). Behind this central idea of the search for a 'fit', Ricœur discerns the hermeneutic principle of 'the mutual interpretation of parts and whole' at work (1995b: 113).

It is thus no great surprise to find again that the 'guess' was at the heart of the first movement characterizing the dialectic explaining/arguing. Resorting to a wording very close to that used in respect of the guess, Ricœur contends, as regards the concept of 'fit':

> [T]he evaluation of a relation of fittingness, of rightness, of adjustment escapes the alternative between demonstrability and arbitrariness. We are on a plane where controversy is certainly possible, but where a critic can claim that one interpretation is better than another, is more probable, more plausible, more acceptable (where all these terms need to be further clarified). (Ibid.)

Similarly, for the essay on explanation and understanding, a reference is naturally added to Kant's reflective judgment, thereby reinforcing the kinship between the essays on general hermeneutics (1995b: 111; 1996: 196) and those on legal hermeneutics. However, Ricœur remarks that while forcefully tackling the 'discretionary power' thesis, Dworkin may have neglected the moment when his theory should have been followed by a genuine reflection on argumentation (1995b: 113–4; 1995d: 183).

For Ricœur, this theory of argumentation must be sought through the work of Atienza and, more specifically, that of Alexy. It rests on the 'claim to correctness' ('*présomption de rectitude*') implied by the final judgment and, beforehand, by the norms governing the exchange of arguments (argumentation process) (Ricœur 1995d: 184). Argumentation is thus inscribed in the larger circle of the *normative practical discourse* – that is, a discourse 'on the whole domain of human interaction', which is 'considered from the point of view of the norms that govern it and that, as norms, make a claim to correctness' (Ricœur 1995b: 116). That is where we witness the encounter and linkage between interpretation and 'justification' (Ricœur 1995d: 184), echoing the polarity between 'guess' and 'procedures for validation' within the dialectic explanation/understanding. The kinship between this 'justification' and the 'procedures for validation' is all the more evident as Ricœur, purporting to illustrate the latter, uses an example drawn from judicial procedure: it 'is an argumentative discipline comparable to the judicial procedures used in legal interpretation, a logic of uncertainty and of qualitative probability' (1971: 155).

How should the 'claim to correctness' be defined? In fact, the correctness and the rightness of the final judgment (or of any normative utterance whatsoever) rely upon the possible universalization of an argument and its aptitude to be taken as acceptable by all the parties concerned (Ricœur 1995b: 117; Habermas 1973: 108). In the language of Habermas's 'consensus theory of truth', it expresses the thesis of the universal consensus or the potential agreement at the level of an unlimited and unconstrained community (universal pragmatics of discourse) (Ricœur 1995b; Habermas 1973). The close link between this argumentative phase and the procedures for validation lying at the core of Ricœur's more general works on hermeneutics leads to the further strengthening of this idea according to which a 'critical moment' is at stake. As Ricœur mentions explicitly:

> [T]he ideal of a potential agreement contains within itself the conditions for a rational critique of more or less empirical agreements, due more or less to

extortion, stemming from coalitions of interests, and in general representative of any factual equilibrium between conflicting powers.

(1995b: 117)

More significant is the fact that this authentic moment of *distanciation* also adopts a *very strong ethical dimension*. To understand it fully, it is of prime importance to underline where Ricœur locates what he calls the 'judiciary circle'. Standing as an intermediate rationality between moral rationality and the rationality of state, 'so bound up with violence', the judiciary circle is a region in which 'the presupposition is precisely the break between discourse and violence'. And, Ricœur adds, 'the trial is, in this regard, the privileged place for an ordered and ritualized discussion' (1995a: 118). This statement undoubtedly comes in the wake of the 'little ethics' formulated in *Oneself as Another* (1990: 169–296). Indeed, in a move that *The Just* substantiates (1995c: xii; see also 1991), Ricœur has endeavoured to frame a province of intermediary rationality personified by a judge placed between moral behaviour and politics (Zaccaria 1998: 135; Lesaar 2003: 552). But let us examine why Ricœur attaches so much importance to the judiciary. In his view, the judiciary is paradigmatic for the law in that it is faced with conflict and must ensure that word prevails over violence. The ethical aim is of paramount importance since the judiciary purports to guarantee social peace and cooperation. In other words, the judicial body reaffirms the fundamental act whereby the political community has made the choice to become a cooperative body (1996: 192). But this is an act that 'has not taken place', 'a contract which has not been contracted', which appears only in 'political awareness, in retrospection, and reflection' (Ricœur 1964: 251–2; see also Ricœur 1990: 197; Abel 1996: 51–2, 81–2). As Christopher Watkin writes, 'there is no community without contract, but also no contract outside community, for the original situation exists only ever as a fictional retrojection from within the community. Between community and contract is an irreducible aporia of time' (2009: 116). This act of foundation has nothing to do with the violent proclamation of a kind of iron law, an 'incontrovertible imperative'. In constant search for its legitimacy, its reassertion, the community must continuously – through the *word* – 'engage in the to and fro of continual challenges to its "just distance"' (ibid.).

It then becomes self-evident as to why so much emphasis is placed on the figure of third-party-ness. The judge in particular, who gives flesh and bones to this idea of the third party, can interpose a just distance – that is, a fair balance between proximity (appropriation) and distance – that we also find in friendship and love relationships (Zaccaria 2003: 544–5; see also Ricœur 1995c: xiii) and therefore can ground, by retrojection, the foundational project of the community.

But this appeal to justice and fairness is all the more important as it directly fills a gap in the monopoly on the use of legitimate violence at the judiciary level. Ricœur is very clear that 'at the point of imposing the sentence, this part of justice [inflicting the sentence] is at the same time a word of force and, hence, in a certain measure, one of violence' (2001c: 229). Insofar as the legitimacy of the political contract and the ethical project of aiming at the 'good life' with and for others in just institutions (Ricœur 1990: 172; Zaccaria 1998: 135) must be continually reaffirmed through proceedings every time 'claims of unjust distribution' are asserted (Watkin 2009: 116), legal interpretation cannot be self-sufficient and *must integrate, for its own sake, the notion of validity*. Without this idea of validity, one leaves the field of the law (Ricœur 1996: 194; 1995b: 120–1).

Now that we are aware of the need for legitimacy at the political and judicial levels, we can return to the rules of universal pragmatics and ask the question as to whether the rule of the proceedings are sufficient to ensure the correctness of a judgment. Let us recall that discourse ethics rests upon only a few rules that are distinguished depending on whether they (1) regulate the entry into discourse; (2) apply to the ongoing discussion itself; or (3) govern the end of the discussion (Ricœur 1995b: 118). Even a superficial review shows that if legal argumentation is a *species* of the *genus* general practical discourse, it has significant limitations with respect to the rules of the universal pragmatics of discourse (Ricœur 2001c: 118). First of all, judicial discussion occurs in a very specific institutional framework (tribunals and courts) in which not every question is open to debate. Second, even if some progress has been made over the past few years through European Court of Human Rights case law, procedural roles are not equally distributed, especially in criminal matters. Third, deliberation is subjected to proceedings rules and must intervene in a very limited time (Ricœur 1995d: 186; 1995a: 118; 1995b: 120; 1996: 195; Zaccaria 1998: 137; 2003: 547). Finally, and most importantly, 'the discussion in the judicial instance does not end with an agreement and does not even aim at one, at least as a first approximation. Judgment means a decision and therefore a separation of the parties, instituting [. . .] a just distance between them' (Ricœur 1995b: 177). Inasmuch as these limitations widen the gap with the rules of universal pragmatics, there is no choice but to introduce a new interpretive step of the law in a very short period of time. Here, says Ricœur, is the time for innovation, *the critical moment where the interpretive part compensates the argumentative part* (2001a: 219). We find again the ultimate distanciation, the unrealization or potentialization of the reader, the distance in the relation *of self to itself* enabling the reinvention (innovation) of ego and a critical appraisal of oneself.

What accounts for the ultimate critical moment in the judicial field? To answer this question, we need to come back to the notion of 'place of justice' – this 'theatre of justice' that constitutes any court: a place defined, first of all, in contrast to revengeful and violent reactions that abolish the space between human bodies (Ricœur 1995c: xi). Conversely, the primary function of the trial process is to 'transfer conflicts from the sphere of violence to that of language and discourse' (Ricœur 2001c: 228). The judicial *praxis* is entirely designed to ensure a *just distance*, insofar as the 'trial is [. . .] the privileged place for an ordered and ritualized discussion' (Ricœur 1995a: 118).

What is more, as a 'web of ritualised relationships', the space of the law court is also a 'space' or web of narratives (Watkin 2009: 109; Lesaar 2003: 554–5) circulating within the trial, sometimes consensual, sometimes conflictual. The challenge is then to untangle this set of tightly woven threads of the history (the so-called 'facts in issue') so that the sentence can separate the protagonists. If it all starts with an 'assault of words and the competition of arguments' (Ricœur 1995a: 118), with the judicial account of the roots of conflict, then come the more general narratives produced by new and hard cases, which are directed at re-establishing a coherence disrupted by conflicts of interpretation (Watkin 2009: 109–10; Ricœur 1990: 322–3). Finally, as Watkin subtly indicates, the judicial ceremony, 'the unfolding ritual of the court itself', structures the proceedings as narrative: 'The form which the courtroom lends to a trial, with a definite beginning, a structured and procedurally constrained deliberation and the outcome (in most cases) of a verdict, itself reflects the coherence of the Aristotelian "well-wrought story"' (2009: 110). If proven correct, these findings show the space of the courtroom as a space of language or, more accurately, as a space of circulation of narratives. Yet these narratives are 'temporally' dependent upon two interpretive judgments, namely the 'judgment of law' and the 'judgment of fact' (ibid.: 110). The real difficulties lie in the former, if only because the space of the court as a web of narratives cannot exist without it. The judgment of law creates a topographic map of the factually possible, just as the text creates a new world (ibid.: 111).

But it remains to be seen 'where' this judgment is from. I have already highlighted that it is, in the first instance at least, a kind of pre-judgment, a pre-understanding, a 'guess' consisting in the grasp (which, at first glance, looks very much like a clumsy gesture) of statutes, precedents, academic writings, etc. (Zaccaria 2003: 548). The outcome is then subjected to the test of argumentation, which 'is meant to descend from the claimed validity of the admitted rules and norms to that of the specific case' (Ricœur 2001c: 227). At this point, we enter the realm of probable reasoning, and Ricœur recalls how the definition given is that of the Aristotelian *dialectic*, which the Stagirite tied with *rhetoric* (Giuliani 1972).

The argumentative step is the crux of the matter inasmuch as it tends to resolve the major issue of foundation or legitimation both of the monopoly of the use of violence by, and the normative power of, the state. Unfortunately, due to the unbridgeable gap between the model of 'open discussion' (universal pragmatics of discourse) and the reality of the proceedings, it is not sufficient in itself to sustain the deprivation of the right to seek revenge as well as the right to inflict a penalty to a wrongdoer. It must be strengthened by an interpretive step, the peak of the innovative aspect of the application of a law. Now, if we draw a parallel with the social contract, whose oblivion (*oubli*) has separated the community from its 'original position' (Ricœur 1989: 25), we can see clearly *where* this innovative interpretation comes from. *Like the community that is formed through the non-space (atopos) of the social contract (the act of foundation appears only by retrojection), the power of posing a 'just distance' emerges from the non-space of interpretation.*

This is the moment when subjectivity is 'placed in suspense', 'unrealized', the moment when *topos* and *atopos* form two planes that 'cannot be mapped in relation to each other' (Watkin 2009: 114); the 'critical moment' *par excellence* since, as Ricœur contends about utopia ('utopia' was coined by Thomas More to designate a 'no-place' – '*οὐ-τόπος*'), 'to imagine the non-judgment is to keep open the field of the possible' (Ricœur 1976c: 430; Watkin 2009: 131, n. 13; see also Ricœur 1976d: 25). This echoes Jacques Derrida's account of what justice is: 'that which must not wait', 'a madness'. The instant of decision is always a rush, a 'right away', an 'urgency' and a 'precipitation' (Derrida 1990: 27). Whatever the time devoted and the care given to the deliberation, the decision will 'be structurally finite', 'acting in the night of non-knowledge and non-rule' (ibid.: 28). The juridico-cognitive deliberation that precedes the judgment is interrupted when the non-space unfolds, where we must 'negotiate without the sort of rule that wouldn't have to be reinvented there where we are cast, where we find ourselves; but we must take it as far as possible, beyond the place we find ourselves and beyond the already identifiable zones of morality or politics or law' (ibid.).

Rooted in narrative identity and tradition, the pre-judgment or guess is immediately followed by the validation process or argumentative step that tests and challenges the outcomes of the 'naive' or 'surface' interpretation. The apex of the *hermeneutic arc* must then be reached to take a position in this retrojected non-space that frees creative imagination – an off-centre position that offers the opportunity to take a critical look at both the interpretative and argumentative steps. Each step is reflected in the philosophical tradition that might serve as a model: the *guess* is hermeneutic; the *argumentative step* is rhetorical; as to the *last step* – atopic, creative and structurally finite (*application of the law*) – it is, as we may put it, poetical (Ricœur 1986: 143; 1995a: 118; see also Watkin 2009: 118). These findings closely mirror the suggestion made by Ricœur, in a note at the end of 'Interpretation and/or Argumentation', to transpose the Kantian reflective judgment to the epistemology of judicial debate (1995b: 126) – what can but lead us seriously to reflect upon the idea of *a legal aesthetic*, the '*beautiful*' in legal hermeneutics (Cananzi 2008). They equally invite us to deepen our understanding of the links between poetics and utopia and therefore between space and non-space, interpretation (*sensu lato*) and atopy.

Endnotes

1 In his essay 'The Paradigm of Translation' (1999), Ricœur recognizes that translation is exemplary of hermeneutics (Davidson 2010). For a reinterpretation of Ricœur's works in the light of his essays on translation, see Jervolino (2008).
2 On the link between Dworkin and the so-called 'hermeneutic turn', see Dworkin (1986: 419–20, n. 15).

Bibliography

Abel, O. (1996) *Paul Ricœur: La promesse et la règle*, Paris: Michalon.

Alexy, R. (1978) *A Theory of Legal Argumentation: The Theory of Rational Discourse as Theory of Legal Justification*, Oxford: Oxford University Press, 2011.

Atienza, M. (2006) *El derecho como argumentación: concepciones de la argumentación*, Barcelona: Ariel.

Benveniste, É. (1969) *Le Vocabulaire des institutions indo-européennes*, vol. I, Paris: Éditions de Minuit.

Cananzi, D.M. (2008) *Interpretazione Alterità Giustizia. Il diritto e la questione del fondamento. Saggio sul pensiero di Paul Ricœur*, Turin: G. Giappichelli.

Dagognet, F. (1973) *Écriture et iconographie*, Paris: Vrin.

Davidson, S. (2010) 'Introduction: Translation as a Model of Interdisciplinarity', in S. Davidson (ed.) *Ricœur Across the Disciplines*, New York: Continuum.

Derrida, J. (1990) 'Force of Law: The "Mystical Foundation of Authority"', trans. M. Quaintance, in D. Cornell, M. Rosenfeld and D.G. Carlson (eds) *Deconstruction and the Possibility of Justice*, London: Routledge, 1992.

Dworkin, R. (1985) *A Matter of Principle*, Cambridge, MA: Harvard University Press.

—— (1986) *Law's Empire*, Cambridge, MA: Harvard University Press.

Frege, G. (1892) 'On Sense and Reference', in P. Geach and M. Black (eds) *Translations from the Philosophical Writings of Gottlob Frege*, trans. M. Black, Oxford: Blackwell, 1960.

Gadamer, H.-G. (1986) *Truth and Method*, trans. J. Weinsheimer and D.G. Marshall, 2nd rev. Eng. edn, New York: Continuum, 2004.

Giuliani, A. (1972) 'The Aristotelian Theory of the Dialectical Definition', *Philosophy & Rhetoric*, 5(3): 129–42.

Grondin, J. (1993) *L'horizon herméneutique de la pensée contemporaine*, Paris: Vrin.

—— (2003) *The Philosophy of Gadamer*, trans. K. Plant, London: Routledge, 2014.

Habermas, J. (1973) *Legitimation Crisis*, trans. T. McCarthy, Boston, MA: Beacon Press, 1975.

—— (1992) *Between Facts and Norms: Contributions to a Discourse Theory of Law and Democracy*, trans. W. Rehg, Cambridge, MA: MIT Press, 1996.

Hirsch, E.D. (1967) *Validity in Interpretation*, New Haven, CT: Yale University Press.

Jakobson, R. (1960) 'Closing Statement: Linguistics and Poetics', in T.A. Sebeok (ed.) *Style in Language*, Cambridge, MA: MIT Press.

Jervolino, D. (2008) 'Rethinking Ricœur: The Unity of His Work and the Paradigm of Translation', in D.M. Kaplan (ed.) *Reading Ricœur*, Albany, NY: SUNY Press.

Kearney, R. (2006) 'Introduction: Ricœur's Philosophy of Translation', in P. Ricœur, *On Translation*, trans. E. Brennan, London: Routledge.

Lesaar, H.R. (2003) 'Judging Action: Paul Ricœur's Contribution to the Legal Interpretation of Facts', in A. Wierciński (ed.) *Between Suspicion and Sympathy: Paul Ricœur's Unstable Equilibrium*, Toronto: Hermeneutic Press.

Pareyson, L. (1961) 'Interprétation et jugement', *Revue philosophique de la France et de l'Étranger*, 151: 221–36.

Ricœur, P. (1964) *History and Truth*, trans. C.R. Kelbley, Evanston, IL: Northwestern University Press, 2007.

—— (1971) 'The Model of the Text: Meaningful Action Considered as a Text', in *From Text to Action*, trans. K. Blamey and J.B. Thompson, New York: Continuum, 2008.
—— (1973) 'Hermeneutics and the Critique of Ideology', trans. J.B. Thompson, in *From Text to Action*, trans. K. Blamey and J.B. Thompson, New York: Continuum, 2008.
—— (1974) 'Science and Ideology', trans. J.B. Thompson, in *From Text to Action*, trans. K. Blamey and J.B. Thompson, New York: Continuum, 2008.
—— (1975a) 'The Hermeneutical Function of Distanciation', trans. J.B. Thompson, in *From Text to Action*, trans. K. Blamey and J.B. Thompson, New York: Continuum, 2008.
—— (1975b) 'The Task of Hermeneutics', trans. J.B. Thompson, in *From Text to Action*, trans. K. Blamey and J.B. Thompson, New York: Continuum, 2008.
—— (1976a) 'Conclusion', in *Interpretation Theory: Discourse and the Surplus of Meaning*, Fort Worth, TX: TCU Press, 1976.
—— (1976b) 'Explanation and Understanding', in *Interpretation Theory: Discourse and the Surplus of Meaning*, Fort Worth, TX: TCU Press, 1976.
—— (1976c) 'L'idéologie et l'utopie: deux expressions de l'imaginaire social', in *Du texte à l'action: Essais d'herméneutique II*, Paris: Éditions du Seuil, 1986.
—— (1976d) 'Ideology and Utopia as Cultural Imagination', *Philosophic Exchange*, 7: 17–28.
—— (1976e) 'Speaking and Writing', in *Interpretation Theory: Discourse and the Surplus of Meaning*, Fort Worth, TX: TCU Press, 1976.
—— (1977) 'Explanation and Understanding', trans. K. Blamey, in *From Text to Action*, trans. K. Blamey and J.B. Thompson, New York: Continuum, 2008.
—— (1983) 'On Interpretation', trans. K. Blamey, in *From Text to Action*, trans. K. Blamey and J.B. Thompson, New York: Continuum, 2008.
—— (1986) 'Rhetoric – Poetics – Hermeneutics', trans. R. Harvey, in M. Meyer (ed.) *From Metaphysics to Rhetoric*, Dordrecht: Kluwer, 1989.
—— (1989) 'Power and Violence', trans. L. Jones, *Theory, Culture & Society*, 2010, 27(5): 18–36.
—— (1990) *Oneself as Another*, trans. K. Blamey, Chicago, IL: University of Chicago Press, 1992.
—— (1991) 'Le juste entre le légal et le bon', in *Lectures 1: Autour du politique*, Paris: Éditions du Seuil.
—— (1995a) *Critique and Conviction: Conversations with François Azouvi and Marc de Launay*, trans. K. Blamey, Cambridge: Polity Press, 1998.
—— (1995b) 'Interpretation and/or Argumentation', in *The Just*, trans. D. Pellauer, Chicago, IL: University of Chicago Press, 2000.
—— (1995c) 'Preface', in *The Just*, trans. D. Pellauer, Chicago, IL: University of Chicago Press, 2000.
—— (1995d) 'Le problème de la liberté de l'interprète en herméneutique générale et en herméneutique juridique', in P. Amselek (ed.) *Interprétation et droit*, Brussels: Bruylant.
—— (1996) 'Conclusioni: Diritto, Interpretazione, Applicazione', *Ars interpretandi*: 191–7.
—— (1999) 'The Paradigm of Translation', in *On Translation*, trans. E. Brennan, London: Routledge, 2006.

—— (2001a) 'Decision Making in Medical and Judicial Judgments', in *Reflections on The Just*, trans. D. Pellauer, Chicago, IL: University of Chicago Press, 2007.
—— (2001b) 'Introduction', in *Reflections on The Just*, trans. D. Pellauer, Chicago, IL: University of Chicago Press, 2007.
—— (2001c) 'Justice and Vengeance', in *Reflections on The Just*, trans. D. Pellauer, Chicago, IL: University of Chicago Press, 2007.
—— (2004) *On Translation*, trans. E. Brennan, London: Routledge, 2006.
Steiner, G. (1998) *After Babel: Aspects of Language and Translation*, 3rd edn, Oxford: Oxford University Press.
Watkin, C. (2009) *Phenomenology or Deconstruction? The Question of Ontology in Maurice Merleau-Ponty, Paul Ricœur and Jean-Luc Nancy*, Edinburgh: Edinburgh University Press.
Weinsheimer, J. and Marshall, D.G. (2004) 'Translator's Preface', in H.-G. Gadamer, *Truth and Method*, trans. J. Weinsheimer and D.G. Marshall, 2nd rev. Eng. edn, New York: Continuum.
Zaccaria, G. (1998) 'Expliquer et comprendre, argumentation et interprétation dans la philosophie du droit de Paul Ricœur ?', in J.A. Barash and M. Delbraccio (eds) *La sagesse pratique. Autour de l'œuvre de Paul Ricœur*, Paris: Centre national de documentation pédagogique.
—— (2003) 'On Paul Ricœur's Philosophy of Law: Reflections on His Latest Works', in A. Wierciński (ed.) *Between Suspicion and Sympathy: Paul Ricœur's Unstable Equilibrium*, Toronto: Hermeneutic Press.

Chapter 6

Dworkin, interpretation and legal change

Paul Yowell

A distinctive feature of Ronald Dworkin's theory of law is that it denies that judges have legitimate power to change the law. Dworkin set forth this argument in different ways from his first essays on jurisprudence in the 1960s and 1970s to the end of his career. This chapter traces the development of that argument from his early work to *Law's Empire* (1986). Here Dworkin introduces the idea of law as an 'interpretive concept', and in making that case relies at a crucial turn on the hermeneutic theory of Hans-Georg Gadamer. Dworkin's theory of law as integrity developed in *Law's Empire* has a number of affinities with Gadamer and contains valuable insights into legal interpretation. I contend, however, that Dworkin is mistaken in trying to find the essence of law in interpretive and adjudicative processes. One symptom of this mistake is his failure to provide an adequate account of legal change.

I

Dworkin's argument that judges lack legitimate power to change the law would not be distinctive in the civil-law world, where it is widely viewed that the legislature is the legitimate source of law and that the judge's role is to apply it (Merryman 2007: 23–4). Whatever leeway judges may have in interpreting the law, orthodox theory holds that this does not amount to a power to change existing law or create new law; as John Merryman notes, however, this theoretical view is not unanimous, and actual practice may depart from theory (ibid.: 46–7). In the common-law world, the notion of 'judge-made law' is often spoken of and implicitly accepted. This is in part because some areas of the common law, including matters such as negligence and murder in English law, have no statutory basis, and in part due to the strong force of precedent (which, to the extent it exists in civil-law systems, operates with weaker force).

It is very widely accepted, in common-law countries today, that judges have some degree of law-making power. But this has not always been the case. For a long time the theory held sway that judges *declare* rather than *make* the law. This is not the place to rehearse the complex history of the declaratory theory, how it came to be seen as a 'fairy tale' (Reid 1972: 22), or to consider arguments in its defence (Beever 2013). My focus is on Dworkin, who aspires to transcend the traditional debate. The theory of law as integrity defended in *Law's Empire* – which will be explored below – does not claim that judges *find* or simply *discover* pre-existing law.

> It insists that legal claims are interpretive judgments and therefore combine backward- and forward-looking elements; they interpret contemporary legal practice seen as an unfolding political narrative. So law as integrity rejects as unhelpful the ancient question whether judges find or invent law; we understand legal reasoning, it suggests, only by seeing the sense in which they do both and neither.
>
> (Dworkin 1986: 225)

Dworkin's claim sounds paradoxical, and it might be questioned whether the paradox is vicious. How can it be that judges *both* find and invent law and that they *neither* find nor invent law? But Dworkin gives this only as a response to a question he finds unhelpful. For Dworkin we should stop asking whether judges find or invent law (a 'false dichotomy' (ibid.: 228)); the question presumes that law exists prior to and outside the interpretive process. I will argue that this attempt by Dworkin to, in effect, step outside of time, by rejecting the question of whether judges find or invent law, is, in the end, unsuccessful.

II

Dworkin's career as a legal philosopher launched with his critique of legal positivism in three seminal articles published in 1967, 1972 and 1975, then collected as Chapters 2–4 of *Taking Rights Seriously* (1977). Dworkin concentrated his attack on H.L.A. Hart, who conceived of a legal system as a set of rules picked out by a 'rule of recognition', a master rule that sets the criteria for the validity of other legal rules. Hart considered legal language to be inherently open-textured, and this meant that certain cases (call them 'hard cases') cannot be resolved by the straightforward application of a rule. Hart said that the judge in such cases has discretion to form a new rule or extend an old one, which amounts to an 'interstitial' law-making power (1961: 259).

Dworkin rejected Hart's view of judicial discretion and the concept of law as a system of rules. He accepted that there are legal rules, which he defined as having an 'all-or-nothing' character, but argued that the law also contains 'principles', which have varying weight and reflect moral judgment or reasoning (1977: 22–8). Such principles need not be picked out as valid by a rule of recognition and do not depend on any other form of positivistic pedigree. These principles serve to guide legal reasoning in hard cases, leading judges to the 'right answer'. Dworkin puts the claim forcefully in the essay 'Hard Cases':

> I shall argue that even when no settled rule disposes of the case, one party may nevertheless have a right to win. It remains the judge's duty, even in hard cases, to *discover* what the rights of the parties are, not to *invent* new rights retrospectively.
>
> (Ibid.: 81, emphasis added)

Note that that the italicised words suppose the dichotomy that Dworkin later calls false in *Law's Empire*. In his early work Dworkin is comfortable asserting that certain legal rights exist *before* a case is brought, even if they have not yet been clearly articulated in legal sources, and that the judge's duty is to *discover* or to find them. Dworkin acknowledged that such discovery is imbued with controversy; there is no 'mechanical procedure' for resolving hard cases, and 'the argument supposes that reasonable lawyers and judges will often disagree about legal rights' (1977: 81). Nonetheless, the aim of the adjudicative process is to find *pre-existing* rights.

Dworkin describes positivism's theory of hard cases as one in which a judge conceals the truth. 'His opinion is written in language that seems to assume that one or the other party had a pre-existing right to win the suit', but according to the positivist, 'that idea is only a fiction. In reality he has legislated new legal rights, and then applied them retrospectively to the case at hand' (1977: 81). Dworkin finds this theory 'inadequate' and firmly rejects retrospective law-making as contrary to the rule of law. The positivist model of judicial discretion, according to Dworkin, entails retrospective law-making and also conflicts with democracy, insofar as judicial discretion might embrace matters of 'policy' whose resolution appropriately belongs to the legislative branch (1977: 84–5).

Dworkin pursues his argument by analysing examples of hard cases, most famously *Riggs v Palmer* 1889, a New York Court of Appeal case in which a man who feared being disinherited murdered his grandfather.[1] The court construed the statute at issue to exclude the man from inheriting even though the statute's express terms contained no such exception; the property went instead to the grandfather's two daughters, who were his legal heirs but not named in his will. The court relied on the principle that one should not profit from his own wrongdoing and on an Aristotelian approach to equitable construction of statutes (in which a court asks what the legislature would say about the case before the court). For Dworkin, it is crucial to conclude that the daughters had a *pre-existing legal right* to inherit under the will; the court recognised and enforced that right and did not – as the positivist view would entail – engage in any law-making act (1977: 23–39).

III

In *Law's Empire*, Dworkin abandons or reworks much of the vocabulary and conceptual apparatus of *Taking Rights Seriously*. He no longer draws a sharp distinction between rules and 'principles', and largely ceases to use the latter in the special sense of the early work. A number of Dworkin's underlying ideas in *Taking Rights Seriously*, including some of his basic strategy in arguing against positivism, can still be seen as reflected in the new theory of 'law as integrity'. But looking back on his early work in light of the later, it can be seen that its conceptual apparatus was beholden to a Hartian or positivist backdrop in which the law is a set of materials existing outside of and prior to the judicial process. Dworkin viewed the law more broadly than Hart and rejected the necessity of any authoritative, positive source. But he saw the law as something to be found, something that the judicial process *operates on*. The theory of *what law is* was distinct from the theory of adjudication (1977: vii–viii).

Law's Empire marks a fundamental shift whereby law is now seen as what emerges within the process of adjudication. The book opens with the sentence 'It matters how judges decide cases' (1986: 1). It continues to be centred around adjudication to the end, where we are told: 'General theories of law, for us, are general interpretations of our own judicial practice' (ibid.: 410). Courts, says Dworkin, are the 'capitals of law's empire, and judges are its princes' (ibid.: 407). Law itself is an 'interpretive concept' (ibid.: 73), subject to a method Dworkin calls *constructive* interpretation (ibid.: 48–68). Constructive interpretation, which for Dworkin applies to law and more generally to social practices, has three stages: (1) a 'pre-interpretive stage' that identifies the 'rules and standards taken to provide the tentative content of the practice'; (2) an 'interpretive stage at which the interpreter settles on some general justification for the main elements of the practice'; and (3) a 'post-interpretive or reforming stage' at which the interpreter 'adjusts his sense of what the practice "really" requires so as better to serve the justification he accepts at the interpretive stage' (ibid: 65–6). What a positivist would consider to be legal sources – or, simply, 'the law' – is in Dworkin's scheme merely 'pre-interpretive' material. For Dworkin, law in its true sense belongs to the interpretive stage.

The court-centred approach of *Law's Empire* can be contrasted with the larger task that Dworkin set for himself and for legal theory in general – in *Taking Rights Seriously*. In the Introduction to that book he aimed to offer a theory of law that is both normative (in providing a moral justification for law) and conceptual (in defining what law is) (1977: vii–viii). Pointing to Bentham as the last Anglo-American philosopher to offer such a general theory, Dworkin says that the essays in *Taking Rights Seriously* provide 'the main structure for a distinct theory of law' (ibid.: viii). The normative part of a general theory of law must include a theory of (1) legislation; (2) adjudication; and (3) compliance – that is, whether and when citizens are obligated to obey the law (ibid.: vii–viii). A theory of legislation includes both (a) arguments that justify the authority of the person or group that creates statutory law and (b) a theory of legislative justice, which 'describes the law they are entitled or obliged to make' (ibid.: viii).

In *Law's Empire*, Dworkin narrows the scope considerably. In the Introduction, he states:

> This book is about theoretical disagreement in law. It aims to understand what kind of disagreement this is and then to construct and defend a particular theory about the proper grounds of law. But of course there is more to legal practice than arguments about the law, and this book neglects much that legal theory also studies.
>
> (1986: 11)

Strikingly, Dworkin suggests that judges and courts are not the most important part of a legal system, in the course of acknowledging that his study overlooks legislators:

> My project is narrow in a different way as well. It centers on formal adjudication, on judges in black robes, but these are not the only or even the most important actors in the legal drama. A more complete study of legal practice would attend to legislators, policemen, district attorneys, welfare officers, school board chairmen, a great variety of other officials who are not called public officials but whose decisions also affect the legal rights of their fellow citizens.
>
> (Ibid.: 12)

This seems in tension with his statement that courts are 'the capitals of law's empire' (ibid.: 407). The latter claim and Dworkin's neglect of the legislature strike an odd note – perhaps especially so for the civilian lawyer for whom the legislated code is the centrepiece of the legal system – and signify an important omission. One consequence of this neglect is that it inhibits Dworkin from developing a general theory of legal change. The legislature is the body responsible for the most important legal changes, in both common-law and civil-law systems, and is the institution with the capacities and competences best suited for creating legal change. The latter point is widely acknowledged by common-law judges, and not infrequently cited as a factor shaping their approach to interpretation and to dealing with precedent (Reid 1972; McKay 1987).

IV

At key points in Chapter 2 of *Law's Empire*, entitled 'Interpretive Concepts', Dworkin discusses Gadamer in developing his theory of constructive interpretation. This, along with a brief invocation of Jürgen Habermas, has prompted a substantial body of commentary connecting Dworkin with hermeneutic theory more broadly (see, for example, Couzens Hoy 1987; Donato 1988; Eskridge 1990). Dworkin's engagement with these authors is rather thin, however, and feels incomplete, making it difficult to determine the extent of his reliance on Gadamer and other authors in the hermeneutic tradition.

Dworkin begins his account of interpretation by analysing courtesy as an example of social practice understood through interpretation. The practice of courtesy might begin in behavioural taboos reflected in a set of rules, but over time an 'interpretive' attitude develops, with two components: (1) an assumption that the practice '*has value*, that it serves some interest or purpose or enforces some principle – *in short, that it has some point* – that can be stated independently of just describing the rules that make up the practice'; and (2) a further assumption that the particular requirements of a practice are not 'not necessarily or exclusively what they have always been taken to be but are instead sensitive to its point, so that the strict rules must be understood or applied or extended or modified or qualified or limited by that point' (1986: 47, emphasis added). The point of a social practice is not permanently fixed. Not only can the rules or requirements be adjusted to fit the point, but the point itself can change – as courtesy itself changes from a posture of deference to feudal superiors to a practice suited to a more egalitarian age (ibid.: 48–9). When the interpretive attitude takes hold within a community, 'the institution of courtesy ceases to be mechanical; it is no longer unstudied deference to a runic order. People now try to impose *meaning* on the institution – to see it in its best light – and then to restructure it in the light of that meaning' (ibid.: 47, emphasis original).

Dworkin distinguishes the domains of interpretation that interest him – social practices and artistic interpretation – from 'scientific interpretation', which is applied to 'data' – that is, to 'events not created by people'. Scientific interpretation is only a metaphor in which the data are 'speaking to' the scientist who strains to understand; the metaphor can be dissolved by eliminating the idea of purpose from scientific explanation (ibid.: 51). Artistic interpretation and interpretation of social practices, however, are both concerned with identifying purpose and are for that reason instances of 'creative' interpretation. Critics 'interpret poems and plays and paintings in order to defend some view of their meaning or theme or point' (ibid.: 50). Creative interpretation is on the one hand distinguished from scientific interpretation, which is not concerned with purpose, and on the other hand distinguished from 'conversational' interpretation. The latter 'assigns meaning in the light of the motives and purposes and concerns it supposes the speaker to have, and it reports its conclusions as statements about his "intention" in saying what he did' (ibid.: 50).

Although such interpretation may be appropriate for interpersonal communication, Dworkin rejects the conversational model of interpretation for social practices. The creative interpretation required in that domain he terms *constructive*.

> Interpretation of works of art and social practices, I shall argue, is indeed essentially concerned with purpose not cause. But the purposes in play are not (fundamentally) those of some author but of the interpreter. Roughly, constructive interpretation is a matter of imposing purpose on an object or practice in order to make it the best possible example of the form or genre to which it is taken to belong. It does not follow, even from that rough account, that an interpreter can make of a practice or work of art

> anything he would have wanted it to be [. . .]. For the history or shape of a practice or object constrains the available interpretations of it, though the character of constraint needs careful accounting, as we shall see. Creative interpretation, on the constructive view, is a matter of interaction between purpose and object.
>
> (Ibid.: 52)

In a long footnote accompanying this passage, Dworkin draws on Dilthey, Gadamer (citing *Truth and Method*) and Habermas (citing *The Theory of Communicative Action*), to consider the relationship between intention, history and interpretation. Dworkin seems to endorse Gadamer's idea of 'historically effected consciousness' which he describes as aiming 'not to look at history from no point of view but to understand how our own viewpoint is influenced by the world we wish to interpret' (1986: 419–20 n. 2). Dworkin then appears to side with Habermas against Gadamer, stating that Habermas criticises the former's 'too-passive view that the direction of communication is one way' and 'makes the crucial observation (which points in the direction of constructive rather than conversational interpretation) that interpretation supposes that the author could learn from the interpreter' (ibid.). This is a misleading simplification of the so-called Gadamer–Habermas debate (see Mendelson 1979; Piercey 2004). Dworkin makes no specific reference to Habermas's work in support of this contention, and fails to mention Gadamer's nuanced discussion of the question of whether an interpreter can 'understand an author better than he understood himself' (Gadamer 1986: 192). Gadamer states:

> As an interpreter [an author] has no automatic authority over the person who is simply receiving his work. Insofar as he [the author] reflects on his own work, he is his own reader. The meaning that he, as reader, gives his own work does not set the standard.
>
> (Ibid.)

In the pages that follow, Dworkin cites Gadamer as an authority for points that support his claim that constructive interpretation 'is a matter of interaction between purpose and object' (1986: 52). In the context of a modern attempt to interpret *The Merchant of Venice*, Dworkin states that that we 'must first notice Gadamer's crucial point, that interpretation must *apply* an intention' (ibid.: 55, emphasis original). A successful portrayal of Shylock must capture 'the complex sense that the figure of a Jew had for Shakespeare and his audience, so his interpretation must in some way unite two periods of "consciousness" by bringing Shakespeare's intentions forward into a very different culture located at the end of a very different history' (ibid.: 55–6).

Dworkin's most direct engagement with hermeneutic theory in the main text of *Law's Empire* (setting aside the footnote considered above) follows his claim that:

> [I]nterpreters think within a tradition of interpretation from which they cannot wholly escape. The interpretive situation is not an Archimedian point, nor is that suggested in the idea that interpretation aims to make what is interpreted the best it can seem.
>
> (Ibid.: 61–2)

In support of this Dworkin states: 'Once again I appeal to Gadamer, whose account of interpretation as recognising, while struggling against, the constraints of history strikes the right note' (ibid.: 62). Gadamer's work lends strong support to the first sentence in the block quotation above, although, as we shall see in the next section, Dworkin does not specifically engage with Gadamer's development of this idea in his discussion of legal hermeneutics. Insofar as Dworkin intends the appeal to Gadamer to support his claim that interpretation aims to make the interpretive object 'the best it can be', his appeal seems odd in light of his previous invocation of Habermas against Gadamer's 'too-passive view'. But given the lack of a fuller discussion by Dworkin of these authors and hermeneutic theory more broadly, it is perhaps best to let the matter lie here. The next section, though, will compare Dworkin's theory of law as integrity with Habermas's account of legal hermeneutics.

V

Dworkin's theory of 'law as integrity' applies his more general theory of 'constructive interpretation' to the domain of legal adjudication. He calls it a 'third conception' of law, distinguishing it from (1) 'conventionalism', which he means to stand broadly for legal positivism, which sees the law in consisting in 'backward-looking factual reports'; and (2) pragmatism, which he means to include American legal realism, characterised as seeing the law as a 'forward-looking instrumental progra[m]' (1986: 225). Law as integrity is a concept applicable principally to judges. They neither *find* nor *make* the law (ibid.); law is what emerges in the act of constructive interpretation:

> The adjudicative principle of integrity instructs judges to identify legal rights and duties, so far as possible, on the assumption that they were all created by a single author – the community personified – expressing a coherent conception of justice and fairness. We form our third conception of the law, our third view of what rights and duties flow from past political decisions, by restating this instruction as a thesis about the grounds of law. According to law as integrity, propositions of law are true if they figure in or follow from the principles of justice, fairness, and procedural due process that provide the best constructive interpretation of the community's legal practice.
>
> (Ibid.)

It is by conceptually linking law to the *present* adjudicative act of constructive interpretation that Dworkin sidesteps the question of whether judges find or make the law. Once a decision is reached, the decision fades into the background of the other past legal and political decisions that will shape other acts of constructive interpretation.

In 'law as integrity' the judge relates the past to the present through two dimensions: *fit* and *justification*. At the pre-interpretive stage, a judge identifies the past legal decisions and other materials that set the frame for eligible interpretations of the law. The proposed interpretations a judge will consider must pass a threshold of fit, which 'will eliminate interpretations that some judges would otherwise prefer'; 'the brute facts of legal history will in this way limit the role any judge's personal convictions of justice can play in his decisions' (ibid.: 255). For example, any plausible approach would admit that there is no general principle in private law that requires the rich to share their wealth with the poor (ibid.).

Hard cases arise, Dworkin says, when a judge perceives that two or more interpretations pass the threshold of fit, thus bringing in the dimension of justification. 'Then he must choose between eligible interpretations by asking which shows the community's structure of institutions and decisions – its public standards as a whole – in a better light from the standpoint of political morality' (ibid.: 256). Whereas in his earlier work Dworkin spoke of a 'right answer', he now describes the goal of the judge as that of the 'best' interpretation.

> Judges who accept the interpretive ideal of integrity decide hard cases by trying to find, in some coherent set of principles about people's rights and duties, the best constructive interpretation of the political structure and legal doctrine of their community.
>
> (Ibid.: 255)

The best interpretation is not chosen solely in light of considerations of political morality; the dimension of fit continues to exert force at the justification stage, and 'any infelicities of fit will count against' a proposed interpretation (ibid.: 256; see also 246–7). Hence the best interpretation is one that rightly balances the values in the dimensions of fit and justification.

These claims have produced an enormous amount of commentary, and the jurisprudential literature contains a wide-ranging critique of many aspects of Dworkin's theory of law as interpretation (Raz 1994: 195–209; Finnis 1987; Henley 1990). It is not my aim in this chapter to enter this broader discussion or to offer a general evaluation of Dworkin's theory of law as integrity. Instead, I focus on what I perceive to be Dworkin's specific failure to account for the nature of legal change in common-law systems. Before reaching that critique in the next section, I pause to consider Dworkin's theory of law as integrity in relation to Gadamer.

Dworkin makes no specific reference to anything in Gadamer's discussion of legal hermeneutics, even though Gadamer seeks to relate historical texts to present judgments in ways that resonate with Dworkin's account in several respects. (Gadamer 1986: 320–36). It is worth noting at the outset that Gadamer's aim is to offer an account of legal hermeneutics, not – like Dworkin – an all-encompassing definition of law itself.

For Gadamer, '[t]he jurist understands the meaning of the law from the present case and for the sake of this present case' (ibid.: 322). Dworkin does allude generally to Gadamer's idea of *applying* an intention (Dworkin 1986: 56), albeit in the context of interpreting Shakespeare; it is possible that Dworkin had in mind passages from Gadamer such as this:

> It is true that the jurist is always concerned with the law itself, but he determines its normative content in regard to the given case to which it is to be applied. In order to determine this content exactly, it is necessary to have historical knowledge of the original meaning, and only for this reason does the judge concern himself with the historical value that the law has through the act of legislation. But he cannot let himself be bound by what, say, an account of the parliamentary proceedings tells him about the intentions of those who first passed the law. Rather, he has to take account of the change in circumstances and hence define afresh the normative function of the law.
>
> (Gadamer 1986: 323)

Dworkin's view that the judge is bound by the threshold requirement of fit, eliminating certain possible interpretations, is similar to the way Gadamer sees a judge as seeking to 'mediate' between the past and present:

> The judge who adapts the transmitted law to the needs of the present is undoubtedly seeking to perform a practical task, but his interpretation of the law is by no means merely for that reason an arbitrary revision. Here again, to understand and to interpret means to discover and recognize a valid meaning. The judge seeks to be in accord with the 'legal idea' in mediating it with the present. This is, of course, a legal mediation. It is the legal significance of the law – and not the historical significance of the law's promulgation or of particular cases of its application – that he is trying to understand.
>
> (Ibid.: 324)

However, Gadamer seems less concerned than Dworkin to insist that judges simply enforce the law without changing it. In the quotation just mentioned, Gadamer thus alludes to 'revision' of the law; elsewhere, he states that 'a judge regards himself as entitled to supplement the original meaning of the text of a law' (ibid.: 336).

> The work of interpretation is *to concretize* the law in each specific case – i.e., it is a work of *application*. The creative supplementing of the law that is involved is a task reserved to the judge, but he is subject to the law in the

> same way as is every other member of the community. It is part of the idea of a rule of law that the judge's judgment does not proceed from an arbitrary and unpredictable decision, but from the just weighing up of the whole. Anyone who has immersed himself in the particular situation is capable of undertaking this just weighing-up. This is why in a state governed by law, there is legal certainty – i.e., it is in principle possible to know what the exact situation is. Every lawyer and every counsel is able, in principle, to give correct advice – i.e., he can accurately predict the judge's decision on the basis of the existing laws.
>
> (Ibid.: 325–6, emphasis original)

Gadamer's argument that the judge is not in a privileged position to know the law in comparison with ordinary citizens stands in contrast to Dworkin's account of Judge Hercules, the ideal interpreter who has perfect knowledge of a community's past legal decisions and of the history that informs them. For Dworkin, this does not mean that the law is accessible only to Hercules, but Hercules is in a substantially better position than others to be able to know the law by working out the 'best interpretation' of past decisions (Henley 1990: 25–7).

Gadamer's discussion of legal hermeneutics relates the point of view of the jurist to that of the legal historian. He denies that there is any fundamental divide between how each one understands the law. The legal historian cannot seek to understand the law merely as a fact about the past isolated from the concerns of legal dogmatics; to understand past law – even that of a legal system no longer in existence – he must put himself in the position of someone applying the law to a case and hence concerned with its normative content. The historian 'cannot disregard the fact that he is concerned with a legal creation that needs to be understood in a legal way. He must be able to think not only historically but also legally' (Gadamer 1986: 324). Gadamer's recognition of the distinct point of view of the legal historian is helpful for understanding the nature of legal change – and is something largely omitted from Dworkin's account. I return to this point in section VII below.

VI

One of Dworkin's main strategies in arguing against legal positivism has been to show how actual cases illustrate his claims (1977: 23–39, 83–6; 1986: 15–30, 130–50). As discussed above, he gave *Riggs v Palmer* as a paradigm case showing that judges use principles to find right answers in hard cases; the court did not make new law but enforced the pre-existing rights of the grandfather's daughters against the grandson who had murdered him. Dworkin returns to the same case in *Law's Empire*, calling it 'Elmer's Case' after the name of the grandson, and recasting its holding in language drawn from law as integrity. Here, instead of focusing on rights, Dworkin makes an argument about how Judge Earl, writing for the majority, construed the statute at issue. Dworkin notes that the court said that:

> [S]tatutes should be constructed from texts not in historical isolation but against the background of what he called the general principles of law: he meant that judges should construct a statute so as to make it conform as closely as possible to principles of justice assumed elsewhere in the law.
>
> (1986: 19)

Judge Earl reasoned, according to Dworkin, that 'since a statute forms part of a larger intellectual system, the law as a whole, it should be constructed so as to make that larger system coherent in principle' (ibid.: 19–20).

A gaping omission in Dworkin's early work as well as *Law's Empire* is his failure to grapple with cases where judges explicitly claim that they have the power to change the law – and on occasion exercise it. One such case is *West Midland Baptist (Trust) Association Inc v Birmingham Corporation* (hereinafter *West Midland Baptist*), a 1970 House of Lords decision.[2] This is an illuminating case in part because the leading speech is by Lord Reid, who two years later authored an influential article, 'The Judge as Lawmaker'. In this article, Lord Reid argued that common-law judges have the power to make the law, though they should use it sparingly. He wrote:

> There was a time when it was thought almost indecent to suggest that judges make law – they only declare it. Those with a taste for fairy tales seem to have thought that in some Aladdin's cave there is hidden the Common Law in all its splendour [. . .]. But we do not believe in fairy tales any more.
>
> (Lord Reid 1972: 22)

Some have interpreted this as a departure from the *West Midland Baptist* case in which Lord Reid wrote: 'We cannot say that the law was one thing yesterday but is to be something different tomorrow. If we decide that [the existing rule] is wrong, we must decide that it always has been wrong' (*West Midland Baptist* 1970: 898–9). Lord Sumption gives this as an example of the central principle of the declaratory theory: that when judges overrule earlier decisions, those decisions 'must always have been wrong' (Sumption 2016: 17). On this view, judges reinstate older law rather than create new law.

A close examination of *West Midland Baptist*, however, reveals that Lord Reid frankly acknowledged that the House of Lords was engaged in changing the law in that case to something new. His views about judicial law-making in the article and in the case are essentially the same. This is worth considering in detail not only because it stands as a stark counter-example to Dworkin's theory, but also because it presents a normatively attractive view of the judge's role as law-maker.

West Midland Baptist centred on a common-law rule which provided that in cases of compulsory purchase of land by public authorities, the value of the land is to be determined on the date of the notice to treat – that is, the date on which a public authority provides the owner with notice that land would be taken. Lord Reid calls this a 'judge-made rule': it was an application of the statute governing compulsory purchase, but not contained in the statute itself (*West Midland Baptist* 1970: 898). The rule, according to Lord Reid, served the purpose of an underlying principle of providing fair compensation. For many years the principle and rule were aligned because (1) the value of money held fairly constant over time and (2) there was rarely any substantial lapse of time between the date of the notice to treat and the date on which the owner was in fact prevented from occupying the land.

The course of events in *West Midland Baptist* revealed a challenge to both factual assumptions. In 1947 the city of Birmingham obtained a compulsory purchase order for the land owned by the West Midland Baptist Association, on which was situated 'The People's Chapel'. This was part of a long-term development plan, and the chapel was allowed to continue in operation for more than a decade. In 1958 the City offered the Association land for a new chapel, which was accepted. Because notice to treat had been effective on the date of the compulsory purchase order, the Lands Tribunal awarded compensation of £50,025, the value of the land in 1947. The Court of Appeal, however, awarded £89,575, the value in 1961, when rebuilding could have commenced.

Lord Reid saw these facts as posing a challenge to the existing law:

> So the question is whether it is proper for this House to re-examine a judge-made rule of law based on an assumption of fact which was true when the rule was formulated but which is no longer true and which now in many cases causes serious injustice.
>
> (*West Midland Baptist* 1970: 898)

He answered the question in the affirmative, announcing an altered rule according to which compensation would, in this case and henceforth, be based on the value at the time when it was reasonably possible for the owner to be reinstated in a different location (*West Midland Baptist* 1970: 899).

In a candid reflection on the nature of the adjudicative endeavour in which he was engaged, Lord Reid noticed the importance of 'not upsetting proprietary or contractual rights' and observed:

> We cannot say that the law was one thing yesterday but is to be something different tomorrow. If we decide that the rule as to the date of the notice to treat is wrong we must decide that it always has been wrong, and that would mean that in many completed transactions owners have received too little compensation. But that often happens when an existing decision is reversed. Here there appears to me to be little or no chance that by reopening the whole matter we would alter the future operation of existing vested rights.
>
> (*West Midland Baptist* 1970: 898–9)

It is important to note precisely what Lord Reid is excluding in the use of 'cannot' in the first sentence above. He is not denying that judges can change the law, and he is not denying that judges can posit new law. It might appear from the next sentence, that he is saying that in changing the law judges can only revert back to some prior, pre-existing law, in the course of admitting that the law being changed 'always has been wrong'. But the surrounding context makes it clear that for several decades the rule requiring valuation on notice to treat was consistent with the underlying principle, and thus in that sense was not wrong. The sense in which the rule was 'wrong' is that it failed to anticipate the changing circumstances, and so for a certain period of time cases were decided in which owners received too little compensation. In adopting the new rule regarding when to value land, Lord Reid did not purport to be reverting to a prior rule or law.

In saying that 'we cannot say that the law was one thing yesterday but is to be something different tomorrow', what Lord Reid is excluding is a mode of legal change that belongs solely to the legislature. The legislature has the power to announce prospective change in the law without retrospective effect. But when the judge changes the law, that has, according to Lord Reid, the unfortunate consequence of having retrospective effect in the case at hand. Lord Reid's view can be clearly seen in a passage in his 1972 article that parallels his reasoning in *West Midland Baptist*:

> And there is another sphere where we have got to be very careful. People rely on the certainty of the law in settling their affairs, in particular in making contracts or settlements. It would be very wrong if judges were to disregard or innovate on what can fairly be regarded as settled law in matters of this kind. When Parliament passes an Act there is always objection to any proposal to make it retrospective. But judge-made law is always retrospective. *We cannot say that the law until yesterday was one thing, from tomorrow it will be something different.* That would indeed be legislating.
>
> (Lord Reid 1972: 23, emphasis added)

The italicised phrase is almost an exact quotation from the case. Lord Reid holds that judges have a kind of law-making power, but one that differs in an important respect from legislating because of its necessary retrospective effects. This leads him to offer considered reflections on the need for judges to use their law-making power cautiously, and to refrain from exercising it where the nature of the issue suggests that the legislature would be in a better position to effect the contemplated legal change (ibid.: 23, 27–9).

How might Dworkin analyse *West Midland Baptist*? Some aspects of Lord Reid's reasoning fit with his work. The discussion of the relationship between rules and principles tracks well what Dworkin writes in *Taking Rights Seriously* (1977). The early Dworkin could argue that the Baptist Association had a pre-existing right to win, because the law encompassed not just the *rule* regarding compensation on the date of the notice to treat but also the *principle* of fair compensation. Thus, even before the decision was reached, it was the case that *the law* – combining both rule and principle – included the right announced in the case. Even so, Dworkin could not easily dismiss Lord Reid's frank acknowledgment that he was changing the law and his assertion of the judge's law-making power. Dworkin had mocked positivists for insisting that judges were concealing their law-making in the face of an opinion 'written in language that seems to assume that one or the other party had a pre-existing right to win the suit' (1977: 81). But if Hart's thesis about judicial discretion is true, a court's silence about it in most cases is consistent with the formal structures of common-law judicial methods, which require a decision once a case is initiated and do not allow judges to decline to rule on grounds that the law is uncertain (Henley 1990: 27). How can Dworkin defend his own view against a judge who positively asserts the power of law-making? Dworkin could contend that Lord Reid simply misunderstood or mischaracterised what he was doing, and attempt to recast his reasoning in the language of law as integrity, arguing that the rule requiring valuation on the date of reinstatement is the 'best interpretation' of the past legal decisions. A difficulty here might be concluding that this rule was an eligible interpretation that passed the threshold of fit, given the long-standing, clear rule requiring valuation on the date of the notice to treat.

Dworkin could also contend that *West Midland Baptist* is an outlier, and that cases such as *Riggs v Palmer* represent the mainstream. It is true that such candid acknowledgment of law-making power as Lord Reid's is uncommon, but *West Midland Baptist* is by no means the only case to do so (the *Kleinwort Benson* case discussed in the next section is another example).[3] It is difficult to know whether judges frequently consider themselves to be changing the law while failing to explicitly acknowledge that. But rather than pursue that question as an empirical inquiry,[4] I think it better to reorient the discussion.

VII

John Finnis has provided a compelling account of the relationship between adjudication and legal change that is consonant with parts of Dworkin's theory of law as integrity but refrains from his insistence that judges do not change the law. In 'The Fairy Tale's Moral', an article commenting on *Kleinwort Benson Ltd v Lincoln City Council* (hereinafter *Kleinwort Benson*), a 1998 House of Lords decision that abrogated a long-standing rule regarding restitution of money paid under mistake of law and adopted a new rule with retrospective effect,[5] Finnis argues that the claim that judges declare rather than make law (Lord Reid's 'fairy tale') is properly understood as a normative point about the responsibility of judges and not a descriptive, historical claim about common-law development (Finnis 1999). The normative point was captured by Lord Goff's statement in *Kleinwort Benson* that 'the change so made must be seen as a development [. . .] of existing principle and so can take its place as a congruent part of the common law' (1999: 378). The affinity with Dworkin's theory of law as integrity is clear.

Finnis contends, however, that we fail to understand law if we try to reduce it either to (1) a descriptive/historical fact about the contents of legal sources or

(2) a normative standard requiring a particular practical decision in the application of a law.

> Law has a double life. It is in force as a matter of fact; historians and contemporary observers can describe – and make predictions about – its content and effect by attending to the opinions and practices prevalent among certain persons and groups, especially courts and their officers. But it has its force by directing the practical reasoning of those persons and groups. And since one engages in practical reasoning to reach normative conclusions (such and such ought to be done, or ought not, or is desirable, or permissible, etc.), facts count in practical reasoning only by virtue of some further, normative premise(s), the source of the reasoning's directiveness for decision and action. Law stated in such reasoning, not least in judicial reasoning, is stated as a norm, and exists as directing one towards or away from decisions and actions, validating or invalidating one's transactions, and so forth, precisely by being itself justified as part of a set of such standards. *Law's existence, force and effect – its life – can always thus be understood as sheer fact (historical or predictable) or alternatively as directive standard.*
>
> (Finnis 1999: 170, emphasis modified)

From the historical perspective an observer can see that the development of the common law in a given area over time as a series of changes in the law. Gadamer's analysis of the complementary points of view of the legal historian and the jurist is consistent with this. From the internal perspective of the judge charged with responsibility over that development, the following is also true:

> [A]djudication involves the duty not to declare and apply a rule unless it can fairly be said to have been all along a legally appropriate standard, more appropriate than alternatives, for assessing the validity and propriety of the parties' transactions. When that can fairly be said, the same rule, having been declared and applied, is clearly the only legally appropriate standard for assessing the *correctness* of the parties' belief in the legal validity and propriety of their transactions.
>
> (Ibid.: 175, emphasis original)

Lord Reid's decision in *West Midland Baptist* is consistent with this principle, but so is his acknowledgment that his act resulted in a change of law. In making that acknowledgment, Lord Reid momentarily stepped outside of the internal viewpoint as a judge and adopted the historical perspective (as did the majority in *Kleinwort Benson*). That perspective was complemented by a theoretical view – made more clear in his extra-judicial writing – that judges should exercise their power to change the law sparingly.

In denying that judges have legitimate power to change the law, Dworkin adopts a too narrowly truncated view of what law is. He finds the very essence of law in the adjudicative process, equating a general theory of law with a theory of how judges decide cases. Although Dworkin's theory of law as integrity offers insights into law as a directive standard for adjudication, his insistence that law is an interpretive concept leads him to deny the perspective from which one can rightly conclude that judges change the law.

Endnotes

1 *Riggs v Palmer*, 115 N.Y. 506 (1889).
2 *West Midland Baptist (Trust) Association Inc v Birmingham Corporation*, [1970] A.C. 874 (H.L.).
3 See also Lord McKay (1987) and cases discussed therein.
4 For a discussion of interviews with judges on this point, see Goldsworthy (2011: 315).
5 *Kleinwort Benson Ltd v Lincoln City Council*, [1999] 2 A.C. 349 (H.L.).

Bibliography

Beever, A. (2013) 'The Declaratory Theory of Law', *Oxford Journal of Legal Studies* 33: 421–44.
Couzens Hoy, D. (1987) 'Dworkin's Constructive Optimism v. Deconstructive Legal Nihilism', *Law and Philosophy*, 6: 321–56.
Donato, J. (1988) 'Dworkin and Subjectivity in Legal Interpretation', *Stanford Law Review*, 40: 1517–41.
Dworkin, R. (1967) 'The Model of Rules', *University of Chicago Law Review*, 35: 14–46.
—— (1972) 'Social Rules and Legal Theory', *Yale Law Journal*, 81: 855–90.
—— (1975) 'Hard Cases', *Harvard Law Review*, 88: 1057–109.
—— (1977) *Taking Rights Seriously*, Cambridge, MA: Harvard University Press.
—— (1986) *Law's Empire*, Cambridge, MA: Harvard University Press.
Eskridge, W.N. (1990) 'Gadamer/Statutory Interpretation', *Columbia Law Review*, 90: 609–81.
Finnis, J. (1987) 'On Reason and Authority in *Law's Empire*', *Law and Philosophy*, 6: 357–80.
—— (1999) 'The Fairy Tale's Moral', *Law Quarterly Review*, 115: 170–5.
Gadamer, H.-G. (1986) *Truth and Method*, trans. J. Weinsheimer and D.G. Marshall, 2nd rev. Eng. edn, New York: Continuum, 2004.
Goldsworthy, J. (2011) 'The Limits of Judicial Fidelity to Law: The Coxford Lecture', *Canadian Journal of Law and Jurisprudence*, 24: 305–25.
Hart, H.L.A. (1961) *The Concept of Law*, 2nd edn, Oxford: Oxford University Press, 1994.
Henley, K. (1990) 'Protestant Hermeneutics and the Rule of Law: Gadamer and Dworkin', *Ratio Juris*, 3: 14–28.
McKay, Lord (1987) 'Can Judges Change the Law?' *Proceedings of the British Academy*, 73: 285–308.
Mendelson, J. (1979) 'The Habermas-Gadamer Debate', *New German Critique*, 18: 44–73.

Merryman, J.H. (2007) *The Civil Law Tradition*, 3rd edn by R. Pérez-Perdomo, Stanford, CA: Stanford University Press.

Piercey, R. (2004) 'Ricœur's Account of Tradition and the Gadamer–Habermas Debate', *Human Studies*, 27: 259–80.

Raz, J. (1994) *Ethics in the Public Domain*, Oxford: Oxford University Press.

Reid, Lord (1972) 'The Judge as Law Maker', *Journal of Public Teachers of Law*, 12: 22–9.

Sumption, Lord (2016) 'The Limits of the Law', in N.W. Barber, R. Ekins and P. Yowell (eds) *Lord Sumption and the Limits of the Law*, Oxford: Hart.

Chapter 7

Taking stories seriously

The place of narrative in legal interpretation

François Ost

As long as the law continues to refer to texts, the question of interpretation will remain an integral part of it. Moreover, this matter itself, as it pertains to 'understanding', comprises many features that concern, for example, its relation to communication, argumentation, translation and narration. In this chapter, I want to emphasize the connection between 'interpreting' and 'storytelling', which I approach by making exclusive reference to its relevance as regards the interpretation of statutes by judges. In the process, I purport to underline an aspect of the 'law and literature' movement within legal theory that has for the most part been ignored.

For at least a century, the 'law and literature' perspective has been well known to US law schools. More recently, it has also been unfolding in Europe. Generally speaking, this outlook helps to elucidate the social dimensions of the law – that is, the human aspects of the workings of justice (Ost 2004: 40–8). However, it remains unusual that the attention directed towards narrative be harnessed with a view to shedding light on the nature of legal reasoning itself. Such is the aim of this chapter: to assert the proximity between the narrative of fiction and a court case; more precisely to show how the treatment of a case, including the mobilization of the legal texts having to be interpreted, intersects in multiple ways with the narratological operation and appeals to creative imagination at various levels. I develop my argument by way of seven propositions. At this stage, these statements largely consist of programmatic orientations within an intellectual undertaking that will warrant amplification in the future.

1. One has learned to take interpretation seriously since the so-called 'linguistic turn', sometimes labelled the 'hermeneutic turn', that materialized in the second half of the twentieth century. Indeed, the idea then asserted itself that there is no pre-established truth, no truth 'as such' that would be extralinguistic, objective and *a priori*. Rather, there are but language approximations calling for constructive interpretations for which one is responsible. For instance, any conception of justice is indebted to an interpretive filter: 'a language game, a tradition, a paradigm, a conceptual scheme, a vocabulary' (Ferrara 2008: 17).

This first thesis leads to a radicalization of interpretation over against all positivisms seeking either to prohibit it or to minimize its extent. In the field of law, illustrations of such strategies of denial have never been in short supply. Thus, Justinian and the Prussian emperor, Frederick II, proscribed interpretation of their legal texts. Also, the Belgian *Cour de cassation* and *Conseil d'État* – the private law and public law 'supreme courts' of Belgium – have long held that a judge cannot be allowed to interpret a legal text if it is clear. Historically, the sovereign also assumed a monopoly over the interpretation of hard cases through a mechanism known as 'legislative reference' (*référé législatif*) whereby judges were forced to solicit a decision from the legislature whenever they believed the interpretation of a statute to be necessary. In France, for example, this procedure was in force from 1790 to 1837 when it was found to be too cumbersome. And then there is the time-honoured principle according to which interpretation must remain exceptional and cannot be permitted if the judge wishes to fill a gap or solve a contradiction in the law. One could also mention the claim whereby to interpret must be to strive to identify the legislator's intention.

But experience with the judges' genuine interpretive practices has long ago demonstrated the futility of these bans and safeguards. One understands nowadays that it is impossible to read a text, even the simplest one, without interpreting it, and one realizes that safeguards such as 'the clear meaning of the text' or 'legislative intent' are evidently notions that themselves call for interpretation. As Wittgenstein has indicated (and as Julia Tanney reminds one in this book), a rule does not regulate its own application. It follows – a point Paul Ricœur well underlines – that it would be wrong to regard the matter of the application of a statute as a minor question vis-à-vis a general theory of law (1995: xxii). Still, there are two currents of thought at least that depreciate the interpretive issue: one that favours a mechanical application of the statute and considers that this process resolves itself strictly as a matter of knowledge, at least in simple cases, which are in the majority; and another that, contrariwise, assumes that the application of legal texts pertains exclusively to the will of interpreters, at least in hard cases, whose unpredictable solutions would be left to the discretionary power of judges. Under these conditions, it becomes urgent to think through what Ricœur calls the '*middle* zone' (1995: xxii, emphasis original) that characterizes the space that the production of the judicial decision really occupies and that has been designated by way of different names such as '*rhetoric*', '*hermeneutic*' and '*poetic*' (ibid., emphasis original). Why 'poetic'? Because, answers Ricœur, 'the invention of an appropriate solution to the unique situation stems from what, since Kant, we have called the productive imagination, in order to distinguish it from the merely reproductive imagination' (ibid.).

2. My second thesis begins with the statement that if everything as regards the question of meaning production is a matter of language, it remains that one must understand in what consists this language. Contrary to received ideas, it is not a tool that would be neutral and available in the service of arguments formulated 'elsewhere' or out of language. In other words, language is not the 'clothing of thought' but its texture itself. One thinks *in* language and *through* its resources,

by way of its limits. Words are not like labels or 'bar codes' that one affixes to ready-made things or ideas and that would exist independently from them. Rather, words are the very construction of these things or ideas (Merleau-Ponty 1969: 4–8; Wittgenstein 1953: §120; Quine 1960; Quine 1962: 139–87).[1] Meanwhile, the act of speaking itself pertains to pragmatics: it very much consists in an activity and not only in the informational unfolding of linguistic considerations. Such an activity falls within various language games that themselves refer to forms of life, all these traits belonging more to the dramatics of narrative than to the semantics of theory. To speak is thus not only to exchange information or ideas but to involve oneself in interactions and therefore to expose one's own responsibility. To speak is to undertake acts of language chosen from within the vast register of forms of life (White 1990: ix).

3. By way of third thesis, I want to contend that these linguistic constructions – I mean these words and the body of explicit and implicit meanings that are associated to them, the sum of connotations that they marshall – are largely the product of cultures at once specific and differentiated. In this sense, linguistic constructions do not assume objectivity but feature at least a kind of non-subjectivity. If it is the case that meaning is not inscribed in the *a priori* reality of the thing or the idea being ascribed significance (these were my first and second theses), it is neither subjective nor contingent either since it appears as the product of a historical and intersubjective construction, as the emanation of a culture and of the language that expresses it. In this sense, the interpretive turn leads neither to sceptical relativism nor to the incommensurability of different interpretations. If perfect commensurability does not exist, and if a plurality of meanings is therefore inevitable, the challenge remains to recapture a form of universality (which, as a matter of law, means a form of predictability and legal certainty) that is plural, contextual and reiterative (Walzer 1990: 183–99; Beck 2004: 50–4; Ricœur 1990: 283–90; Jullien 2008: 115–20, 137–9 and 171–2).

4. Umberto Eco is right to recall – such is my fourth thesis – that as a matter of communication and interpretation, one uses encyclopedias more than dictionaries (1984: 46–86). What I mean is that while a dictionary conveys the formal meaning of the word by producing definitions according to genus and species – for example, by stating that a 'cat' is a mammal of the Felidae family – the encyclopedia, contrariwise, rekindles all the implicit connotations and the secondary meanings that the history of the word in the French language has linked to 'cat'– for instance, references to sexuality or witchcraft. Thus, Eco explains that to interpret can never be reduced to the uncoding of an encrypted message with the help of a closed vocabulary list (such as Berlitz's *1000 French Words*). To interpret consists also in reconstructing the complex meaning of a message with the assistance of the set of connotations conveyed by language as encyclopedia.

Consider the illustration of a municipal ordinance prohibiting the access of dogs to platforms in railway stations. Apparently, the meaning of this text is clear, and if one were to base oneself on a dictionary and on the accompanying lexical conception of language, there should not be any difficulty in the interpretation and thus in the application of these words. But it is enough to imagine the predicament of the stationmaster in the two following situations to appreciate how this legal text can rapidly find itself obscured. What if a blind individual arrives at the station under the guidance of a faithful Labrador? (Or – a variation on this question – what if an anti-drugs police squad comes to the station accompanied by sniffer dogs?) And what if a circus entertainer appears at the ticket office with the bear or tiger with which he performs a winning duet? One must conclude that, as regards the practical judgments under consideration that the stationmaster must reach, the interpretation that carries is the encyclopedical rather than the lexical one: a Labrador and a sniffer dog are not necessarily 'dogs', while, in the eyes of the law (here, the municipal ordinance), it may happen that a bear or a tiger must be regarded as a dog.

What matters in these cases is less the lexical definition 'by genus and species' than the scenario that has prompted the adoption of the municipal ordinance. In effect, the scenario is the micro-narrative, the lived experience that persuaded the decision-makers that dogs, on account of their potential aggressivity or because of their excrements, could bother or irritate travellers. However, another micro-narrative would have convinced decision-makers of the usefulness for blind individuals of being guided by their faithful Labrador. In the event, the micro-narrative of reasonable justice leads one to decide that the second scenario must carry over the first. It is good that blind individuals should be able to use public transportation though provoking the fear of certain travellers. But a complementary lesson from experience also teaches one that this fear is itself ill-founded given that Labradors are well known for their kindness.

And the narratives thus come after one another all the way to infinity according to the movement of universal *symbiosis*: one does not stop interpretation, the construction of scenarios, any more than one stops the flux of experience (Eco 1984: 1–3). Accordingly, one could also say that in India, for example, because of the tradition that makes the cow a sacred animal, one cannot imagine a regulation that would prohibit the cow's access to railway platforms any more than a judicial or administrative interpretation that would lead to this result.

5. To turn to my fifth thesis, the interpretation of a text entails taking hold of the script, the scenario or the pattern underlying the statute and adjusting it to the narrative that the litigants tell the judge and that the file reflects. One often forgets, as one offers a schizophrenic presentation of this operation, that interpretation is a two-dimensional process. It bears as much on the complex of 'facts' to be selected and 'assembled' (in a cinematographic sense) with a view to reaching a certain legal result as on the complex of available legal texts in a position to account for the facts and 'do justice' in the specific case. Bernard Jackson, a specialist in legal semiotics, reminds us that the law aims to offer 'narrative models' that the judge applies to the narrative built from the facts of the case (the facts themselves not being the reflection of a given reality, but a construction). More broadly, Jackson also observes that to understand and apply

the law is to put to work a set of narrative typifications burdened with the normative evaluations that legal institutions attach to them and that interact with the innumerable narratives that social practice generates (1988: 1–6, 89–129).[2] It is therefore clear that the 'report' that the judge offers of the facts of the case is akin to a narrative that is axiologically oriented and 'assembled' with a view to reaching the legal solution that is wanted.[3]

In her book *Poetic Justice*, Martha Nussbaum shows well the variety of these narratives and their decisive influence upon the outcome of the trial. Does a court want to condemn behaviour that it judges to be deviant? It will then adopt an attitude at once distanced and abstract that epitomizes a refusal to inquire about the motivations of the accused and the context of the matter, and it will keep to an official narrative regarding legal texts and authoritative commentaries. To illustrate her claim, Nussbaum refers to Chief Justice Warren Burger's concurring opinion in *Bowers v Hardwick* (1986) (Nussbaum 1995: 114).[4] In this case, the court refused to recognize the constitutional right of consenting adults to engage in sodomy. In Chief Justice Burger's words, '[t]o hold that the act of homosexual sodomy is somehow protected as a fundamental right would be to cast aside millennia of moral teaching' (*Bowers v Hardwick* 1986: 197). Nussbaum contrasts this type of official and 'distancing' narrative (1995: 114) with the one Adam Smith recommends to the 'judicious spectator' (ibid.: 72–8), a character Smith regards as the paradigm of public rationality. Constantly basing himself on the model of the reader or of the spectator at a theatrical representation, Smith solicits a reading that concerns itself with details rather than with fixed rules and that focuses its attention on the singularity of individuals instead of confining itself to dehumanizing stereotypes. For Smith, the issue is the reconstruction of a narrative with empathy but without partiality, with imagination but without sentimentalism, with responsibility but without complacency. If it be well implemented, this standpoint of the impartial spectator,[5] inspired by a narrative of fiction, far from being an *ad hoc* reasoning pursuing an interested goal, appears quite to the contrary as the condition for a rational moral point of view and as the way to reach a generalizable solution, which is precisely what is expected of a judicial decision (Smith 1790).[6]

To be sure, it may be that the official narrative of the judicial institution and of the statutes that judges apply will be largely foreign to lay people. In such cases, as Jean-François Lyotard well explains, one is no longer concerned with *litigation*, since in such an instance both protagonists share at least an understanding of the rule that will lead to a decision between them, but with a *differend* whereby the solution ultimately reached will appear to one of the parties, in the absence of a shared narrative, as an unbearable violence being visited on him (1983: 9–10). Literature is replete with rewritings of trials of this type in the course of which the defendant, having been brought to (in?)justice, has the feeling that his story interests no one (that it literally cannot be *coded*) so that he is reduced to screaming for revenge – which is a way to recall the archaic story of the talion, a far cry from the modern official history of justice by a third party (Ost and Ost 2015).

I note in passing that this 'narrativist' representation of the act of judgment, that leads to adjust the narrative of facts with the narrative of laws, also usefully relativizes the unduly stark opposition between 'is' and 'ought' that still dominates classical legal thought. As Ricœur has tirelessly underlined, storytelling stands as an intermediary figure – better still, as a dialectical operator – between description and prescription (1990: 152–63). In other words, the narrative is the register allowing for the passage from fact to law and, on the way back, from law to fact. Without narrative, one could hardly understand how the law can have a grip on reality or how facts can inform the legal decision. Everything happens as if the narrated fact is already pre-assessed and as such turned towards the law, while, on the contrary, the applied law is necessarily inserted within a scenario that opens it to the facticity of reality.

6. I turn to my sixth thesis. Taking one step further, Jackson explains that in court the narrative does not concern only the substance of the facts or of the rules that are mobilized for the treatment of the case. Before all else, it involves the totality of the pragmatic operations conducted by legal agents to reach a solution. Jackson thus distinguishes between 'the story in the trial' and 'the story of the trial' (Jackson 1988: 127).[7] This narrativization of the pragmatic has to do with the interrogation of witnesses, the pleadings of the lawyers, the deliberations of the court or the reasons of the judgment. It also addresses scholarly work which, through professionalization and specialization, has progressively detached itself from the originary narratives whence the rules came (ibid.: 106–10). There is in this secondary operation (the narrative of the process of narrativization) a set of discursive strategies governed by the interests, the values and the representations of the different agents implicated in the great game of justice.[8] Thus, the 'history' of the conventions that are generally accepted in such and such a branch of the law or by such and such a category of professionals of the law plays a determining role in the selection of the rules applicable to the litigation – the 'rule of recognition' and the 'internal point of view', in H.L.A. Hart's vocabulary (1961: passim). A matter of 'tradition', the construction of this vulgate is also the focus of a permanent power play, for instance, between those who favour continuity and those who defend the idea of an opening. It is itself the object of procedural regulation and the cornerstone of professional ethics.[9]

7. I want to embark on my seventh thesis by observing that *a fortiori* the narrative plays a central role in hard cases – that is, when the matter is not simply about a faulty rule but concerns the default of a rule. Thus far, I have assumed the existence of legislative texts capable of qualifying the complex of facts and of bringing to bear a normative solution. But it is well known that such is not always the case. And talking of the case, it is indeed the case that the life of the law does not reduce itself to the application of ready-made legislative texts to a reality that would docilely conform to them. Even though this observation is not easy to state for jurists trained in the civil-law tradition, it appears that the law arises as much from cases as from rules.[10] The case stands for the unforeseen configuration, the event that happens and that entails perplexity since it calls into question the

classical cognitive frames that allow to grasp proximate and standard situations. Under such conditions, the judge is indeed sometimes (or is it often?) faced with 'singular configurations' or 'cases' that no anterior solution seems to have contemplated. It thus falls to him to locate the generalizable criterion that will lead to the rule, as of yet unformulated, of which the instant case is but an illustration. Kant termed this paradoxical and backward reasoning 'reflecting judgment' as opposed to what he called a 'determining judgment' that confines itself to the application of the pre-existing rule to the case at hand (1793: 15).[11] Kant explains that the judgment that 'reflects' in exploratory and hesitating fashion essentially applies one's capacity for imagination as it works by analogy from *exemplary narratives* (ibid.: §32).[12] Here also, the narrative imagination lies at the heart of the heuristic process that leads to the elaboration of a solution.

Following upon Ricœur and Hannah Arendt, one must note the paradoxical temporal dimension that characterizes the putting to work of the reflective judgment. Indeed, to the extent that the reflective judgment nurtures a regulatory aim for the future (the *idea* of what still remains without a concept such as the idea of 'humanity' or of a 'cosmopolitan constitution') based on the substance of significant historical *examples*, one can speak of a kind of *prophetic history*, of a reconstruction of the history of humanity based on an eschatological hope.[13]

In truth, the mobilization of the creative imagination on the occasion of the reflective judgment must not be understood as a kind of necessary evil or a solution of last resort in the 'pathological' cases where the law would be defaulting. Quite to the contrary, it appears that these cases are multiplying nowadays on account of the network articulation of the law and of the multiplication of legal sources so that, even when it is served by an inventive argumentation, the interpretation of texts reaches its limits. The jurist is then led to demonstrate creativity and to take an active (and responsible) part in the process of the law's production through 'an effort of extrapolation and anticipation using the resources of the imagination and by producing new representations endowed with active strength' (Chevallier 2016).

One better understands therefore the deep link that is forged between the interpretation of the problematical rule and the narrative of an inspiring example. And this is why Dworkin is well advised to say of judges that their daily interpretive work can be understood as the writing of a 'chain novel' (1986: 228–32) and in effect to cast judges as the moral storytellers of the nation. It indeed pertains to them to do justice on the occasion of particular cases while keeping the totality of the law in mind, a law envisaged as a coherent whole whether from the standpoint of its ideological consistency or its historical continuity. The idea of law as a coherent story is a cornerstone of Dworkin's thesis of 'law as integrity' (ibid.: 227–8). According to Dworkin, it is the judge's responsibility to present the law and its underlying values, which have evolved through the nation's constitutional developments from its origins until the present, in a way that will make it 'as good as it can be' (ibid.: 239) or display its most positive implications for today. Accordingly, judges are the spokespeople for the community's values in the way the successive statutes and judicial decisions have progressively configured them. It is as if they were transmitting to one another, from hand to hand and from generation to generation, the pen serving to write the great book of adjudication, each judge having at heart the wish to contribute to the continuation of this great narrative in coherence with the past but also by introducing the transformations demanded on account of present concerns. Regardless of whether one adheres or not to Dworkin's 'right-answer' thesis (incidentally later relativized in terms of the 'best-answer' thesis, as Paul Yowell reminds one in this book), what matters here is the accentuation of the narrativist approach. Indeed, everyone knows how much, whether in the lawyers' arguments or the judges' reasons, the construction of the meaning of the law operates as the outcome of a painstaking work of rewriting of the history of precedents. There is nothing more instructive in this regard than the juxtaposition of a majority opinion with the dissenting or even the concurring judgments that accompany it. One then witnesses 'live' the clash of narratives, each narrative being introduced as more ancient or resting on more solid foundations than the others.

Whether one considers the history of the sedimented meanings of words that is constitutive of language as 'encyclopedia', the legal scenario to be viewed in relation to a file's factual synopsis, the treatment of a case starting from the standpoint of reflective judgment, of the faculty of imagination and of exemplary narratives, interpretation as the writing of a chain novel and judges as moral storytellers of the nation, the relations between narration and interpretation, as can be seen, are numerous and decisive. Here are so many issues on which to work with a view to the edification of a general theory concerning the place of narrative within *jurisdictio*. There is the narrative of words constitutive of the interpretation of texts, the narrative of facts constitutive of the singularity of the case, the narrative of the history of preceding interpretations constitutive of the legal order as a whole and finally the narrative of the judgment that I deliver, here, today, under my responsibility, which is the combination of the other three narratives.[14] In a word, to interpret is less to deduct a meaning from a text and a dictionary than it is to reconstruct a credible meaning – a meaning that is suitable, desirable, reasonable – starting from a virtually infinite set of elements contributed through tangled stories.

Recall that I have only reasoned thus far about the interpretation of statutes by judges in the courtroom, a paradigmatic though reductionist example. But one ought also to evoke thousands of other circumstances in the course of which the law develops: in notarial offices when families tear themselves apart regarding the interpretation of a will (thus awakening so many family stories), in the muted offices of banks as they seal gigantic corporate takeover operations, in the deliberations of a university examinations committee where the fate of a student will depend on the interpretation of a given section of the relevant regulation. These are so many legal laboratories – in French, Latour talks about '*fabrique[s] du droit*'[15] (factories of law) – where stories, small or large, become intermingled as they determine the construction of legal texts.

Are these 'micro-narratives' capable of integrating themselves into a wider history that would not be unrelated to Global History – which, according to Hans-Georg Gadamer and the hermeneutic tradition, presides over the 'fusion of horizons' (1986: 305–6) in terms of its efficacy, of 'the efficacy of history' (ibid.: 300)? Would this history not also be that of the juridical reason of the type suggested by the cover of Hobbes's *Leviathan* as it exhibits the sovereignty of the *res publica* (the commonwealth) whose laws are assumed to relay the people's will? If such a reason ever existed, its history no longer matters nowadays in the context of globalization (which Simone Glanert addresses in this book) and of the network articulation of the law which thus connects with multiple and competing sources (Ost and van de Kerchove 2012).

The task of judges as the moral storytellers of the nation is made all the more difficult given that '[t]he grand narrative has lost its credibility' (Lyotard 1979: 37) and because of the disappearance of the character of the storyteller heralded by Benjamin (1936: 143–66). It is certainly not that there are no more stories being told in contemporary culture. Indeed, 'formidable storytelling machines' are fully operational and '[s]tories are invading newspaper columns, legal arguments, and computer screens' (Salmon 2007: vii, ix). The question that arises – which must already have been that of Plato's law-makers who at times rejected poets out of the city (Plato 380 BCE: bk II, 377b–378a; bk X, 600e–601b, 604a–605c) and at other times sought to imitate them (Plato 348 BCE: bk VII, 817a–d) – is therefore to ascertain what separates this bogus imaginary from narrative that tells one's experience, in court for instance, and thus gives meaning to one's life. This distinction is one more reason to take stories seriously.

Translated from the French by Pierre Legrand

Endnotes

1 Quine's 1962 text is included in the proceedings of the fourth 'Colloque de Royaumont' that gathered Anglophone and French philosophers in 1958. Quine spoke and published in French.

2 One thus finds oneself far removed from the model of the judicial syllogism whereby the statute would be applied to the facts, from the conception of truth as 'correspondence' and from the 'referential' conception of language. For Jackson, the application of a statute is a matter of 'greater or lesser proximity, in terms of human experience' (1988: 89).

3 The 1977 English Court of Appeal decision in *Miller v Jackson*, as it addresses the hitting of balls on the property of a cricket club's neighbours, offers an illustration of this point involving the famous judge, Lord Denning (Jackson 1988: 94–7).

4 *Bowers v Hardwick*, 478 U.S. 186 (1986).

5 While Nussbaum uses the word 'judicious', Smith has 'impartial'.

6 Nussbaum refers to a Judge Richard Posner opinion as illustrating a judgment by a 'judicious spectator' (1995: 109). The case, *Carr v Allison Gas Turbine Division, General Motors*, 32 F.3d 1007 (7th Cir. 1994), involved a complaint of sexual

harassment by a GM worker who had quit her job on account of a situation she had come to find unbearable after many years of fruitless complaints. Nussbaum credits Posner J. with having demonstrated imagination in attempting to compare the plaintiff's circumstances with those of persons finding themselves in similar situations of social inequality (ibid.: 108). While Posner J.'s irritation is genuine, Nussbaum underlines how it remains firmly based on the facts of the case (ibid.: 110). In the end, 'his opinion does what good satire of the Juvenalian or Swiftean kind does: it inspires indignation through the mordant portrayal of human venality and cruelty' (ibid.: 110–1).

7 More generally speaking, this insistence on the pragmatics of 'storytelling', which interferes with the semantics of 'what is being storied', captures the ambivalence of the word 'history' itself as it evokes at once the narrative and the process of narrativization, the dramatic production as such.

8 For many very well-documented illustrations of the practice of the French *Conseil d'État* in this respect, see Latour (2002). For example, Latour refers to the following public reporter's speech to the *Conseil d'État* (note that until 2009, the public reporter was known as the 'government commissioner'): 'Let us admire the beauty of this address in the second person plural: "It is open to *you*". It is the case that the [government commissioner] never ceases to remind this great virtual body of what it has meant to say and adjudicate over two hundred years by way of this immense corpus consisting of hundreds of thousands of decisions. It is as though he were addressing himself to a sphinx that no longer knew quite what it thought and for whom administrative law formed like a sort of penumbra or unconscious with the commissioner bearing the burden of highlighting in this darkness well-drawn paths and straight lines, reminding him always of what is the law, of what is the state, of what is the general will, of what is the deep thought – always to be reworked, to be re-interpreted – of the [*Conseil d'État*]' (ibid.: 166, emphasis original, translation modified). A fully fledged member of the *Conseil d'État*, the public reporter is entrusted with the task of mastering the file and of intervening during the proceedings to suggest, in view of the public interest, a resolution of the dispute and reasons justifying the recommended outcome.

9 From a cognitive standpoint, this process of narrativization is regulated by a type of 'narrative coherence' that negotiates the greater or lesser similarity between scenarios and as such proves less constraining than logical or analytical coherence, without being uncontrolled for all that.

10 For an exploration of this topic within both the civil-law and common-law traditions, see the essays by Jérémie van Meerbeeck, Jeremy Perelman, David Fennelly and François Ost in the 2014/2 issue of the *Revue interdisciplinaire d'études juridiques* (No. 73) devoted to legal thought by cases.

11 For an authoritative commentary, see Arendt (1982).

12 For a theorization of this notion of 'exemplarity' showing that the example is the model for that with which it claims to align itself thus suggesting a 'bootstrapping' phenomenon whereby it becomes self-carrying or even self-founding, see Ferrara (2008: 37). In my language, I talk of 'auto-transcendence' and of 'performative effect': the example realizes what it heralds in saying it, in giving it a form, in presentizing it. See also ibid.: 117, where Ferrara observes that the exemplary is 'a law unto itself' in the sense that it is not the example of something that pre-existed it but the putting into form of what it heralds. It acts as a force that

mobilizes energies and inspires behaviour (ibid.: 119). One can refer to the Nuremberg trial that applies for the first time the idea of 'humanity' (in order to adjudicate on 'crimes against humanity') in unprecedented cases that, literally speaking, are beyond belief. This idea was not a universal 'given' that existed before the judgment. On the contrary, it is the case that allowed for inhumanity to come into existence and thus also revealed the default of the law. There, the judgment operated in 'reflective' fashion by making happen the first concrete elements pertaining to this idea of 'humanity' then under elaboration. This 'reflective' construction rests on three elements: the performative strength of the legal verb and deed (in the present), the attractive force of the regulatory idea thanks to its imaginative anticipation (in the future) and the recollection of exemplary narratives (in the past).

13 Quoting Kant and his writings on the French Revolution, Ricœur writes that '[1789] was indeed [. . .] a question of "the prophetic history of the human race"' (1995: 106). He adds that '[t]he retrospective signs for reflective judgment are prospective as regards those projections authorized by the "disposition" with which nature has endowed human beings as destined to strive for a cosmopolitan state' (ibid.). Compare Ricœur's views to Ronald Dworkin's: '[The judge] [. . .] begins in the present and pursues the past only so far as and in the way its contemporary focus dictates. It does not aim to recapture, even for present law, the ideals or practical purposes of the politicians who first created it. It aims rather to justify what they did (sometimes including [. . .] what they said) in an overall story worth telling now, a story with a complex claim: that present practice can be organized by and justified in principles sufficiently attractive to provide an honorable future' (1986: 227–8). In her discussion of Dworkin's argument, Julie Allard notes that '[t]his aspect of justification proper to law sheds light on the Kantian idea according to which judgment is not an imitation but an inheritance' (2001: 146). In referring to a *preceding* example, one does not reproduce it but draws from the same sources.

14 Observe in passing that the way in which common-law judges reason their opinions often resembles the writing of a first-person narrative.

15 The original French title of Latour (2002) is *La Fabrique du droit*.

Bibliography

Allard, J. (2001) *Dworkin et Kant: réflexions sur le jugement*, Brussels: Éditions de l'Université de Bruxelles.

Arendt, H. (1982) *Lectures on Kant's Political Philosophy*, R. Beiner (ed.), Chicago, IL: University of Chicago Press.

Beck, U. (2004) *The Cosmopolitan Vision*, trans. C. Cronin, Cambridge: Polity Press, 2006.

Benjamin, W. (1936) 'The Storyteller', in *Selected Writings*, H. Eiland and M.W. Jennings (eds), trans. H. Zohn, vol. III, Cambridge, MA: Harvard University Press, 2002.

Chevallier, J. (2016) 'Qu'est-ce qu'un bon juriste?' (unpublished; on file).

Dworkin, R. (1986) *Law's Empire*, Cambridge, MA: Harvard University Press.

Eco, U. (1984) *Semiotics and the Philosophy of Language*, Bloomington, IN: Indiana University Press.

Ferrara, A. (2008) *The Force of the Example*, New York: Columbia University Press.
Gadamer, H.-G. (1986) *Truth and Method*, trans. J. Weinsheimer and D.G. Marshall, 2nd rev. Eng. edn, New York: Continuum, 2004.
Hart, H.L.A. (1961) *The Concept of Law*, 3rd edn, L. Green (ed.), Oxford: Oxford University Press, 2012.
Jackson, B.S. (1988) *Law, Fact and Narrative Coherence*, Roby, UK: D. Charles.
Jullien, F. (2008) *On the Universal, the Uniform, the Common and Dialogue Between Cultures*, trans. M. Richardson and K. Fijalkowski, Cambridge: Polity Press, 2014.
Kant, I. (1793) *Critique of the Power of Judgment*, P. Guyer (ed.), trans. P. Guyer and E. Matthews, Cambridge: Cambridge University Press, 2000.
Latour, B. (2002) *The Making of Law*, trans. M. Brilman and A. Pottage, Cambridge: Polity Press, 2010.
Lyotard, J.-F. (1979) *The Postmodern Condition*, trans. G. Bennington and B. Massumi, Minneapolis, MN: University of Minnesota Press, 1984.
—— (1983) *The Differend*, trans. G. Van Den Abbeele, Minneapolis, MN: University of Minnesota Press, 1988.
Merleau-Ponty, M. (1969) *The Prose of the World*, C. Lefort (ed.), trans. J. O'Neill, Evanston, IL: Northwestern University Press, 1973.
Nussbaum, M.C. (1995) *Poetic Justice*, Boston, MA: Beacon Press.
Ost, F. (2004) *Raconter la loi*, Paris: O. Jacob.
—— and I. Ost (2015) 'Representing the Unrepresentable: Making Law Anyway', *Pólemos*, 9: 199–219.
—— and Kerchove, M. van de (2012) *Pyramide ou réseau? Pour une théorie dialectique du droit*, Brussels: Presses de l'Université Saint-Louis.
Plato (380 BCE), *The Republic*, 2nd edn, H. Bloom (ed.), trans. H. Bloom, New York: Basic Books, 1991.
—— (348 BCE), *The Laws*, T.L. Pangle (ed.), trans. T.L. Pangle, Chicago, IL: University of Chicago Press, 1988.
Quine, W.V.O. (1960) *Word and Object*, Cambridge, MA: MIT Press.
—— (1962) 'Le mythe de la signification', in L. Beck and J. Wahl (eds) *La Philosophie analytique*, Paris: Éditions de Minuit.
Ricœur, P. (1990) *Oneself as Another*, trans. K. Blamey, Chicago, IL: University of Chicago Press, 1992.
—— (1995) *The Just*, trans. D. Pellauer, Chicago, IL: University of Chicago Press, 2000.
Salmon, C. (2007) *Storytelling*, trans. D. Macey, London: Verso, 2010.
Smith, A. (1790) *The Theory of Moral Sentiments*, K. Haakonssen (ed.), Cambridge: Cambridge University Press, 2002.
Walzer, M. (1990) *Thinking Politically*, D. Miller (ed.), New Haven, CT: Yale University Press, 2007.
White, J.B. (1990) *Justice as Translation*, Chicago, IL: University of Chicago Press.
Wittgenstein, L. (1953) *Philosophical Investigations*, 4th edn, P.M.S. Hacker and J. Schulte (eds), trans. G.E.M. Anscombe, P.M.S. Hacker and J. Schulte, Oxford: Wiley-Blackwell, 2009.

Part III

Variances/discrepancies

Chapter 8

Wittgenstein on rule-following and interpretation

Julia Tanney

I. Introduction

Sections 201 and 202 of Wittgenstein's *Philosophical Investigations* (1953) are probably the most discussed and disputed passages of twentieth-century philosophy. In what follows, I shall give my own reading of the argumentative strategy contained in these important remarks.

First, let us take a look at the famous passages:

> §201. This was our paradox: no course of action could be determined by a rule, because any course of action can be made out to accord with the rule. The answer was: if *any* action can be made out to accord with the rule, then it can also be made out to conflict with it. And so there would be neither accord nor conflict here.
>
> It can be seen that there is a misunderstanding here from the mere fact that in the course of our argument we give one interpretation after another; as if each one contented us at least for a moment, until we thought of yet another standing behind it. What this shews is that there is a way of grasping a rule which is *not* an *interpretation*, but which is exhibited in what we call 'obeying the rule' and 'going against it' in actual cases.
>
> Hence there is an inclination to say: any action according to the rule is an interpretation. But we ought to restrict the term 'interpretation' to the substitution of one expression of the rule for another.
>
> §202. And hence also 'obeying a rule' is a practice. And to *think* one is obeying a rule is not to obey a rule. Hence it is not possible to obey a rule 'privately': otherwise thinking one was obeying a rule would be the same thing as obeying it.
>
> (Wittgenstein 1953, emphasis original)

Next, let us take a quick look at the major steps of the argument that (in my view) underlie these remarks.

A. Let us stipulate what we shall call a 'rule' to be that which imposes conditions of correctness or acceptability on a particular action, step, or move within a practice. A move, then, might be judged acceptable, admissible, permissible, correct, or not, in so far as it accords with or falls afoul of the rule. A 'tool' is an instrument that allows us to implement the rule.

B. There are innumerably many different ways of acting in the light of a rule or making use of tools that implement it *correctly*, depending upon the particular circumstances.

C. Suppose the correct way to implement a rule in any particular situation can be spelled out by instruction. This constitutes what we will call an 'interpretation' of the rule: in this context, an interpretation is a fuller expression or higher-order specification of the rule, intended to facilitate understanding of how it is to be applied.

D. Any higher-order specification (interpretation) of how a rule is to be obeyed will also be subject to innumerable ways of obeying it correctly, depending upon the circumstances, *ad infinitum*.

E. Given C and D, nothing determinate is prescribed or proscribed by any given rule. Thus, we arrive at a point where there is neither accord nor conflict.

F. But this conflicts with A.

G. After an examination of what we call 'obeying a rule' and 'going against it' in actual cases, we see that, contrary to what is suggested above, we do not appeal to ever higher-order specifications of rules. Justifications come to an end until the only response left is an appeal to what we, as a matter of practice, do.

H. Hence 'obeying a rule' is a practice.

I. 'It seems to me to be correct' qualifies as a justification neither for a move that purports to accord with a rule nor for the correct use of higher-order instructions to facilitate the move. Thus, it cannot be possible to obey a rule privately.

In what follows I shall discuss and argue for these points in some detail. Before I do, however, let us take a look at the purpose of these remarks. The target is a mythical picture – bringing in its train metaphysical and epistemological predicaments – that needs resisting.

This mythical picture supposes that what is used in the teaching of practices, consulted in the course of them, or read off by an observer, are mere expressions of rules: the real rules are something at which these expressions only gesture. Once grasped, apprehended, or intuited by a participant in these normative activities, there is no rational option but to do as the rule requires: apprehension of the rule is sufficient to determine and thus to explain how the one who grasps it acts as it mandates. According to this mythical picture, when expressions of the rules are not used in the learning or teaching of the activity, nor within the practice itself, those who have mastered it can be credited with more than knowledge by wont of the relevant standards of correctness: they have (somehow) come into cognitive contact with rules that determine these standards, unexpressed or unrepresented though they may be, which (somehow) guide them and thus (somehow) explain their ability to act as they mandate. A 'cavalierly' *realist* version of this myth supposes that the real rule, shorn of its expression, exists independently not only of any particular individual's grasp and propensity to act in accordance with it, but independently of human practices altogether: the rule consists in steps that are already drawn in advance.

A variation on this mythical picture is that anyone who issues a command, who means something by an utterance, or who intends that his expression be taken in a certain way *has in mind* the way his command, meaning, or expression of intention should be acted upon in all possible circumstances, extending indefinitely into the future. As if the successful implementation of his command, or uptake of his meaning or intention, follows steps already drawn – in his mind – in advance and independently of the particular circumstances of his utterance.

The reach of this mythical picture extends to most of the debated topics in philosophy today. Its attraction, as well as its metaphysical mysteriousness, is due to its seeming to accommodate the *objectivity* as well as the *force* of that which we hold most dear. For 'rules' we can substitute 'reasons', 'principles of morality', 'linguistic meaning', and 'mathematical truths', to name a few. Moreover, if a person's acting morally, with reason, intentionally, or with knowledge of any kind is a matter of her having a private grasp of these rules, as the mythical picture suggests, then the *epistemology* of rule-following brings in tow further wonders about how we could ever know that one is to be credited (or not) with acting in any of these ways. This picture is responsible for a great number of conundrums that occupy professional philosophers today in almost all of its various sub-disciplines.

Wittgenstein's discussion of rules should put this myth and its attendant metaphysical and epistemological problems to rest. Although he was, in the passages we are regarding here, particularly interested in the idea that in speaking and understanding a language one is operating a calculus according to fixed rules, the arguments here extend far beyond.

With this by way of introduction, let us move on to how I interpret the argument contained in Wittgenstein's famous remarks, taking them step by step.

II. The argument in detail

> A. Let us stipulate what we shall call a 'rule' to be that which imposes conditions of correctness or acceptability on a particular action, step, or move within a practice. A move, then, might be judged acceptable, admissible, permissible, correct, or not, in so far as it accords with or falls afoul of the rule. A 'tool' is an instrument that allows us to implement the rule.

Consider the various kinds of tools we use to apply rules in the sense above, both in our everyday and technical practices: rulers, diagrams, signposts, maps, colour charts, recipes, mathematical formulae, and even images are just a few of those we make use of, either in learning the moves in question, within the practice when we need to avail ourselves of them for checking that our moves accord with the standards, and afterwards, for example, in order to correct or defend our actions. I mean by 'practice' here such things as taking measurements, drawing or building, travelling to a destination, choosing a colour, cooking, calculating, and so on. We are investigating such basic and banal situations in order to dispel some of the mystery that tends to cloud our understanding when the topic is morality, law, rationality, mathematics, and language.

When Wittgenstein invents his 'primitive language games', he is, in effect, describing his own rule-governed (i.e. normative) practices: ones in which he stipulates what moves count as correct, appropriate, permissible, and so on. For example, he tells us in the language game of §2 that when the builder calls out the name of a stone, the assistant is to bring a stone with that name to him. What counts as a correct move in this primitive normative practice is an action performed by the assistant: namely, his bringing the required stone when asked. In the language game of §1, the action required is more complicated. Here, the shopkeeper is to consult the paper (on which is written 'five red apples') and he is to open the drawer marked apples, consult his colour chart to find the word 'red' and the sample opposite, and then count out five apples to give his customer. Notice that in this particular primitive language game, the shopkeeper uses a device of the kind we have described above. He consults a colour chart to help him determine which apples to pull out of the drawer. The chart, then, imposes a rule in the sense described: it sets conditions on what is to count as an appropriate move in this particular practice – here, what is to count as red for the purposes of choosing apples.

> B. There are innumerably many different ways of acting in the light of a rule or making use of tools that implement it *correctly*, depending upon the particular circumstances.

This is a phenomenon with which we are all familiar. Consider, for example, the simple instruction 'Add three eggs'. In the context of a recipe for brownies, we would use raw chicken eggs, crack them open, and pour their contents into a bowl. In the context of preparing Easter baskets, however, we would use either hard-boiled or 'blown' – that is, hollow – decorated chicken eggs or chocolate ones and add them to the basket *without* cracking them open. In the context of an arithmetic lesson, we would, for example, choose three eggs and add them to whatever other items we are using in our calculation. Whether these are raw, cooked, chicken, or chocolate eggs does not matter. Indeed, they might be models or even pictures of eggs. The question of cracking them open or leaving them intact does not arise.

Of course, the same sorts of variations in how we correctly go by a rule apply to diagrams (such as for flat-pack furniture), for signposts (such as arrows), for maps, and for mathematical formulae. This can be brought home with the realization that one has to learn how to use these tools in different situations. Because it often comes so naturally *how* we are to use them once we have been trained, it may be worth reminding ourselves of the fact that different situations call for different uses of the very same instruments.

Notice in the case of the shopkeeper game described above, we can readily imagine how the colour chart is to be used. But *must* it be followed in any particular way? We were asked to imagine that opposite the word 'red' is a patch of colour. But 'opposite' itself signifies a relation that admits of a great deal of variability. If we were not trained or naturally inclined to read these charts in more or less the same way, then we might need instruction in how to use them in particular circumstances.

Wittgenstein also discusses whether mental images are necessary in determining the meaning of a word. Suppose, if I am unsure about the meaning of 'cube', a picture of one is handed to me. This may help. But I would need to know what to make of it, since there are various methods of projection from the image to the use of the word 'cube'. To bring this point home, let us acknowledge that any representation of a cube will involve details that strictly speaking are not essential – its size and colour, for example. And so, too, will it leave out certain essential aspects, such as, for example, the cube's three-dimensionality. So, even if we do use images to help determine the meaning of a word, there must be a method of projection from the representation to the use of the word. This method of projection – which shows us how it is to be used – is an integral part of the tool if it is to do the job required.

This is perhaps even easier to see for those of us who, not mathematically inclined, are presented with an algebraic formula to determine the continuation of a series, or one expressing a natural law of, say, the melting temperature of a precious metal. You may be the proud owner of a Cy Twombly painting with tokens of equations scribbled all over the canvas. But this does not, unfortunately, give you knowledge of a mathematical formula or a law of nature unless you know what to do with it: how to apply it to the situation at hand.

> C. Suppose the correct way to implement a rule in any particular situation can be spelled out by instruction. This constitutes what we will call an 'interpretation' of the rule: in this context, an interpretation is a fuller expression or higher-order specification of the rule, intended to specify how it is to be applied.

Plenty of rules come replete with clues as to how they are to be acted upon. Consider, for example, the key or legend that accompanies a map, or a glossary that accompanies a dictionary. Wittgenstein examines such higher-order specifications when he discusses the instructions for following a table:

> 86. Imagine a language-game like (2) played with the help of a table. The signs given to B by A are now written ones. B has a table; in the first column

> are the signs used in the game, in the second pictures of building stones. A shews B such a written sign; B looks it up in the table, looks at the picture opposite, and so on. So the table is a rule which he follows in executing orders. – One learns to look the picture up in the table by receiving a training, and part of this training consists perhaps in the pupil's learning to pass with his finger horizontally from left to right; and so, as it were, to draw a series of horizontal lines on the table.
>
> Suppose different ways of reading a table were now introduced; one time, as above, according to the schema:
>
> 
>
> another time like this:
>
> 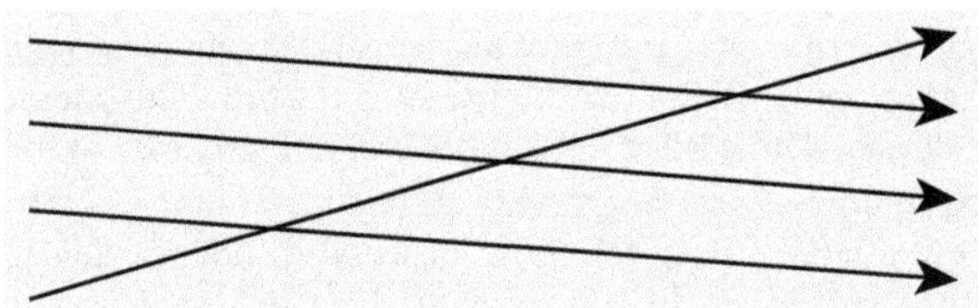
>
> or in some other way. – Such a schema is supplied with the table as the rule for its use.

He goes on to ask:

> Can we not now imagine further rules to explain *this* one? And, on the other hand, was that first table incomplete without the schema of arrows? And are other tables incomplete without their schemata?
>
> (Wittgenstein 1953, emphasis original)

Yes, of course we can imagine further rules to explain this one. Would they help? They may do. But they may not. Even if they do, this does not mean that either set of rules was incomplete without the aid of further, higher-order specifications.

> D. Any higher-order specification (interpretation) of how rule is to be obeyed will also be subject to innumerable ways of obeying it correctly, depending upon the circumstances, *ad infinitum*.

Let us return to the recipe for brownies. Suppose we add a specification for the instruction 'Add three eggs'. In order to add three eggs, we might say, you should count out three chicken eggs, crack them open, and pour their contents into the bowl. Someone who has never baked or cooked eggs may go astray here in a way that is *incorrect* in the context of baking brownies, but would not be incorrect in some of the other circumstances we examined above. In other words, just as there are different appropriate responses to the instruction 'Add three eggs', if we vary the circumstances or the practices we are pondering, there may be different acceptable responses to the higher-order directive 'Count out three chicken eggs' or 'crack the eggs open' or 'pour their contents into the bowl'. In the context of baking, it is correct to remove the shells before pouring the contents in the bowl. What counts as the eggs' contents, in this situation, is the (unfertilized) yolk and white. Different contents (two yolks, a foetus, blood, or jelly beans) would not do. In order to spell this out in an attempt to make the instructions more exact, however, we would certainly introduce new possibilities, which may themselves need further elaboration. (If the two yolks are small enough, or if the fertilized egg is less than a day old, this may be permissible, but not otherwise.)

Going through examples such as these, again and again Wittgenstein reminds us that pictures, linguistic expressions, signs, maps, diagrams, and so on – the tools we use to implement standards of correctness – have a fair amount of flexibility built into them as to how they are to be employed: particular occasions call for different uses, each of which may be correct for the situation at hand. So adding further, higher-order pictures, linguistic expressions, signs, maps, diagrams, or formulae will simply iterate this variability, even if doing so might be helpful in particular cases.

This simple exercise – reminding ourselves how things are or might have been different – is important when we are tempted by the thought that the rule itself dictates how it is to be applied.

Some people feel the case of mathematical formulae is different: that there is only one way to follow the instruction 'Add two' when continuing a series. But perhaps this is because we have in mind a particular series – for example, the natural numbers. But in the context of the days or months in a calendar, or the hours, minutes, and seconds of a day, then what will count as adding two *correctly* will be different.

If this sort of reasoning is on the right track, then we might conclude:

> E. Given C and D, nothing determinate is prescribed or proscribed by any given rule. Thus, we arrive at a point where there is neither accord nor conflict.

This will not do, however, for:

> F. This conflicts with A, which stipulates a rule to be that which imposes conditions of correctness or acceptability on a particular action, step, or move within a practice.

So something is wrong.

Before going further, it may be worth pausing here to contemplate a natural response. Perhaps the meaning of – or how we are to follow the instruction –'Add three eggs' depends upon the intention of the one giving the orders. When we obey the order correctly, it is because we interpret correctly the intentions of, say, the recipe writer or the one who prepares the Easter basket.

The philosophically tendentious thought behind this response is that when a person means something by an utterance, has a thought, or expresses an intention with a particular content, or when I understand the utterance, thought, or intention of another, we both 'grasp' a proposition which, as it is understood in this context, determines the conditions in which it (the thought, utterance, or intention) is true or will be satisfied in every possible circumstance of its tokening. Just as, according to the mythical picture, the meaning of an utterance (including the conditions of its satisfaction or its truth) is laid out in advance of all possible circumstances and determines in advance its logical implications, so, too, for any possible thought content. For such a 'content' is none other than a proposition in this sense.

It should be clear, however, that introducing the notion of meaning, intention, or thought into this discussion takes us no further in the dialectic, for it serves simply to reintroduce the mythical picture that we are resisting.

We can in all innocence invoke the intentions of one, say, giving an order or laying down a law, but in so doing we are not assuming that *there is a determinate* answer as to how the intention should be respected in every possible future case. To suppose so is to reintroduce the idea that natural language expressions (and the thoughts they express) lay down determinate truth or satisfaction conditions independently of the context, circumstances, or practices in which they figure. But as our examples so far have shown, no rule that we are familiar with – including those expressed in images, diagrams, formulae, or natural language – does any such thing. Such expressions are pliable. They are put to various uses like tools in a toolbox. But their efficacy for any particular task is not hampered as a result.

There is much more to be said about the notion of meaning, thought, and intention. But let us now continue with the argument.

> G. After an examination of what we call 'obeying a rule' and 'going against it' in actual cases, we see that, contrary to what is suggested above, we do not appeal to ever higher-order specifications of rules. Justifications come to an end until the only response left is an appeal to what we, as a matter of practice, do.

Let us go back to our everyday examples. Anyone making brownies fails to act upon the instruction 'Add three eggs' correctly when she plops them whole, shells intact, into her batter. The market stall owner fails to implement the instruction 'Add three eggs' appropriately when he cracks them open and discards their contents into the basket of the customer containing bread, cheese, and milk.

It should have become clear by now that when we concluded that nothing determinate is prescribed or proscribed by any given rule considered independently of the circumstances of its use, we were asking too much of our tools. We were certainly asking more than we normally do of them, for when we examine their uses in the various situations in which they normally function, they in fact *do* prescribe or proscribe various moves.

The instruction 'Add three eggs' in the context of baking brownies, for example, requires removing the yolk and the white from the egg and discarding the shell before adding them to the batter. The instruction 'Add three eggs' in the middle of a shopping trip, when communicated to the market stall owner, demands that he put three eggs in a basket, say, without cracking them open first. Those of us *au fait* with these practices know how to use the recipes, maps, diagrams, pictures, signposts, and formulae in question, and we act as required. When clarification is needed – for example, by a further specification or interpretation how the rule is to be obeyed – we usually have no trouble understanding how that specification or interpretation should be put into action and, again, we perform as expected.

Whether or not we need higher-order instructions for how to use a tool depends on several factors: perhaps, as in cracking eggs open, we will learn by demonstration; in the case of mathematical formulae, by drill. In other cases – such as following an arrow or a pointed finger – we (and some dogs) will (but a cat will not) find it natural to look or turn in the indicated direction.

Do we need to use a tool or rule to guide us in the first place? That, too, depends on the situation. In the shopkeeper game, it was specified that the shopkeeper was to use the chart to determine the colour of the apple. In other words, it was set up as part of the practice that the device specifying what is to count as red be used. We can, of course, imagine other practices in which a shopkeeper, for example, would not need to use a chart to ascertain which apples are red. If a builder can reliably determine a metre length by sight, then presumably he would only need a ruler when convincing others (or himself, if he has doubts) that he is right. We do not normally consult dictionaries when speaking languages in which we are fluent unless we need to check a difficult word or convince another that our use of the word was appropriate. Similarly, we would not need to use a recipe for brownies if we were able to make them without one.

The situation is different when we are teaching, learning, and perhaps even persuading others. The teacher may not only be required to be able to *do* and to *show*, but also to *tell* by giving instruction. And those who teach teachers may have at their disposal even higher-order specifications as their tools of their trade.

The story, as it is unfolding, appears to subordinate what we are calling 'rules' to the practices which they serve. They are implemented by tools, as it were, to be used as needed. But now the sense in which rules 'determine' correct or incorrect moves within a practice is in need of clarification. For it is not as though the rules come first, logically speaking, and the moves that accord with them come later. This picture – part of the mythical one we are questioning – has been rejected with the realization that if we consider the rules independently of any particular practice or circumstances of their use, then they prescribe or proscribe any number of different moves. This is what led to the 'paradox' that there would be neither accord nor conflict.

Instead, if we regard the expression of rules – recipes, charts, diagrams, instructions – as tools that we are naturally equipped or trained to use correctly given the situation, then they 'determine' correct or incorrect moves only with this presupposition in place. Only someone who is not completely lost will benefit from the instruction about how to add three eggs. He will already need to know what the yolks and whites are, what to do with the shells, and what it means, in the circumstances, to 'add' them to the bowl. Any further specification (as we have seen) will simply reintroduce further possibilities of misinterpretation, so, again, the instruction, if it is to be helpful, presupposes prior knowledge of what actions are required, ending with basic abilities that are presupposed of our would-be chef.

Suppose one were to ask: Why do we obey the rule or put the instruction into action in one way rather than another? There may be an answer: perhaps one way is easier, or more practical. Or we might recognize that it could have been done or still could be done in any number of ways. Sometimes there may just be a shrugging of the shoulders. Justifications come to an end. Perhaps the answer is simply: 'This is what we do.'

H. Hence 'obeying a rule' is a practice.

To say that obeying or following a rule is a practice is to emphasize that justification as to why we should act in one way rather than another reaches bedrock with the response that it is just our custom or practice to do it this way rather than another. This allows us to preserve the idea that there can be accord or conflict with the rule: a way of acting in accordance with it and going against it even when justifications have come to an end and all we can do, if we are pushed, is advert to what we do.

This is consistent with the thought that although interpretations can be given – that is, higher-order specifications of how lower-order rules are to be obeyed – these higher-order rules only determine correct moves because they too belong to (higher-order) normative practices. Eventually, these practices also reach bedrock with the admission that *this is what we do*.

With this admission, a certain philosophical picture of what it is to engage in rule-following practices (in particular, to speak and understand language) is overturned. It has been held, for example, that meaning-rules determine the truth conditions of the expressions of natural languages 'from above' as it were. Their nature was thought to be timeless, eternal, unchanging, and far-reaching. We do not understand our expressions until we grasp (traditionally: by an act of intuition) the word-meanings (concepts) or sentence-meanings (propositions) which they supposedly express. This picture becomes replaced by one in which having mastered an ability or knowing how to proceed is logically prior to the ability to appeal to rules that determine that, or to give justifications as to why, one ought to proceed in such and such a way.

One who is credited with the ability to participate in a practice knows how to make the kinds of moves that accord with the standards of correctness, acceptability, or truth. He or she may also be required to know how to correct, challenge, or justify any given move in the light of standards by appealing to the rules that enshrine them. Of course, this higher-order activity – challenging or justifying – is interpersonal at its core. Thus, for any practice or activity in which standards for correctness *are* in place, one answer that will not count as an appropriate justification is: 'because it seems to me that this is correct'. Indeed, the move from what *seems to be* right to what *is* right is the very one that the rules were introduced to determine in the first place.

In other words, as long as these are norm-governed practices – there are moves that count as correct or incorrect – we must preserve the possibility that any one person or participant in the practice may be mistaken as to whether she has acted correctly (or, if she is following a rule for acting, whether she is following the rule correctly). And a satisfactory justification cannot be that it seems to her as if she has.

Given this thought, then it cannot be possible to follow a rule privately: for if it were, the distinction between following a rule correctly and merely thinking one is doing so would collapse.

QED.

Bibliography

Wittgenstein, L. (1953) *Philosophical Investigations*, trans. G.E.M. Anscombe, 3rd bilingual edn, Oxford: Blackwell, 2001.

Chapter 9

Derrida's Gadamer

Pierre Legrand

> There is [. . .] a dissemination [of meaning] that is irreducible to hermeneutics in the sense of Gadamer.
>
> Jacques Derrida

While French, German or Italian philosophers consider that they practise 'philosophy', Anglophone philosophers deem them to be engaged in '*Continental* philosophy'. Approaching 'Continental philosophy' as a discipline, one observes that, as is the case with other fields, it reveals a specific history. Indeed, in the words of intellectual historian Peter Gordon, '[i]nsofar as Continental philosophy today can still claim to be a coherent intellectual tradition, its identity is bound to history and is therefore burdened by the memory of events' (2010: 358). Some of Continental philosophy's milestones consist in celebrated disputations, arguably none as famous as the encounter between Ernst Cassirer and Martin Heidegger, a two-week philosophical conversation consisting of lectures and debates that took place in Davos, Switzerland, in March and April 1929. This *Auseinandersetzung* immediately assumed great philosophical significance and continues to be viewed in philosophical memory as a defining argumentative moment casting, on one hand, a world-view that posited the primacy of human agency and, on the other, an understanding of the human being confining him to a largely receptive position. In other words, Davos opposed the ideas of 'spontaneity' and 'thrownness' as they stood for two countervailing models of man and of the extent to which man is conditioned by his worldliness (Gordon 2010: 363),[1] as they epitomized two apprehensions of how much human finitude is to be envisaged as 'a permanent and incorrigible feature' of the constitutive condition of human being (ibid.: 76).

In the *Frankfurter Zeitung* dated 22 April 1929, a philosopher writing for the newspaper is said to have observed that the *Internationale Davoser Hochschulkurse*, the host organization, had staged 'not merely an academic quarrel between professors', but 'a confrontation between representative envoys of two epochs' – although the two speakers were in fact only fifteen years apart (ibid.: 329). Emmanuel Levinas, in attendance in Davos as a budding philosopher, recalled the moment in spectacular terms: 'A young student could have the feeling that he was witnessing the creation and the end of the world' (Poirié 1987: 78). In the words of the late Professor of Philosophy and Judaic Studies Steven Schwarzschild (1924–1989), '"Davos" was like a medieval morality-play, in which each of the two antagonists represented great ideas or virtues' ([no date]: 2). Gordon remarks that 'for several critics, the difference of historical and philosophical perspective was so immense that it prohibited genuine dialogue' (2010: 330). In this regard, he notes that 'each [philosopher] spoke a unique language with terminology so distinct as to defy the possibility of mutual translation' (ibid.: 189), while Levinas referred to 'an unsurpassable antinomy' (Poirié 1987: 77). Heidegger bore no small responsibility for this communicative impasse as he had basically redrafted the language of philosophy in ways that his critics would not hesitate to call 'abstruse' (Cassirer 1948: 187).[2]

Secondarily, the clash was one of personalities. Heidegger was a vehement, conflictual, passionate, at times lyrical thinker, already admired by many young German academics for his innovative readings of the philosophical tradition and for a style of interpretation that could turn a text somewhat violently on its head with a view to unearthing its (allegedly) concealed content. Also, Heidegger strongly defended his country roots, in effect holding the idiosyncratic view that 'only in the country side was genuine reflection truly possible' (Gordon 2010: 112). Whereas for Heidegger it seemed, as the academic saying goes in some quarters, that if it was not rude it was not worth it, Cassirer very much appeared in the garb of a wise old man set in the classical philosophical mode, a discreet and well-mannered thinker with more than a touch of patrician demeanour, a civilized humanist who exuded urbanity and espoused moderate and rationalist thought, a pacifist who eschewed polemics, an erudite whose blandness in fact went so far, it is reported to have been said with regret by Karl Jaspers, as to fail to inspire (ibid.: 86). Perhaps unsurprisingly, Cassirer, who valued philosophical amity, often indicated throughout the Davos encounter how ultimately similar Heidegger's views and his own actually were. Meanwhile, Heidegger, who did not seem to care for philosophical friends unless they were his disciples, incessantly emphasized the sharp differences between Cassirer and himself (ibid.: 346). As Schwarzschild perspicuously frames the matter, Davos pitted against one another 'the gentleman and the peasant-in-arms' ([no date]: 2).

Just over fifty years later, in April 1981, another highly consequential discussion took place, which again involved two European philosophical giants. Over three days, the Paris *Goethe-Institut* thus staged an argument under the banner 'Text and Interpretation' between Hans-Georg Gadamer (1900–2002), one of Heidegger's closest and most influential students, and Jacques Derrida (1930–2004), a thinker also deeply indebted to Heidegger but who, though readily acknowledging his intellectual dues (1972c: 18, 73; 1980a: 70), refused to style himself a disciple (2002a: 41), forged his distinctive intellectual path and transformed key Heideggerian insights along the way. Indeed, Derrida would refer to Heidegger as '[his] *contremaître*' – that is, as the master against whom he was thinking and writing in the very name of loyalty to Heideggerian contrarianism (1999a: 57, emphasis added): 'I am all the time in the process of disobeying a Heideggerian injunction that, nonetheless, I feel within me' (Janicaud 2001: 115).[3] In Paris, in line with the philosophical labels that had come to be attached to their work, Gadamer and Derrida were perceived to be presenting a confrontation between 'hermeneutics' and 'deconstruction' (Bertram 2002; Angehrn 2003; Kapsch 2010; Silverman 1994; Greisch 1977; Jankovic 2003).

On the occasion of their debate, Gadamer unmistakably appeared, like Cassirer half a century earlier, in the guise of the elderly, courteous, reasonable and consensual interlocutor. For his part, Derrida, three decades younger than his opponent, adopted the role of the philosophical firebrand who boldly, at times pugnaciously, questioned the eminent texts and chastised what he deemed their fustiness and the unduly conservative readings that were being made of them. A combative and contentious thinker boasting a huge following in academic ranks mainly in the United States but elsewhere also, a philosopher not at all adverse to literary or lyrical inflexions, Derrida was at pains to affirm his basic differences with his debater just as Heidegger had done in Davos. And Derrida very much remained an outsider from the standpoint of mainstream French philosophy, not unlike the way Heidegger had been marginal vis-à-vis classical German philosophy in the Cassirerian mould,[4] although it would be a mistake to overemphasize the analogies between the two philosophers. Quite apart from the fact that one was a Jew and the other a Nazi,[5] Derrida lived in something like self-imposed exile for all of his adult life and was a restless world traveller whose peripateticism could not have been at greater variance with Heidegger's determined sedentariness.

As in Davos, the Paris meeting was structured around presentations and conversations. Echoing the reactions to the Davos controversy, commentaries on the Paris encounter underline the notable character of a contest that went beyond mere philosophical disagreement to address 'two radically different interpretations of interpretation, of writing, even of language itself' (Michelfelder and Palmer 1989: 1). Also, writers such as Richard Bernstein and Jean Grondin remark how Gadamer and Derrida spoke such different languages that, in the end, '[a] genuine dialogue between [them] [. . .] never t[ook] place' (Bernstein 2002: 276); how there happened at best 'a dialogue of the deaf' (Grondin 2011b: 97) – an impasse just as had materialized in Davos. It cannot have helped that, like Heidegger, Derrida never seemed to hesitate in crafting neologisms that could leave even benevolent audiences baffled.

Beyond the fact that '[t]he differences between Gadamer and Derrida – in temperament, vocabulary, style, and thematic concerns – seem so radical that one may despair of finding anything in common [. . .] we can say that both [were] passionately concerned with the subtleties of language and the interpretation of texts' (Bernstein 2002: 275). With respect to commonalities, one could readily add that by 1981 both philosophers had actively participated in the so-called 'linguistic turn' – that is, to put the matter as succinctly as one can, in a movement emphasizing the power of language that began in philosophy and spread through the humanities, language's stated 'position of primacy in the inquiries we undertake and the ways we make sense of things and of ourselves' inscribing 'a fundamental break with methodologies and ontologies that for more than three centuries [had] privileged the internal mental states of a disembodied knowing subject' (Kompridis 2014: xv). And one could also mention that Gadamer and Derrida rejected the idea of the subject's unrestricted self-enactability that would exercise unalloyed authority over the world and engage in world-producing, object-determinative activity (Gadamer 1986a: 281; Derrida 1967b: 335). In the same vein, neither thinker was persuaded by the merits of method (Gadamer 1986a: 306; Derrida 1972a: 303) – indeed, the two philosophers remained unconvinced by anything smacking of programmability or calculability and deployed, more generally, anti-positivist and anti-scientistic stances. Incidentally, this accumulation of interfaces has led John Caputo, one of Derrida's most learned analysts, to praise deconstruction as a 'radical hermeneutics' (1987).

Yet these intersections, prompting Derrida himself to style hermeneutics as a form of deconstruction (1972b: 162–3), cannot dispel the disagreements that obtain concerning the primordial matters of alterity and textuality, some of which were on display in Paris not least because Derrida cast his conversation with Gadamer in a resolutely adversarial light, evoking the undisguised acerbity that Heidegger had visited on Cassirer. Although there is evidence that Gadamer had long been interested in Derrida (Grondin 2012: 377) – indeed, that he had been reading him as far back as 1962 (Grondin 2011a: 457, n. 1) – and further proof that he was willing to learn from Derrida (Grondin 2003: 116–8) with a view to questioning hermeneutics – for instance, by ultimately envisaging that hermeneutics may have been too sanguine as regards the feasibility of understanding and agreement (Gadamer 1988: 142) – Derrida neither intimated a disposition to reap from Gadamer nor any eagerness to investigate deconstruction hermeneutically – an 'asymmetry' that Grondin describes as 'blatant' (2011b: 101). Specifically, Derrida's talk at the *Goethe-Institut* did not address Gadamer's philosophy and refused to mention him at all (1981: 58–71).[6] Indeed, if one reviews Derrida's work from the time of his first publications in the mid-1960s up to the Paris debate, one observes that on the few occasions when hermeneutics made a noteworthy appearance, it was stigmatized as a sort of search engine destined to elucidate and fixate the real or true sense of texts, to bring to light through a brand of consensus somehow allowing the *interpretans* to reach the *interpretandum*,[7] a unitary, complete and stabilized meaning.

In his most caustic observations, Derrida thus decried hermeneutics as a 'basically traditional' venture (1972c: 118), 'sheltering behind a given and stable institution' (1990a: 424) and in thrall to the 'deciphering' or the 'decrypting of a meaning or a truth' (1972b: 392), to 'the true meaning of a text' (1978: 86), a 'discourse on truth' (1980a: 470). He attacked it as 'semantic' or 'formalistic' (1972c: 118; see also 1980a: 460), even assimilating it to an 'exegetical method' (1972c: 86). Chastising the fact that it idolized and idealized the text (1988: 29), that it postulated the existence of 'an accomplished signified' (1972c: 86), and regretting an 'appropriati[ng]' (1988: 29), indeed a 'totalizing' (1987: 116) enterprise, what he called 'hermeneutic mastery' (1978: 110), Derrida castigated 'the hermeneutic temptation' (2005: 25) for its 'somnambulism' (1978: 104) or its 'aestheticizing and obscurantist reaction' (1978: 112) to the matter of interpretation. Condemning 'the hermeneutic space of the question of truth' (1978: 94), Derrida held that hermeneutics's 'default' (2005: 25) cast a 'veil' (1978: 107) over the interpretive enterprise, that hermeneutics was like a piece of cloth that one had to 'pierce' (1978: 107). By the same token, in word-play expressly aimed at Friedrich Schleiermacher, a nineteenth-century German philosopher closely associated with hermeneutics' modern revival, Derrida opposed 'all veil-makers' (1978: 108). Derrida's stated goal was a 'deconstruction of a certain hermeneutics' (1990a: 454) – that is, of a hermeneutics that is ultimately certain of itself, 'assured of its horizon' (1978: 107), in search of 'an only originary meaning' (1986b: 50). In sum, Derrida advocated alterity or textuality's resistance to 'the hermeneutic exhaustion' (1986b: 50), to a reading that would be definitive, complete, exhaustive – to an interpretation that would be *fixed*.

These determinedly unconciliatory accounts of hermeneutics over the years would plausibly have to do with the fact, as Grondin surmises, that throughout the 1960s and 1970s Gadamer's work was largely unknown in France where the idea of 'hermeneutics' rather evoked Paul Ricœur. Indeed, Derrida was Ricœur's assistant at the Sorbonne in the early 1960s and debated with him in Montreal in 1971 (Grondin 2012: 361, n. 12). To the extent that Ricœur's hermeneutics is more structuralist and more methodical than Gadamer's, more exegetical also, that it insists more upon the autonomy of the text (thereby de-emphasizing the role of history), that it is more directed towards recovery of meaning and that it is particularly attuned to the idea of 'conciliation', not to mention the fact that it discloses a transcendental dimension,[8] one can imagine how Derrida, not having yet familiarized himself with Gadamer's publications, might have too hastily concluded that hermeneutics was hermeneutics, whether the particular model bore the signature 'Ricœur' or 'Gadamer'.[9] Interestingly, Gadamer himself thought that Derrida's critique of hermeneutics was very much a commentary on Ricœur's philosophy (Risser 1989: 179).

Be that as it may, it is a highly sceptical view of hermeneutics that Derrida took with him to the Paris *Goethe-Institut* in April 1981, a re-presentation Grondin has branded a 'caricature' (1999: 14) – another commentator going one step further and depicting Derrida's understanding as an 'appalling caricature' (Davis 2010: 33). Yet one can find passages in Gadamer's Paris intervention (as indeed in his foremost *Wahrheit und Methode* or in his other writings) that, once his 'torturous formulations' have been elucidated (Vandevelde 2010: 294), lend credence to Derrida's critique. For example, in Paris Gadamer did say that ultimately in interpretation '[t]he interpreter [. . .] vanishes, and the text speaks' (1983: 360), that '[t]he interpreter has no other function than this, to vanish completely into the realization of understanding' (ibid.: 350). He did maintain also that '[t]he discourse of the interpreter is therefore not a text, but *serves* a text' (ibid.: 350, emphasis original). And in *Wahrheit und Methode*, Gadamer does contend that 'one means *to understand the text itself*' (1986a: 392, emphasis original) and that a text is to be understood 'appropriately' (ibid.: 314). Moreover, he does write of the 'hermeneutic challenge' in terms of 'strangeness and its conquest' (ibid.: 391), adding that one is 'to appropriate what is said in the text' (ibid.: 392). Elsewhere, Gadamer mentions 'the unity of meaning that belongs to the text' (1986b: 428), insists that 'univocity inheres of necessity to all discourse' (ibid.: 429), considers that '[e]very possibility of double understanding is an offense' (1983: 359) and gestures towards the idea of interpretation as 'correctness' (1986b: 440).

During the three days of the Paris meeting, Derrida's long-standing writerly defiance towards hermeneutics – his objection *ad rem*, so to speak – took an *in personam* twist in focusing on Gadamer as the placeholder of what he, Derrida, thought hermeneutics to be and of everything that he, Derrida, saw as being inadmissible about hermeneutics. Interpretations of Derrida's behaviour on the Paris stage vary. At best, it is said that he refused to involve himself in a conversation worthy of the name with Gadamer. At worst, it is reported that he displayed 'agressivity' towards Gadamer – which, incidentally, is the view Derrida's first significant biographer holds, although he invokes an accumulation of serious personal and professional problems as mitigating factors (Peeters 2010: 402–3). In any event, Derrida used his Paris forum to make a formal intervention that pointedly ignored hermeneutics in general and, as I have indicated, avoided Gadamer's views in particular as if these simply did not deserve his attention. Instead, Derrida talked about Heidegger's reading of Nietzsche (Derrida 1981: 58–71). Derrida then took advantage of the roundtable discussion to launch a frontal attack on Gadamer's most primordial assumptions. This dual approach, indifference and belligerence – or was it 'petulan[ce]' squared (Davis 2010: 34)? – left Gadamer at once perplexed and irritated (Grondin 2011b: 103).

Derrida's express challenge to Gadamer took the form of three 'questions' (I use quotation marks advisedly for the record shows that these 'questions' consisted largely of statements). Derrida's three-pronged retort addressed the following issues.

First, Derrida rejected Gadamer's basic idea that interlocutors must 'have the goodwill to understand one another' (Gadamer 1983: 343). For Derrida, the idea of the 'will', no matter how 'good', is not a secure, self-evident postulate in as much as it cannot be dissociated from a Nietzschean will to power and from a Kantian metaphysics of the subject, a subjectivism that, in the end, would be unacceptably self-affirmative and all-determinative. Pursuant to Derrida, hermeneutics is therefore devoted, more or less consciously, more or less openly, to a strategy of arraignment or of appropriation of the other, an instrumentalization that he cannot countenance. Derrida thus earnestly disagrees as Gadamer impels one '[t]o recognize one's own in the foreign' and claims that 'to become at home in [the foreign] is the basic movement of spirit' (Gadamer 1986a: 19–20). Not only is this projection of the self into the other in vain – 'there are only islands', says Derrida (2002c: 31) – but it is reprehensible to the extent that it would structure an appropriation of the other, that it would marshall knowledge of the other with a view, finally, to assimilating it to the self so as to achieve, say, a deeper knowledge of the self. For Derrida, a manifestation of the will to appropriate and assimilate the other to the self is tantamount to what he calls an 'interpretive totalization' and, as such, inadmissible (1986b: 50). And Gadamer's 'will' cannot be justified because it would pertain to 'goodwill'. According to Derrida, Gadamer's motions simply do not acknowledge the recognition and the respect that are owed alterity or textuality as a matter of justice. Rather, they enact 'the oppression and the totalitarism of the same' (Derrida 1967b: 136).

Second, Derrida objected to Gadamer's key idea of 'dialogue' and to the accord it pursues that it assumes to be realizable, though 'mirac[ulously]' (Gadamer 1986a: 297, 316 and 347). For Derrida, 'dialogue' supposes that two interlocutors, or an interpreter and a text, are speaking the same language. However, Derrida argues, the language one hears or reads is always already *another* language. And there is, there can be, no bridge across languages: each language is 'monologue'; it speaks '*lonesomely*' (Heidegger 1959: 265, emphasis original).[10] To use Derrida's own illustrations, 'Pierre' is not 'Peter' (1998b: 209) and '*deux*' is not 'two', which is not '*zwei*' (2002b: 241, emphasis modified). In effect, Derrida challenges the idea of 'translatability', arguably the *raison d'être* of the hermeneutic enterprise, by claiming for instance that 'my here-now is absolutely untranslatable and [. . .] the world in which I speak is absolutely heterogeneous'; he adds that '[b]etween two "here", there is a properly infinite irreducibility, an infinite heterogeneity' (1998a: 247). Whereas Gadamer holds that '[s]trangeness, that which makes a text incomprehensible, must be suppressed by the interpreter' (1983: 350), Derrida takes the view that 'the difference between one world and the other will always remain unsurpassable' (2002b: 31) and accepts that the other – for example, the text – will, agonistically, be the enduring repository of a secret, a 'singularity forever encrypted' (2003a: 41), permanently inaccessible in its withdrawal from presence, a 'radical resistance to the light of phenomenality' (Derrida and Ferraris 1997: 51).[11] 'What guides me', remarks Derrida, 'is always untranslatability' (2004b: 26) – an observation that is not without recalling Beckett as the playwright exclaims, 'what is the word? What the wrong word?' (1989: 51).

Crucially, Derrida feels no need to regret this epistemic gap, quite to the contrary in fact, since any conciliation, whether on the basis of a Gadamerian gathering or after a Hegelian fashion, say, through appeasement or mediation, involves a totalization, which must entail an assimilation of the other to the self and therefore the other's ultimate effacement. As he writes that 'it must be that at some point the other remains as other', that 'if he is the other he is other' (1986a: 82), Derrida unreservedly maintains that any elimination of the other must be infinitely deferred. For Derrida, it is indeed key that the self, far from seeking to assimilate the other, ought to 'keep a close watch on the otherness of the other' (2000: 218). In sum, incommensurability appositely acts to safeguard alterity's very existence and to grant it a future as a focus of interpretation. It follows that Derrida himself values his enisled condition, that he dislikes both the word 'community' – it 'sickens' him (Peeters 2010: 361) – and the entity itself (Derrida 1992: 366). Like Beckett again, he believes that 'all groups are horrible' (Beckett 1939: 660), be they linguistic, national, political, philosophical or literary (Derrida and Ferraris 1997: 25).

Conversely, according to Gadamer:

> One must search the word and one can find the word that will reach the other person; one can even learn the strangeness of the language of the other, of his [language]. One can cross over into the language of others in order to reach the other. All of this, language as language can achieve it.
>
> (1985: 364)

Arguably, Gadamer thus purports to expunge singularity: 'The interpreter of texts, like the interpreter of divine or human discourse, has to [. . .] make appropriation possible' (1965: 419), with a view to ensuring that 'in the end, understanding succeeds again and again' (Gadamer 1986a: 221). But Derrida refutes this Gadamerian/Hegelian 'fusion of horizons', or '*Horizontverschmelzung*' (literally, 'horizon-melting'), that hermeneutics pursues even if the other is remarkably different (Rosen 1997: 207–18).[12] As Derrida makes sense of the matter, the Gadamerian '*Aufhebung*' – which, Gadamer himself insisted, is a lesser '*Aufhebung*' than Hegel's on account of the (Heideggerian) insight that the coming to language of being never reaches completion (Eberhard 2004: 104–5) – suggests that the differentiation of horizons is merely a transitory phase destined to 'sublate' itself in agreement. Meanwhile, Derrida asserts that sameness between *interpretans* and *interpretandum* cannot be envisaged (not even as a 'miracle', to use Gadamer's word once more).[13] There is only 'iterability' (even what is repeated is never the same) and 'differance' (even what signifies or is signified never has a fixed or fixable meaning) – two idiosyncratic and transversal notions within deconstruction that allow one to open oneself to the idea of the singularity of the other or of the text and to the further idea of the strangeness of the other or of the text – that is, to the decolonization of difference coercitively assimilated to sameness. Any contention in favour of a 'fusion of horizons' betrays interpretive confusion.

Although Gadamer refers to 'the meaning of the text' as 'the thing itself' (1986a: 469), for Derrida there is neither *the* meaning nor *the* text – the other can never be shown 'as such' or 'in and of itself' (2003b: 198) – and 'equivocity is in fact always irreducible' (1954: 106): 'Of no text can one say that one knows what it contains and what it does not contain' (1980b: 51–2). Still in Derrida's own words, 'the self-identity of the signified is always withdrawing and displacing itself' (1967a: 72). Meaning exists but as infinite dissemination, as a tropological structure infinitely circulating through the advent of supplementary sense at every turn (1972a: 290). And the way meaning undergoes an infinite process of dissemination because of how the other is structured, on account of a 'structural necessity inscribed in the text' (Derrida ibid.: 252), lies at the heart of Derrida's interpretive strategy. There is 'the endless multiplication of folds, unfoldings, foldouts, foldures, folders, and manifolds' (ibid.: 301), the possibility of 'the incessant supplement of an extra turn' (ibid.: 290): meaning can never be contained, finished or framed; it does not have borders. In Derrida's language, to deconstruct is to discern '*plus d'une langue*', which means, as one reads the other or the text, to disclose at once more than one language only and no more of one language only (1988: 38, emphasis original). Observe that this basic motion of heteronomic confidence is enacted productively: 'Deconstruction always presupposes affirmation [. . .]. [. . .] [D]econstruction is, in itself, a positive response to an alterity that necessarily calls, summons or motivates it. Deconstruction is therefore vocation – a response to a call' (Derrida 1995: 167–8).

Reacting to Gadamer's configuration of reconciliation and coherence as key interpretive values, Bernstein notes that '[i]n the fusion of horizons, there is a tendency to gloss over the heterogeneities and abysses that confront us' (2002: 281). And responding to Gadamer's 'commit[ment] to the notion that understanding is always in principle possible', to his view that beneath the differences that separate individuals there is to be found a commonality making mediation possible, Monica Vilhauer sounds a thoughtful warning (2010: 89, 87–91). This is why Derrida is more preoccupied with misunderstandings and takes the view that 'we never quite achieve the moments [*sic*] of coherence and fusion that is the aim of hermeneutics' (Bernstein 2002: 277). Indeed, he finds that the logic of *similarization* is 'deeply imperialistic' (ibid.). Along the way, the interpreter fails to do justice to the singularity of the other. For Derrida, there is – and there must be – the other's untameable singularity. Again, the epistemic stakes concern recognition, respect and justice. Note that according to Derrida, difference, which is irreducible as long as there is more than one (1990b: 253), means – a point he expressly made in Paris – that 'the experience [of the] "well understood" in dialogue or the success of confirmation' (Derrida 1984: 343) is utopian. To be sure, the very notion of 'dialogue' is a key trope in Gadamer's theory. Thus, Gadamer writes that '[l]anguage is dialogue' (1992: 369) and that 'language has its true being only in dialogue' (1986a: 449) – in German, the relevant passages read '*Sprache ist Gespräch*' and '*die Sprache [hat] erst im Gespräch [. . .] ihr eigentliches Sein*'. For Derrida, however, 'dialogue' assumes that two interlocutors, or an interlocutor and a text, are speaking the same language. But in fact, he argues, the language one hears or reads is always already *another* language so that one is better advised to talk of a 'negotiation' (Derrida 1986a: 85).[14] The only approach to alterity that can be had is not dialogue and consensus, but negotiation and dissensus – two terms that, meaningfully, incorporate the idea of 'power' (ibid.).[15] Only this economy of negotiation, this other economy, captures untranslatability as the negative moment necessary to the recognition and to the survival of the idiomatic that exceeds one's grasp, and that must, to which one's response can therefore be neither passive reproduction nor simple meaning transfer.

It is not, as can be too readily accepted, that Derrida is not concerned with the idea of 'fidelity'. Indeed, he writes how '[reading] cannot legitimately transgress the text toward something else than itself' (1967a: 222). For Derrida:

> The text of the other must be read, mercilessly interrogated but therefore respected and, primarily so, in the body of its letter. I can interrogate, contradict, attack, or simply deconstruct a logic of the text that came before me, in front of me, but I cannot and must not change it.
>
> (2001: 373–4)

And Derrida refers to 'the law of the other text, [. . .] its injunction, [. . .] its signature' (1998a: 262). Again, though, according to him, there never is the immediate, full presence of the text – of the other – there, before one, as object. Such presence is a mirage. Interpretation is therefore fated to '*produce*' a 'signifying structure' (ibid.: 227, emphasis original). It ensues that interpretation is 'active' – that it *does* something, and that it *does* something to that which it interprets, to the other or to the text (Derrida 1967b: 427). Interpretation intervenes as a counter-signature and thus proceeds, in effect, to write *towards* alterity or textuality (rather than on it, since there is no 'object', there). One obstinately *countersigns* the other or the text in a manner that both confirms the signature of alterity, of the other's text, and simultaneously compromises that alterity, that textuality, through a re-presentation mediating between self-surrender and self-affirmation (Derrida 2004a: 7–42).[16] Importantly, there is no loss because there never was 'the' meaning of the other or of the text in the first place. It is thus left to Derrida to assert 'the joyful affirmation of the play of the world' (ibid.) – the thrill of the diversity of sense, of the dissemination of meaning, what Beckett styled 'the excit[ement] [of] the failure to express' (1960: 377): 'A thousand possibilities will always remain open even as one understands something of that sentence which makes sense' (Derrida 1990b: 122).[17] There shall be no *monotony*.

Third, Derrida contested Gadamer's classical appreciation of 'understanding', which relies on the relation between interlocutors, or between an interlocutor and a text, as being characterized by continuity or seamlessness – to the point where it has been said that, for Gadamer, 'an understanding of the other becomes a mere instance of understanding ourselves' (Littau 1996: 111). Gadamer's insistence on the value of propinquity seems beyond controversy: 'The interpreter of texts [. . .] has to cancel strangeness' (1965: 419). For hermeneutics, 'the other in his otherness can be recognized only from the starting-point of linguistic commonality' (Cesare 2009: 276). And Gadamer indeed refers to understanding as 'a participation in a common meaning' (1986a: 297). Whereas Gadamer defends the priority of understanding – 'One has to recognize that an understanding is more primordial than misunderstanding' (1970: 187) – Derrida holds that '[i]n the beginning difference, there is what happens, there is what has already happened, *there*' (1987: 44, emphasis original), and refuses to condone a strategy openly seeking to eliminate everything having to do with singularity – that is, with difference. And for Derrida, human existence remains marked by an infinite array of unbridgeable gaps across individuals.

In his report on the Paris debate, Grondin gives a good account of how Derrida envisages 'not-understanding' as he assails hermeneutics' merit. According to Derrida, I do not hear the other when I claim to understand him since 'the will to understand [constrains] the other to yield, to conform himself to the schemes of thought that I urge upon him and that by-pass, by this very fact, *his* specificity' (Grondin 2011b: 103, emphasis original). Understanding is thus always, despite itself, structurally so to speak, a prisoner of schemes and signs. 'To understand' is inevitably to integrate the other *nolens volens* into one's system. For Derrida, it follows that the only way to preserve the other's otherness, to allow the other to exist as other, must involve not so much a continuous relation but rather 'the interruption of the relation', 'a certain relation of interruption', 'the suspension of all mediation' (1984: 343). While not doing away with the term altogether, Derrida thus urges a re-signification of 'understanding' as 'interruption' of the relation. This *disrelation* must manifest itself as 'the condition of understanding' (Derrida 2003a: 21). Derrida's basic point is that discord between worlds must be appreciated – indeed, that it must be valued – and that it cannot be camouflaged. Interpretation must accept the exteriority of what is being interpreted. Metaphorically, Derrida's goal could be framed thus: to get the interpreter, when his already encoded eye gazes at alterity and is able to discern the contours of a unicorn, to avoid asking if by any chance it is not a gazelle.[18]

In addition to Levinas, always an important source of inspiration for Derrida, I am reminded of Barthes, who would approach otherness through the motif of the 'not-to-want-to-grasp', or '*non-vouloir-saisir*' (1977: 285–7). For Derrida, the other who would have been straightforwardly 'understood' would have become part of the same, of the self. And it would have thereby ceased being an other, an outcome that Derrida cannot allow. In the end, the acceptance of distance and of *misunderstanding* as the principle of all interpretation is a matter of doing justice to the other or to the text, of not distorting its existential claim, of beholding its entitlement to be recognized and respected as other or as text. According to Derrida:

> The risk of misunderstanding, the wandering of an answer that misses the question, there is what must always remain possible in this exercise of rightness. There would be no rightness, no ethics of discussion otherwise. [. . .] The *possibility* of this evil (misunderstanding, miscomprehension, mistake) would be in its way an opportunity. [. . .] There cannot fail therefore to be the 'there cannot fail' of failure, and that adequacy remains *impossible*. [. . .] Because an interpretation without failure, an understanding by itself totally adequate [. . .] would render everything *impossible*, both the event and

> the advent of the other, the advent to the other – and thus the answer, the very 'yes' of the answer, the 'yes' *as* answer.
>
> (2001: 306–7, emphasis original)[19]

Having protested against Gadamer's appreciation of what it means to undertake to make a text intelligible, possibly taking his cue from Beckett – 'Friendly or not it's all misunderstanding' (1962: 513) – Derrida ended his Paris rejoinder by claiming for himself 'another thought of the text' (1984: 343). For Derrida, as I have indicated, the Gadamerian thesis rests on 'goodwill', 'dialogue' and 'understanding'. Also, still in Derrida's eyes, Gadamer's argument hyperbolizes the materiality of the text. Now, Gadamer's views and Derrida's own contentions pertaining to the irreducibility of the differend and to the idea that a text does not feature a 'content' existing 'as such' are, in Derrida's words, 'absolutely irreconcilable' (1967b: 427). Derrida thus proceeded to leave the conversation with Gadamer in an impasse that analysts (mostly reproaching Derrida) have been deploring for the past thirty years or so, using words like 'disappointment' and 'embarrassment' (Marshall 1989: 206).[20] For his part, Grondin has framed the Gadamer/Derrida debate as an encounter between 'confidence' and 'suspicion' (2011b: 93). And if such was the end of the story, one could maintain that it suited Derrida's philosophical interest that the Paris debate should have unravelled in hermeneutic failure, as resistance to willed consensus, as impediment to dialogue or as hindrance to understanding, that in his refusal to engage Gadamer on the Paris stage, Derrida was effectuating his theory of interruption, that his philosophy had purposefully taken a performative slant (Jay 1993: 513, n. 74).[21] In fact, though, the narrative of the Derrida/Gadamer transactions includes two more instalments.

The first episode concerns Gadamer and his preparedness, in the years following his Paris meeting with Derrida, to continue to take an interest in deconstruction to the point, Grondin reports, of nuancing his views on the occasion of some late writings and even of amending the fifth edition of his *Wahrheit und Methode* released in 1986 (Grondin 2011b: 105–6). But the second occurrence is the one that principally interests me, and it involves Derrida. In particular, it concerns Derrida's apparent delineation of another Gadamer seemingly at odds with the pre-1981 and Paris Gadamer – the historical Gadamer – whom he, Derrida, had basically cast as a misguided theoretician of interpretation trapped in various metaphysical conceits.

To Grondin's 'amazement' (2012: 368), Derrida, in two texts published after Gadamer's death, would at long last have embraced words like 'dialogue' and ideas such as 'uninterruption', claimed that Gadamer had been right all along and branded him his 'Cicerone', at least according to the German translation of one of Derrida's two papers (2003a: 7). It would appear, then, that Derrida would have ultimately articulated a Gadamer at variance with the one he had seemingly long been excoriating. Derrida would have devised another Gadamer whom he was willing to regard, this time, as having much in common with himself (including a joint attraction to the poetry of Paul Celan), a new Gadamer. Although neither the four public meetings that the two philosophers held after Paris – in 1988, 1993, twice, and 2001 (Grondin 2012: 366–8) – nor the correspondence they occasionally exchanged between 1981 and 2002,[22] the year Gadamer deceased, herald such a turn in the relationship between the two philosophers, I accept that Derrida's two texts, which Grondin calls 'extremely generous and conciliatory' (ibid.: 369), could be taken to suggest, *on the face of them*, that he was prepared finally to acknowledge Gadamer as an ally, perhaps even as a guide, that he was at length willing to concede Gadamer's interpretive leadership.

'Derrida [. . .] not [being] someone to let death get in the way of a discussion' (Davis 2010: 43), his purportedly placatory writings appeared first within days of Gadamer's passing and then nearly a year later. I maintain that a close reading of Derrida's argument in both texts shows him *not* to be detracting from the antagonistic stance he had taken vis-à-vis Gadamer and hermeneutics in Paris in April 1981, and indeed long before that time. Behind the exudence of sorrow and warmth, I find that Derrida's two texts of alleged appeasement did not, in effect, soften his substantive views. Specifically, they continued to characterize Gadamer's conception of interpretation as ill-informed in fundamental ways. In other words, despite the impression that may have been created, there was no 'second' Gadamer for Derrida. On careful analysis, the late Gadamer who would have been fashioned into an associate was not different from Derrida's early Gadamer, whom the French philosopher had so clearly cast as an opponent. For Derrida, there was always but one Gadamer only, and it was a Gadamer with whom he profoundly disagreed about how to make sense of alterity or textuality.

I contend that Derrida's two eulogies are palimpsestic: they each affirm more than one text. In particular, I claim that both commendations are informed by an intertextual contradiction, and I want to emphasize various passages where Derrida's praise effectively does something other than what it seemingly says, where his words articulate themselves in a manner that goes against his apparent intention. There is more. As Derrida expresses his views, I maintain that far from being insignificant, his critique of Gadamer in fact usurps the main role. In other words, I argue that a close reading of Derrida's two essays reveals a tension that is not at all meaningless, that cannot be understood as a fault or mistake, that ought not to be resolved or sublated into a higher unity and thorough coherence of meaning by showing, say, how it marks a point of development from one position to another so that the writing could eventually pretend to an ideal of freedom from paradox. Indeed, as Derrida himself would arguably have maintained, a text's lines of rupture – the places where it enters into conflict with itself – are a text's most revealing aspects.

My concern, then, is Derrida's other text – and because of my focus, I shall not spend time rehearsing the laudatory passages that immediately strike the reader even as one is content to peruse the two writings casually only. Suffice it to recall that the first piece, a brief newspaper article published in the leading German daily

Frankfurter Allgemeine Zeitung ten days after Gadamer's death, is entitled, in Derrida's original French, 'Comme il avait raison!' (2002d: 87–91).[23] And suffice it to add that the other text, the transcription of a conference given in February 2003, eleven months after Gadamer's death, on the occasion of a university celebration of Gadamer's life in Heidelberg, his academic home for over sixty years, talks in the very first few lines of 'admiration', 'gratitude' and 'affection' (Derrida 2003a: 9).[24] In order to support my argument, I wish to consider, in particular, Derrida's discussion of Celan in the published version of his Heidelberg conference. I claim that a conscientious examination of Derrida's meditation shows him to be staunchly holding to his anti-Gadamerian and anti-hermeneutics stances, perfunctory intimations of rapprochement notwithstanding.

In his observations on the Celan poem he addresses, Derrida underlines that the very idea of 'reading' assumes how a text must not be 'saturated or closed by a certitude' (ibid.: 35–6). On three occasions, Derrida emphasizes the value of 'indecision', which he expressly links to the idea of 'interruption' (ibid.: 38). For Derrida, 'indecision' ensures the future of a text by keeping attention awake and by informing questions that, far from paralyzing the text, keep it in motion, indeed in 'an infinite motion' (ibid.: 37–8). 'Immediate unreadability', according to Derrida, is a resource in as much as it offers 'infinite reading chances' (ibid.: 40, 46). And, still discussing Celan, Derrida notes that unreadability connects to the fact that a text inevitably contains an 'excess' that always 'withdraws from any gathering within a hermeneutics' (ibid.: 47), a remainder that is properly speaking 'irreducible' (ibid.) or inexhaustible (ibid.: 48). While a hermeneutic analysis – which Derrida continues to associate with formalism (ibid.: 47) – is in the end 'hardly risky' (ibid.: 54), one must be faithful to 'that singular otherness that takes [the hermeneutic demand] [. . .] out of itself, [. . .] beyond itself' (ibid.: 57). Again, the fact that full access to Celan's poems should be forever withheld means the gift of the poem to all its readers and counter-signatories who, operating under the poem's law – '*there is the law of the other text*' (Derrida 1998a: 262, emphasis added) – will be carried, infinitely, towards another reading or counter-reading (Derrida 2003a: 66–7) – a 'carrying' that, Derrida expressly indicates, must exclude appropriation, inclusion or comprehension within the self (ibid.: 76). It follows that an interpretation can only ever offer but 'a simulacrum of conclusion' (ibid.: 71).

Hermeneutics is unable to account for what Derrida understands as the necessary remainder of the other or of the text, what can never be elicited, what must be the other or the text's *secret* allowing it to exist in its otherness – that is, permitting it to exist at all. Gadamer, for instance, is interested in a correct interpretation of Celan that, he thinks, can be had – and that he thinks he himself can have (1973: 7). Writing on another Celan poem under different circumstances in the early 1970s, Gadamer thus ultimately took the view that he had 'adequately understood' Celan (1986b: 428); indeed, he felt that he had understood him 'well' (1991: 468).[25] But Gadamer's motions, as they purport to nullify the alterity of the text, aim to cancel it as other text and, ultimately, as text.

Despite any Gadamerian assertion to the contrary, however, Derrida holds that any claim to understanding would demand 'hours and years' (2003a: 60) – which is to say, practically speaking, that it cannot happen.

One thus appreciates why Derrida, in his Heidelberg homage, refers to a Celan interpretation by Gadamer as having been formulated 'perhaps too hastily' (2003a: 49). Note that whereas Gadamer wants the interpreter to make way and let the 'understood' poem speak, Derrida is of the view that the poem needs the interpreter to expose it to minute scrutiny so that the text comes to suscitate evermore searching interrogations from its readers and yield an ever finer elicitation of meaning (Davis 2010: 54). For Derrida, at no point ought the interpreter to be released from his interpretive duties lest the poem be deprived of the unceasing analysis it solicits in order to exist as meaningfully as is possible – which, because it is language that speaks rather than the author, includes existing in ways the poet may himself not have envisaged (2004c: 26), a good illustration of the manner in which meaning for Derrida can never be *arrested*.[26] In the words of a critic having painstakingly studied the Derrida/Gadamer confrontation, 'Derrida's approach here is anything but Gadamerian' (Davis 2010: 54). The same author contrasts Gadamer's 'shadowing [of Celan's] poem in a faithful commentary' (ibid.) with Derrida's bringing to bear neither 'a sense of the commentator's inferiority nor a fear of falsifying the work' (ibid.), but rather an 'anxiety about being inadequate in face of the poem's exorbitant call' (ibid.). Contrary to Gadamer, Derrida displays 'the urgency of encountering in [the poem] something which is singular and unrepeatable' (ibid.). Indeed, Derrida adds that 'even [once] translated, [the untranslatable] remains untranslatable' (2003a: 77).

Having noted in the German daily article that Gadamer and he read Celan 'differently' (2002d: 89), Derrida continues to assimilate the German philosopher to the idea of 'certainty' (ibid.: 88) – presumably bearing in mind assertive statements on Gadamer's part such as '[t]hese words [of Celan's] are indeed to be understood thus' (1975: 456). Meanwhile, it is trite to recall how Derrida abhorred certainty, a notion against which he built much of his philosophical thinking (Mikics 2009: 40). To Derrida, meaning is 'necessarily equivocal' (1993: 43) or refragable, so that he always forcefully opposed those purporting 'to determine one meaning through a text, to decide it, to decide that it is a meaning and that it is meaning, a posited meaning, positable or transposable as such' (1972a: 276). Playing with words as was his wont, Derrida exclaimed in Heidelberg: 'I am sure [. . .] that no one has here the right to be sure of anything' (2003a: 45). Accordingly, in the text for the German newspaper he readily harnessed the idea of 'interpretation' to what he analyzed as the much more open-textured and forward-looking notion of 'promise' (2002d: 88). Later, in his Heidelberg accolade, Derrida offered ten possible translations of a four-word verse of Celan's (2003a: 46), not-closing the list with the abbreviation 'etc.'. For Derrida, Celan's words offer 'infinite reading opportunities' (ibid.). Indeed, in order to do them justice one would have to continue reading 'endlessly' (ibid.: 43), a strategy Derrida describes as 'an ethics or a politics of reading' (2004c: 24).

In Derrida's words, Gadamer and he were separated, and 'no doubt [. . .] still' are, by 'abysses of misunderstanding' (2002d: 88). For good measure, in Heidelberg Derrida noted the '[i]mmediacy of the abyss' between self and other (2003a: 76). In his commitment to maintaining the other as other, that is, to approximating otherness's unspeakable singularity most advantageously without falling for any attempt at assimilation or totalization that would more or less eventually consign otherness to oblivion, in insistently defending his view that 'there is no shared world, only a profusion of inscrutable singularities' (ibid.: 55), Derrida, even as he celebrated Gadamer's memory in the German newspaper, persisted, as he had consistently done for decades, in calling for 'the necessary interruption to "dialogue"' (Derrida 2002d: 89). Note that Derrida writes the word 'dialogue' in quotation marks. This inscription indicates, as I read Derrida's text, the inadequacy of the term as far as he is concerned. In the process, Derrida adopts a strong assertive stance, which incidentally allows him to resist any charge of nihilism: '[T]he interruption between self and other [. . .] ensures that *something happens*, even if what happens might not readily be described as understanding' (Davis 2010: 55, emphasis original). And it ensures that something will continue to happen: 'The future of interpretation [connects with] a pensive and suspensive interruption' (Derrida 2003a: 36).

In a December 2003 interview – that is, but a few months after his Heidelberg homage – Derrida addressed the reading of others and of texts, the matter of their meaning, in terms that resolutely reiterated his long-standing position: 'There is therefore a dissemination that is irreducible to hermeneutics in the sense of Gadamer' (2004c: 24). If any hesitation remained regarding a Derridean revisitation of Gadamer's hermeneutics, I find it very hard to imagine how it can survive this blunt expression of dissentience. This is especially the case since Derrida indicates that when he had been claiming in the German daily that Gadamer had been right, he, Derrida, had been 'play[ing]' with Gadamer 'this game of approval' (ibid.: 24). Presumably, Derrida did not intend 'play' in strictly lusive terms. Still, the vulpine reference to 'game' in conjunction with the word 'approval' hardly suggests compelling seriousness of purpose. Indeed, in the two encomia he wrote after Gadamer's death, his panegyrizing tone nothwithstanding, Derrida's ostensible 'contest[ation]' effectively acted to 'confir[m]' his familiarly adversarial Gadamer (Derrida 2003a: 73). In deconstruction's language, Derrida '*countersigned*' his contradictor (ibid.).

What would be one important lesson for law understood as an interpretive enterprise? As deconstruction is applied to the regional discipline of legal scholarship, as is importantly though only occasionally being done (Goodrich and others 2008; Ville 2011; Legrand 2014: 581–98), it must not be assumed that Derrida recanted aspects of his interpretive strategy as regards alterity or textuality, in deference to hermeneutics. Despite a strong expression of melancholia towards Gadamer in the days and months following upon the German philosopher's death (such is the leitmotiv in Derrida [2002d and 2003a]), a sadness perhaps informed by an awareness of the terminal illness that would lead to his own death a year or so later, Derrida's commitment to deconstruction held, as did his indictment of hermeneutics. It follows that Derrida's law-school allies need not reconsider the terms of their allegiance to deconstruction's tenets as they learned them from the Derrida they read, the Derrida of the 1960s, 1970s, 1980s and 1990s. Although academic fashion (or is it opportunism?) can be prompt to identify the emergence of 'turns', one must resist the view that there would have taken place a Derridean 'turn' with respect to Derrida's appreciation of Gadamer's hermeneutics. Rather, Derrida persevered in his view that meaning cannot be assembled unitarily, teleologically, totalizingly, in a way that would fixate alterity or textuality as truth. Instead, any limit, any enclosure, any saturation is irreducibly and productively fracturable as ever-contingent and ever-provisional meaning emerges through a process of dissemination (1972c: 62–3).

A commentator on the controversy between Gadamer and Derrida relevantly outlines the paradigmatic dichotomy in these terms: 'Hermeneutics would like to bring interpretation to a close, at least provisionally, though it knows it may not be able to; deconstruction would like not to stop, though it knows it will have to' (Davis 2010: 55). Lawyers and other interpreters will predictably differ as to whether the deconstructive steadfastness I have explained deserves to be welcomed.

Endnotes

1 'What Cassirer calls spontaneity is for Heidegger merely a metaphysical conception of the human being that underwrites the drive to technological domination. What Heidegger calls thrownness is for Cassirer merely a primitive and mythic conception of humanity destined to be surpassed' (Gordon 2010: 363).
2 The word is a translation from Toni Cassirer's German, which is also 'abstruse' ('*Die abstruse Sprache von Heidegger*'). Quite apart from being married to Ernst, Toni is reported to have been a formidable cerebral force in her own right. Indeed, she is said to have been her husband's 'intellectual equal' (Gordon 2010: 335).
3 Gadamer expressly considered that he and Derrida were two 'free-standing developers of the Heideggerian impulses' (1988: 138). For his part, Rorty refered to 'Gadamer's right-wing and Derrida's left-wing Heideggerianism' (1986: 751).
4 Even marginalization, however, manifests itself within limits. According to Derrida himself, for instance, '[a]n institution is not only walls and exterior structures that surround, protect, guarantee or constrain the freedom of our work, it is also and already the structure of our interpretation' (1990a: 424). For a thoughtful essay on the institutional control of interpretation, see Kermode (1983: 168–84).
5 Heidegger's diaries, published as volumes 94 to 97 of his 'Complete Works', or '*Gesamtausgabe*' (Heidegger 1931–1948), reveal persistent intimations of his hostile disposition against Jews (Farin and Malpas 2016). The quarrel continues to rage between those who take the view that Heidegger's works should be restricted to the totalitarian propaganda shelf, Emmanuel Faye being a leading

exponent of this position (2005), and Heidegger's partisans who, though they deplore their philosophical mentor's unjustifiable political engagement, either argue that his philosophy remains untainted or that the philosophical advances he allows are so significant as to warrant a measure of intellectual redemption. Derrida is firmly in the latter camp as he observes how Heidegger fell prey to 'the most banal of anti-semitisms' (the word 'banal' is also in Gordon [2014: 28]) while noting the absence of 'anti-semitical philosophical text' (Derrida 2002a: 35). A Sephardic Jew, Derrida suffered on account of his Jewishness during the Nazi occupation of France, in particular when he was expelled from public school in 1942. He was then twelve. He often recounted this childhood experience as traumatic and maintained that it had made him extremely sensitive to any demonstration of anti-Semitism (1999b: 13–16). Even as he talked of his 'extreme ambivalence' and of his 'thwarted admiration' vis-à-vis Heidegger (Janicaud 2001: 103), Derrida often expressed his 'respect' or 'gratitude' for his predecessor's work (ibid.) and claimed to be operating 'under his gaze' (ibid.: 115).

6 Grondin observes that, though Derrida's text appeared in English and German translations, the French original was never released (2012: 361–2). In the bibliography, I indicate the English version.

7 Gadamer repeatedly refers to a 'miracle' (1986a: 297, 316 and 347). He uses the German word '*Wunder*'.

8 Gadamer's work is also informed by theology. For example, see Arthos (2009). Cf. supra note 7.

9 Detailed comparative examinations of Gadamer's and Ricœur's hermeneutics include Frey (2008), Mootz and Taylor (2011) and Vallée (2012).

10 Beckett refers to 'the simple and necessary and yet so unattainable proposition that their way of being we, [is] not our way and that our way of being they, [is] not their way' (1946: 277).

11 'There is no communication because there are no vehicles of communication' (Beckett 1931: 539).

12 For recognition of a Hegelian influence on his thought, see Gadamer (1986a: 312). For a critique of the idea of 'fusion of horizons', see Vitkin (1995: 57–76). Even advocates of hermeneutics acknowledge that '[a] potential danger of Gadamer's Hegelian model of mediation is that everything may dissolve into an overarching universal perspective' (Makkreel 2015: 39).

13 Supra note 7.

14 Pierre Legendre remarks that 'dogmatic systems as such do not dialogue, [. . .] they can only negotiate' (1988: 183, emphasis omitted).

15 '[C]ritics have justifiably charged that [. . .] Gadamer ignores the power relationships inherent in any socially mediated text or social exchange. Since language itself is not a neutral instrument, Gadamer's dialogical model, his ideal communication between past and present as conversation between two speakers, is both a distortion of what really occurs in understanding, and itself an ideological ploy serving to obfuscate the concrete social relations within which communication occurs. [. . .] [H]is failure to integrate a social perspective into his general theoretical framework remains a weakness in his work. Like Heidegger, he seems able to admit historicality only on an abstract theoretical level' (Holub 2003: 44–5). For Derrida, 'the very notion of communicative consensus disguises a

repression of differences between incommensurable language games' (Bowie 2001: 127). Indeed, Derrida challenges the very idea that the word 'communication' would carry one meaning only (1972b: 367).

16 Derrida never released the French original of the text I mention. In the bibliography, I indicate the English version.

17 Far from being unalloyed, this joy must compose with the fact that a reading is 'an anxious interpretation, quavered or quavering' (Derrida 2003a: 26). I am moved to recall George Steiner's childhood recollection: 'I felt a peculiar dread. Detail could know no end' (1988: 5).

18 An illustration of Gadamer's assumed commonality is in Charles Taylor. As he refers to the conquistadores, the Mass, the Catholic Church and Spanish society, on one hand, and to the Aztecs and human sacrifices, on the other, Taylor writes as follows: 'The fruitful supposition is that what went on atop those pyramids reflected a very different construal of an X, which overlaps with what Christian faith and practice is a construal of in Spain' (2002: 294). Taylor suggests that 'X' stands for 'aspect of the human condition' (ibid.). He then proceeds to claim that 'we can ultimately find our feet in Aztec sacrifice, because it's a way of dealing with a human condition we share' (ibid.). *Quaere*: on what basis is *an* 'overlap' posited and on what ground is *this* 'overlap' posited? To his credit, Taylor specifies that his 'presupposition' is 'challengeable' (ibid.). Indeed, it strikes me – and, as I read him, this contention would be Derrida's also – that no matter how optimally archaeological and how thoughtfully genealogical one's investigation, it is implausible to argue that one can even begin to make sense – except, of course, on one's own terms – of what it meant for an Aztec to perform what one now calls a 'human sacrifice'. There is a differend separating today's inquirer from the Aztec, and this differend is properly unsurmountable. Taylor's wishful thinking and transcendental tropism notwithstanding, there is no ascertainable (epistemic) commonality.

19 In response, Gadamer writes: 'I, too, say that understanding is always understanding differently' (1988: 141). Indeed, in his *Wahrheit und Methode*, Gadamer states that '[i]t is enough to say that one understands *differently, if one understands at all*' (1986a: 296, emphasis original) and elsewhere he writes that '[u]nderstanding is always an other-understanding' (1988: 141). But '[i]n spite of his insistence on difference, Gadamer [. . .] maintain[s] identity [. . .] in the sense of a primacy of identity over difference' (Behler 1987: 209). Gadamer's different understanding is thus an understanding that differs from meaning in a context where meaning is taken to be ascertainable and fixable. It is an understanding that differs on the way to a fusion of horizons. Indeed, even as Gadamer is at pains to disclaim that he holds any idea of identification between self and other, he associates understanding with the capability 'to step into the place of the other' (1988: 141). Although one could claim that on a literal reading of Gadamer on differential understanding there is nothing for Derrida to refute, it remains that in the end Derrida's 'difference' is not Gadamer's. For Derrida, 'what the text says is not a content that could be located' (Vandevelde 2010: 295). If you will, the difference between the two differences concerns 'the view that there is one correct interpretation' and 'the view that there may be equally valid interpretations of the same text' (ibid.: 298) or 'a vertical enterprise of recovering the author's intention' and 'the horizontal

adventure of producing a text along another text' (ibid.: 290). Otherwise said, the differend opposes a 'quest for rational consensus' and 'agonistic respect between interlocking and contending constituencies' (Connolly 2002: x). 'I cannot be in the place of the other', says Derrida (2004c: 23).

20 'But if the conversation does not really get off the ground, the fault is not one-sided' (Bernasconi 1989: 237). Costache thus takes the view that '[Gadamer] was [. . .] never really open to what Derrida might have to say' (2016: 113).

21 Arguably, Gadamer's talk was no less performative in as much as he repeatedly claimed to understand Derrida (Davis 2010: 42).

22 For a helpful reproduction of Gadamer's three letters to Derrida in German and French (or in French only when he wrote in that language) and of Derrida's five letters or postcards to Gadamer in French, see Grondin (2012: 376–90). Gadamer's letter of 9 March 1977 mentions an earlier meeting between the two philosophers (ibid.: 378), which indicates that the 1981 Paris encounter was not the first time they had crossed paths.

23 In the German newspaper version dated 23 March 2002, the French title becomes 'Wie recht er hatte! Mein Cicerone Hans-Georg Gadamer'. The words 'Mein Cicerone' can roughly be translated as 'My guide'. It is unclear who inscribed this addition, why it was felt necessary and whether Derrida was apprised before publication. Correspondence with the newspaper has proved fruitless.

24 Derrida paid his Heidelberg tribute to Gadamer two more times in Paris in the course of 2003 (Palmer 2007: 373).

25 The German word is '*gut*'. Gadamer fails to specify what he matches his interpretation against in order to reach the conclusion he does.

26 Note that to interpret a text beyond the author's intention can enhance its aura. It can invest the text with a powerful charge that a 'mere' (attempted) replication of the author's view might lack. Derrida's point, then, is not necessarily antithetical to the idea of 'conservation', of maximizing the strength of the text. In other words, even this brand of interpretation, audacious as it may seem, remains centripetal rather than interfering: it focuses on deploying, unfurling the text. Although it 'changes' the text, Derrida's reading preserves it.

Bibliography

Angehrn, E. (2003) *Interpretation und Dekonstruktion*, Weilerswist (Germany): Velbrück Wissenschaft.

Arthos, J. (2009) *The Inner Word in Gadamer's Hermeneutics*, Notre Dame, IN: University of Notre Dame Press.

Barthes, R. (1977) *Fragments d'un discours amoureux*, in *Œuvres complètes*, vol. II, É. Marty (ed.), 2nd edn, Paris: Éditions du Seuil, 2002.

Beckett, S. (1931) *Proust*, in *The Grove Centenary Edition*, vol. IV, P. Auster (ed.), New York: Grove Press, 2006.

—— (1939) *The Letters of Samuel Beckett*, vol. I, M.D. Fehsenfeld and L.M. Overbeck (eds), Cambridge: Cambridge University Press, 2009.

—— (1946) 'The Capital of the Ruins', in *The Complete Short Prose*, S.E. Gontarski (ed.), New York: Grove Press, 1995.

—— (1960) *The Letters of Samuel Beckett*, vol. III, G. Craig and others (eds), Cambridge: Cambridge University Press, 2014.

—— (1962) *The Letters of Samuel Beckett*, vol. III, G. Craig and others (eds), Cambridge: Cambridge University Press, 2014.
—— (1989) *Ill Seen Ill Said*, in *Company/Ill Seen Ill Said/Worstward Ho/Stirrings Still*, D. Van Hulle (ed.), London: Faber and Faber.
Behler, E. (1987) 'Deconstruction Versus Hermeneutics: Derrida and Gadamer on Text and Interpretation', *Southern Humanities Review*, 21: 201–23.
Bernasconi, R. (1989) 'Seeing Double: *Destruktion* and Deconstruction', in D.P. Michelfelder and R.E. Palmer (eds) *Dialogue and Deconstruction: The Gadamer–Derrida Encounter*, Albany, NY: State University of New York Press.
Bernstein, R.J. (2002) 'The Constellation of Hermeneutics, Critical Theory, and Deconstruction', in R.J. Dostal (ed.) *The Cambridge Companion to Gadamer*, Cambridge: Cambridge University Press.
Bertram, G.W. (2002) *Hermeneutik und Dekonstruktion*, Munich: W. Fink.
Bowie, A. (2001) 'The "German-French" Debate: Critical Theory, Hermeneutics and Deconstruction', in C. Knellwolf and C. Norris (eds) *The Cambridge History of Literary Criticism*, vol. IX, Cambridge: Cambridge University Press.
Caputo, J.D. (1987) *Radical Hermeneutics*, Bloomington, IN: Indiana University Press.
Cassirer, T. (1948) *Mein Leben mit Ernst Cassirer*, Hamburg: Meiner, 2003.
Cesare, D. Di (2009) *Gadamer – Ein philosophisches Porträt*, Tübingen: Mohr Siebeck.
Connolly, W.E. (2002) *Identity/Difference*, 2nd edn, Minneapolis, MN: University of Minnesota Press.
Costache, A. (2016) *Gadamer and the Question of Understanding*, Lanham, MD: Rowman & Littlefield.
Davis, C. (2010) *Critical Excess*, Stanford, CA: Stanford University Press.
Derrida, J. (1954) 'Introduction', in E. Husserl, *L'Origine de la géométrie [Der Ursprung der Geometrie]*, trans. J. Derrida, Paris: Presses universitaires de France, 1962.
—— (1967a) *De la grammatologie*, Paris: Éditions de Minuit.
—— (1967b) *L'Écriture et la différence*, Paris: Éditions du Seuil.
—— (1972a) *La Dissémination*, Paris: Éditions du Seuil.
—— (1972b) *Marges*, Paris: Éditions de Minuit.
—— (1972c) *Positions*, Paris: Éditions de Minuit.
—— (1978) *Éperons*, Paris: Flammarion.
—— (1980a) *La Carte Postale*, Paris: Flammarion.
—— (1980b) 'Débat', in P. Lacoue-Labarthe and J.-L. Nancy (eds) *Les Fins de l'homme: à partir du travail de Jacques Derrida*, Paris: Hermann, 2013.
—— (1981) 'Interpreting Signatures (Nietzsche/Heidegger): Two Questions', trans. D.P. Michelfelder and R.E. Palmer, in D.P. Michelfelder and R.E. Palmer (eds) *Dialogue and Deconstruction: The Gadamer–Derrida Encounter*, Albany, NY: State University of New York Press.
—— (1984) 'Bonnes volontés de puissance (Une réponse à Hans-Georg Gadamer)', *Revue internationale de philosophie*, 38: 341–3.
—— (1986a) *Altérités* (with P.-J. Labarrière), Paris: Osiris.
—— (1986b) *Schibboleth*, Paris: Galilée.
—— (1987) *Ulysse gramophone*, Paris: Galilée.

—— (1988) *Mémoires*, Paris: Galilée.
—— (1990a) *Du droit à la philosophie*, Paris: Galilée.
—— (1990b) *Limited Inc*, É. Weber (ed.), Paris; Galilée.
—— (1992) *Points de suspension*, É. Weber (ed.), Paris: Galilée.
—— (1993) *Spectres de Marx*, Paris: Galilée.
—— (1995) 'Deconstruction and the Other', in R. Kearney (ed.) *States of Mind*, New York: New York University Press.
—— (1998a) 'Fidélité à plus d'un', *Cahiers Intersignes*, 13: 221–65.
—— (1998b) *Psyché*, vol. I, 2nd edn, Paris: Galilée.
—— (1999a) *La Contre-allée* (with C. Malabou), Paris: La Quinzaine littéraire.
—— (1999b) *Sur parole*, Paris: Éditions de l'Aube, 2005.
—— (2000) *Le Toucher, Jean-Luc Nancy*, Paris: Galilée.
—— (2001) *Papier Machine*, Paris: Galilée.
—— (2002a) *Au-delà des apparences* (with A. Spire), Latresne: Le Bord de l'eau.
—— (2002b) *La Bête et le souverain*, vol. I, M. Lisse, M.-L. Mallet and G. Michaud (eds), Paris: Galilée, 2008.
—— (2002c) *La Bête et le souverain*, vol. II, M. Lisse, M.-L. Mallet and G. Michaud (eds), Paris: Galilée, 2010.
—— (2002d) 'Comme il avait raison!', *Cahiers littéraires Contre-jour*, 9: 87–91, 2006.
—— (2003a) *Béliers*, Paris: Galilée.
—— (2003b) *Voyous*, Paris: Galilée.
—— (2004a) 'Countersignature', trans. M. Hanrahan, *Paragraph*, 27(2): 7–42.
—— (2004b) 'Du mot à la vie: un dialogue entre Jacques Derrida et Hélène Cixous' (with A. Armel), *Magazine littéraire*, April, 22–29.
—— (2004c) 'La vérité blessante ou le corps à corps des langues: entretien avec Jacques Derrida' (with É. Grossman), *Europe*, May, 8–28.
—— (2005) *Déplier Ponge*, G. Farasse (ed.), Villeneuve d'Ascq: Presses universitaires du Septentrion.
—— and Ferraris, M. (1997) *'Il gusto del segreto'*, Bari: Laterza.
Eberhard, P. (2004) *The Middle Voice in Gadamer's Hermeneutics*, Tübingen: Mohr Siebeck.
Farin, I. and Malpas, J. (eds) (2016) *Reading Heidegger's Black Notebooks 1931–1941*, Cambridge, MA: MIT Press.
Faye, E. (2005) *Heidegger: l'introduction du nazisme dans la philosophie*, Paris: A. Michel.
Frey, D. (2008) *L'Interprétation et la lecture chez Ricœur et Gadamer*, Paris: Presses universitaires de France.
Gadamer, H.-G. (1965) 'Hermeneutik und Historismus', in *Gesammelte Werke*, vol. II, Tübingen: Mohr Siebeck, 1993.
—— (1970) 'Sprache und Verstehen', in *Gesammelte Werke*, vol. II, Tübingen: Mohr Siebeck, 1993.
—— (1973) 'Vorwort', in *Wer bin Ich und wer bist Du?*, Frankfurt: Suhrkamp.
—— (1975) 'Sinn und Sinnverhüllung bei Paul Celan', in *Gesammelte Werke*, vol. IX, Tübingen: Mohr Siebeck, 1993.
—— (1983) 'Text und Interpretation', in *Gesammelte Werke*, vol. II, Tübingen: Mohr Siebeck, 1993.

—— (1985) 'Destruktion und Dekonstruktion', in *Gesammelte Werke*, vol. II, Tübingen: Mohr Siebeck, 1993.
—— (1986a) *Wahrheit und Methode*, 5th edn, Tübingen: Mohr Siebeck.
—— (1986b) 'Wer bin Ich und wer bist Du?', in *Gesammelte Werke*, vol. IX, Tübingen: Mohr Siebeck, 1993.
—— (1988) 'Dekonstruktion und Hermeneutik', in *Gesammelte Werke*, vol. X, Tübingen: Mohr Siebeck, 1995.
—— (1991) 'Phänomenologischer und semantischer Zugang zu Celan?', in *Gesammelte Werke*, vol. IX, Tübingen: Mohr Siebeck, 1993.
—— (1992) 'Heimat und Sprache', in *Gesammelte Werke*, vol. VIII, Tübingen: Mohr Siebeck, 1993.
Goodrich, P. and others (eds) (2008) *Derrida and Legal Philosophy*, New York: Palgrave Macmillan.
Gordon, R.E. (2010) *Continental Divide*, Cambridge, MA: Harvard University Press.
—— (2014) 'Heidegger in Black', *The New York Review of Books*, 9 October, 61(15): 26–8.
Greisch, J. (1977) *Herméneutique et grammatologie*, Paris: Éditions du C.N.R.S.
Grondin, J. (1999) 'La définition derridienne de la déconstruction', *Archives de philosophie*, 62(1): 5–16.
—— (2003) *Le Tournant herméneutique de la phénoménologie*, Paris: Presses universitaires de France.
—— (2011a) *Hans-Georg Gadamer: une biographie*, Paris: Grasset.
—— (2011b) *L'Herméneutique*, 3rd edn, Paris: Presses universitaires de France.
—— (2012) 'Le dialogue toujours différé de Derrida et Gadamer', *Les Temps modernes*, 67(669–70): 357–75.
Heidegger, M. (1931–1948) *Gesamtausgabe*, vols XCIV, XCV, XCVI and XCVII, P. Trawny (ed.), Frankfurt: V. Klostermann, 2014 (vols XCIV, XCV, XCVI) and 2015 (vol. XCVII).
—— (1959) *Unterwegs zur Sprache*, Stuttgart: G. Neske.
Holub, R.C. (2003) *Reception Theory*, 2nd edn, London: Routledge.
Janicaud, D. (2001) *Heidegger en France*, vol. II, Paris: A. Michel.
Jankovic, Z. (2003) *Au-delà du signe: Gadamer et Derrida*, Paris: L'Harmattan.
Jay, M. (1993) *Downcast Eyes: The Denigration of Vision in Twentieth-Century French Thought*, Berkeley, CA: University of California Press.
Kapsch, E. (2010) *Verstehen des Anderen*, Berlin: Parodos.
Kermode, F. (1983) *Essays on Fiction*, London: Routledge.
Kompridis, N. (2014) 'Turning and Returning: The Aesthetic Turn in Political Thought', in N. Kompridis (ed.) *The Aesthetic Turn in Political Thought*, London: Bloomsbury.
Legendre, P. (1988) *Le Désir politique de Dieu*, Paris: Fayard.
Legrand, P. (2014) 'Derrida/Law: A Differend', in Z. Direk and L. Lawlor (eds) *A Companion to Derrida*, Oxford: Wiley-Blackwell.
Littau, K. (1996) 'Incommunication: Derrida in Translation', in J. Brannigan, R. Robbins and J. Wolfreys (eds) *Applying: To Derrida*, New York: St Martin's Press.
Makkreel, R.A. (2015) *Orientation and Judgment in Hermeneutics*, Chicago, IL: University of Chicago Press.

Marshall, D.G. (1989) 'Dialogue and *Ecriture*', in D.P. Michelfelder and R.E. Palmer (eds) *Dialogue and Deconstruction: The Gadamer–Derrida Encounter*, Albany, NY: State University of New York Press.

Michelfelder, D.P. and Palmer, R.E. (1989) 'Introduction', in D.P. Michelfelder and R.E. Palmer (eds) *Dialogue and Deconstruction: The Gadamer–Derrida Encounter*, Albany, NY: State University of New York Press.

Mikics, D. (2009) *Who Was Jacques Derrida?*, New Haven, CT: Yale University Press.

Mootz, F.J. and Taylor, G.H. (eds) (2011) *Gadamer and Ricœur: Critical Horizons for Contemporary Hermeneutics*, New York: Continuum.

Palmer, R.E. (2007) 'Hermeneutics Tracking the Trace (On Derrida)', in H.-G. Gadamer, *The Gadamer Reader*, R.E. Palmer (ed.), trans. R.E. Palmer, Evanston, IL: Northwestern University Press.

Peeters, B. (2010) *Derrida*, Paris: Flammarion.

Poirié, F. (1987) *Emmanuel Levinas: qui êtes-vous?*, Paris: La Manufacture.

Risser, J. (1989) 'The Two Faces of Socrates: Gadamer/Derrida', in D.P. Michelfelder and R.E. Palmer (eds) *Dialogue and Deconstruction: The Gadamer–Derrida Encounter*, Albany, NY: State University of New York Press.

Rorty, R. (1986) 'From Logic to Language to Play', in *Proceedings and Addresses of the American Philosophical Association*, 59: 747–53.

Rosen, S. (1997) 'Horizontverschmelzung', in L.E. Hahn (ed.) *The Philosophy of Hans-Georg Gadamer*, LaSalle, IL: Open Court.

Schwarzschild, S. (no date) 'Franz Rosenzweig and Martin Heidegger: The German and the Jewish Turns to Ethnicism', unpublished typescript, 83 pp.

Silverman, H.J. (1994) *Textualities: Between Hermeneutics and Deconstruction*, London: Routledge.

Steiner, G. (1988) *Errata*, New Haven, CT: Yale University Press.

Taylor, C. (2002) 'Understanding the Other: A Gadamerian View on Conceptual Schemes', in J. Malpas, U. Arnswald and J. Kertscher (eds) *Gadamer's Century*, Cambridge, MA: MIT Press.

Vallée, M.-A. (2012) *Gadamer et Ricœur: la conception herméneutique du langage*, Rennes: Presses universitaires de Rennes.

Vandevelde, P. (2010) 'What Is the Ethics of Interpretation?', in J. Malpas and S. Zabala (eds) *Consequences of Hermeneutics*, Evanston, IL: Northwestern University Press.

Vilhauer, M. (2010) *Gadamer's Ethics of Play*, Lanham, MD: Rowman & Littlefield.

Ville, J. de (2011) *Jacques Derrida: Law as Absolute Hospitality*, London: Routledge.

Vitkin, M. (1995) 'The "Fusion of Horizons" on Knowledge and Alterity', *Philosophy & Social Criticism*, 21: 57–76.

Chapter 10

Habermas, law and the European Union

William Outhwaite

Jürgen Habermas's exchange with Hans-Georg Gadamer in the late 1960s and early 1970s (Habermas 1971a: 45–56) is one of his more substantial, along with those with Niklas Luhmann, who had been Theodor Adorno's temporary replacement (Habermas and Luhmann 1971), and later, in the 1990s, with John Rawls (Finlayson and Freyenhagen 2011). These contrast with the largely missed opportunities with Michel Foucault, Jean-François Lyotard, Jacques Derrida (until close to the end of his life) (Borradori 2003) and Pierre Bourdieu who had briefly analysed law (1986). Even in the exchange with Gadamer, although they were personally friendly and Gadamer had encouraged Habermas's career in a variety of ways (Müller-Doohm 2014), they tend to caricature each other's positions, with Gadamer stressing Habermas's 'leftism' and Habermas Gadamer's 'conservatism' (Mendelson 1979; How 1985; 1995; Susen 2007).

It is worth remembering that Habermas's initial discussion, in *Zur Logik der Sozialwissenschaften* (1967a; 1967b), formed part of an argument about interpretive sociology which moved from Alfred Schütz's 'phenomenological sociology' through Peter Winch's Wittgensteinian reworking of idealist hermeneutics (Winch 1958), and invoked Gadamer in the service of what Habermas presented more fully in another book of 1968, *Erkenntnis und Interesse*: a critique of the 'latent positivism' of Wilhelm Dilthey's hermeneutics (Harrington 2000; 2001).

Alfred Schütz's major work of 1932, *Der sinnhafte Aufbau der sozialen Welt*, translated in 1967 as *The Phenomenology of the Social World*, was subtitled '*Eine Einleitung in die verstehende Soziologie*' ('An Introduction to Interpretive Sociology') and can be understood as answering the question how an interpretive sociology of the kind advocated by Max Weber is possible (1932a; 1932b). Schütz's answer, in a nutshell, is that the 'ideal types' of understandable human action used by the Weberian social scientist are based on processes of typification carried out in everyday social life by ordinary members of society. The social world is 'constructed' out of action based on these typifications, as when you go into a shop and correctly distinguish between the sales assistants and the other customers. The phenomenological sociology of everyday life, which has affinities with the earlier and continuing pragmatist tradition of symbolic interactionism, was continued and developed, by Harold Garfinkel and others, in 'ethnomethodology' and 'cognitive sociology' (Garfinkel 1967; Cicourel 1973).

From Wittgenstein, via Winch, comes the related notion of discrete 'language games' embedded in forms of life, studied holistically in ethnographic field-work of the kind favoured by Winch. Finally, Gadamer's reinterpretation of hermeneutics stresses the element of existential encounter involved in understanding texts or other people: a 'fusion of horizons' between our background assumptions and theirs (1986: 305–6). In Habermas's analysis, each of these approaches goes beyond or transcends the previous one(s). In the phenomenological approach to the constitution of meaning in everyday life, '[l]anguage has not yet been understood as the web to whose threads the subjects cling and through which they develop into subjects in the first place' (Habermas 1967b: 117). Similarly, Winch's linguistic approach neglects the Gadamerian requirement to mediate between alternative frameworks. Winch seems to envisage that the linguistic analyst, '[f]rom his free-floating position [. . .] can slip into the grammar of any language game without himself being bound by the dogmatism of his own language game' (ibid.: 136).

The phenomenological and linguistic variants of interpretive sociology are often loosely described by sociologists as 'hermeneutics' and they certainly seem, at first sight, to correspond to the requirements of a hermeneutically orientated approach to the social world. They are, however, Habermas argued, vulnerable to a broadly based hermeneutic critique which claims, in essence, that their conception of meaning is too restricted and that they do not do justice to the hermeneutic basis of social theory.

Symbolic interactionism, for example, focuses, as the term implies, on interaction; consequently, structural aspects of social life are overlooked. In the 'phenomenological' tradition, the focus is on interpretations of reality, the relation between different typifications, such as that the whole enterprise comes to resemble a sociology of knowledge and, in Peter Berger and Thomas Luckmann's book, *The Social Construction of Reality* (1966), is explicitly presented as such. The approach recommended by Winch and following Wittgenstein brings out more sharply one of the problems that arise here: a 'form of life' with its associated view of the world is not a cab which one can get in and out of at will. The hermeneutic process is not the replacement of the interpreter's 'horizon' by that of the object of study, but a dialogical process in which the two horizons are fused.

So far so good, from Gadamer's point of view; where they diverge is with Habermas's critique of what he called 'hermeneutics' claim to universality' (Habermas 1970: 293–319). The upshot of the hermeneutic critique of interpretive sociology is that it must broaden its concept of meaning and recognize the importance of interactively constructed frameworks of meaning. In other words, hermeneutic theorists object to an exclusively subject–object-focused conception of science. Yet even a broadened hermeneutic approach is not enough on its own.

'Hermeneutic consciousness remains incomplete as long as it does not include a reflection upon the limits of hermeneutic understanding' (ibid.: 302, translation modified). These limits are of two related kinds. First, there is the general problem of 'linguistic idealism' ('*Idealismus der Sprachlichkeit*') built into hermeneutics, which neglects the fact that language is not just a means of communication which mediates our experience of the world, but '*also* a medium of domination and social power' (Habermas 1967b: 172, emphasis original). 'Sociology may therefore not be reduced to interpretive sociology' (ibid.: 174). This limit to hermeneutic interpretation manifests itself at a more specific level in relation to what Habermas calls 'systematically distorted communication', exemplified in the psychoanalytic concept of repressed motives. 'In deciphering repressed intentions as unconscious motives, linguistic analysis transcends the dimension of subjectively intended meaning and cultural tradition' (ibid.: 186). Habermas believes that this specific problem of distortion can and must be generalized into an awareness of the dependence of language and language-use on broader social processes. 'Hermeneutic experience, encountering this dependence of symbolic context on actual [*faktische*] relationships, becomes a critique of ideology' (ibid.: 172).

This is the approach that Habermas puts forward in a book published in the following year, *Erkenntnis und Interesse* (*Knowledge and Human Interests*) (1968a; 1968b), in which he develops more fully a critique of what he calls the 'secret positivism' of Diltheyan hermeneutics. The broader context, in terms of the history of philosophy, emerges retrospectively in Habermas's preface to *On the Logic of the Social Sciences*: his '[a]ppropriation' of hermeneutics and linguistic analysis had convinced him 'that critical social theory had to break free from the conceptual apparatus of the philosophy of consciousness [*Bewusstseinsphilosophie*] flowing from Kant and Hegel' (1967b: xiii). In Gadamer's metacritical comments, while welcoming the fact that Habermas had 'made visible' the contribution of hermeneutics to the social sciences (Gadamer 1967: 79), he rejects the distinction between 'culture' and 'material factors' and closes with a dismissive reference to the idea of freedom from domination as an 'anarchist utopia' (ibid.: 82).[1]

Before moving on to Habermas's later account of law, I should stress another aspect of these two books of the late 1960s. Both are presented as what he later called 'reconstructions'. This can be understood both in the informal sense of a mode of argumentation which we might loosely call Hegelian – one which moves through a variety of authors and ultimately incorporates their positive insights into his own theoretical models – and in his later, more precise, notion of reconstructive science. It is clear from Habermas's early discussion of Marx in *Theory and Practice* in 1963 that he was already struck by the parallelism between Marx's critique of idealism and Critical Theory's rejection of positivist social theory: 'that a critical self-enlightenment of positivism leads into the same dimension into which Marx was led from, so to speak, the opposite direction' (Habermas 1971b: 172). He uses a similar image in an interview in 1981:

> In retrospect, I sometimes have the impression that a student can recreate a segment of the critical theory of the thirties if he systematically works his way from Kant through Hegel, including Schelling, and then approaches Marx via Lukács.
>
> (Habermas 1981a: 96–7)

This mode of approach is later formalized in Habermas's 'reconstructive' account of communicative action, dominated by the analogy of linguistics, which reconstructs in formal terms, such as those of generative grammar, rules, which we initially absorb and observe informally as language learners and speakers. This conception is first presented, I think, in his postscript to *Knowledge and Human Interests* (1968a; 1968b), in the context of the distinction he draws there between two types of reflection. After completing *Knowledge and Human Interests*, he realized that the term 'reflection' is traditionally used to refer both to a subject's reflection on what makes it possible for him or her to perform certain actions and to a more critical insight into the distortions built into these and other processes. The first of these processes Habermas now calls 'rational reconstruction', where what is reconstructed is the pre-theoretical knowledge ('knowing how', in Gilbert Ryle's sense) of actors. Reconstructions, such as Noam Chomsky's linguistic theory, do not necessarily affect our practice. 'By learning logic or linguistics I acquire theoretical knowledge, but in general I do not thereby change my previous practice of reasoning or speaking' (1971b: 23). In this idea of the retrospective reconstruction of contexts of which we are initially unaware, it is perhaps not too far-fetched to see an echo of Gadamer's stress on 'what happens to us over and above our wanting and doing' (1986: xxvi). It is this reconstructive concept of reflection which is the focus of my discussion here.

At this stage in Habermas's work, law appears mainly in the form of natural law, which he had discussed in conference papers from 1962, reprinted in 1963 in *Theory and Practice*. In this book, he also argues that in modern welfare-state mass democracies

> [b]oth of these aspects – fundamental norms of political action for which a scientific legitimation can no longer be found, and scientifically rationalized methods of purely technical control over social processes, which methods, as such, are devoid of practical orientation – have become separated in an abstract manner.
>
> (Habermas 1971b: 115)[2]

The problem is still framed very much in the early Habermas's terms as one of technocracy, but the tension between different aspects of law, which both Habermas and Luhmann stressed in their different ways, is foreshadowed in this early work.[3] We should also note, however, that the way in which Gadamer's hermeneutics directs attention to questions of application – for example, in theological or legal hermeneutics – may pave the way for Habermas's own – later – focus on law and the prominent place played there by 'discourses of application'.[4]

In Habermas's work of the 1970s, law appears most systematically in a structural role as part of his reconstruction of historical materialism (1976) and his account of modernity in the second volume of *The Theory of Communicative Action* (1981b; 1981c). In 1976 he presents the notion of 'reconstruction' in the informal sense of 'taking a theory apart and putting it back together again' (Habermas 1976b: 95), although he also introduces his later conception of a 'rational reconstruction' ('*rationale Nachkonstruktion*') (ibid.: 168) in the context of structural analyses in anthropology, developmental psychology and linguistics. Law is analysed as a part of his two-track evolutionary model of social development, where the advance of the productive forces is complemented by a separate advance in the regulation of social relations. As he puts it in *The Theory of Communicative Action*:

> Marx [. . .] fails to recognize the *intrinsic* evolutionary *value* that media-steered subsystems possess. He does not see that the differentiation of the state apparatus and the economy *also* represents a higher level of system differentiation, which simultaneously opens up new steering possibilities *and* forces a reorganization of the old, feudal, class relationships. The significance of this level of integration goes beyond the institutionalization of a new class relationship.
>
> (1981c: 339, emphasis original)[5]

This is the context for Habermas's discussion of law in part of the final chapter of *The Theory of Communicative Action* (ibid.: 301–73). In modern societies, formal economic and legal-political systems are differentiated out from the lifeworld: 'The institutionalization of a new level of system differentiation requires reconstruction in the core institutional domain of the moral-legal (i.e., consensual) regulation of conflicts' (ibid.: 173). Moreover, 'higher levels of social integration cannot be established in social evolution until legal institutions develop in which moral consciousness on the conventional, and then postconventional, levels is embodied' (ibid.: 174–5).

This is the benign side of law; the other side is what Habermas calls '*Verrechtlichung*', in which law intrudes damagingly into more and more domains of social life. Modern law is not just an institution, formalizing practices of reconciliation and agreement with an origin in the lifeworld, but a 'medium' like money and political power which comes to dominate and 'colonize' the lifeworld. (The prenuptial contract, for example, may dominate, degrade or even undermine the prospective wedding.) The dichotomy in the case of law between institution and medium parallels that in sociology between social integration and system integration (Cooke 1994: 134). The latter concerns how well the parts of a social system fit together, the former how well people get on with one another. (In the case of the European Union, we may contrast diagnoses of its malaise which stress the misfit between the different institutions and those which focus more on the lack of a European demos or public sphere.)

This is not the place to go into the critical response to *The Theory of Communicative Action*,[6] which was followed by Habermas's much fuller engagement with law in what became his next major book, *Faktizität und Geltung* (*Between Facts and Norms*) (1992a; 1992b). This tension between 'facticity' and 'validity', he stresses, is central to his theory of communicative action, and more generally to any sociology which takes hermeneutic issues seriously (Habermas 1992b: 19). Whereas traditional practical reason directly yielded norms for action, communicative action does so only indirectly, via the participants' acceptance of the implications of their actual attempts to come to an understanding.

> A set of unavoidable idealizations forms the counterfactual basis of an actual practice of reaching understanding, a practice that can turn critically against its own results and thus *transcend* itself. Thus the tension between idea and reality breaks into the very facticity of linguistically structured forms of life.
>
> (Ibid.: 4, emphasis original)

The same tension between 'facticity' and 'validity' pervades the study of politics and law, 'between normative approaches, which are constantly in danger of losing contact with social reality, and objectivistic approaches, which screen out all normative aspects' (ibid.: 6). And the law itself 'borrows its binding force, rather, from the alliance that the facticity of law forms with the claim to legitimacy' (ibid.: 38–9). Law, in other words, must be both compulsory and compelling, combining '[t]he threat of an avenging power and the force of bonding convictions' (ibid.: 24). The idea of the '*Rechtsstaat*' ['state of law'] is designed to meet the need to 'legalize' the force underlying the law, in an institutionally differentiated form in which citizens prescribe laws for themselves (ibid.: 39). Recalling his central claim in *The Theory of Communicative Action* about the coexistence of social integration via communicatively structured practices in the lifeworld, on the one hand, and system integration via markets and administrative power, on the other, Habermas notes that law is implicated in all three means of societal integration, as well as being exposed to demands from a variety of sources. 'The tension between the idealism of constitutional law and the materialism of a legal order [. . .] finds its echo in the drifting apart of philosophical and empirical approaches to law' (ibid.: 41).

These tensions, however, achieve a remarkably harmonious resolution in *Faktizität und Geltung*. In modern conditions, structured by the interaction of competing moral and legal principles, only political democracy can legitimate the law:

> For without religious or metaphysical support, the coercive law tailored for the self-interested use of individual rights can preserve its socially integrating force only insofar as the addressees of legal norms may at the same time

> understand themselves, taken as a whole, as the rational *authors* of those norms. To this extent, modern law lives off a solidarity concentrated in the value orientations of citizens and ultimately issuing from communicative action and deliberation.
>
> (Ibid.: 33, emphasis original)

Habermas concedes that this may seem a little optimistic. Modern democracies are, undoubtedly, imperfect, but broadly speaking, in his view, up to the job. The anxieties about *Verrechtlichung* seem to have dissipated, to the disappointment of partisans of critical legal studies. Habermas's overall vision seems resigned, even irenic. A review in *La Repubblica* concluded that 'Habermas abandons Marx and shifts to the right' ('*Habermas lascia Marx e si sposta a destra*') (Sorge 1992).

Again, I shall not go into the details of the critical discussion, but focus instead on the way in which Habermas treats the question of legal interpretation. Despite his attention to questions of application, following Robert Alexy and Klaus Günther, Habermas tends to stress legal discourse and argumentation rather than interpretation (although the two are intrinsically related). 'This theory starts with the socially integrating force of rationally motivating, hence noncoercive processes of reaching understanding' (Habermas 1992b: 6).

The core of the book is in a sense the 'discourse principle', linked to the 'democracy principle'. We must, says Habermas, distinguish between *two types of action norms: moral and legal.* According to Habermas's 'discourse principle D', 'those action norms are valid to which all possibly affected persons could agree as participants in a rational discourses' (ibid.: 107). Yet, whereas post-traditional moral norms merely represent 'a form of *cultural* knowledge' (ibid., emphasis modified), albeit one which may make universalistic claims (ibid.: 108), law is also binding on an *institutional* level (ibid.: 107). Habermas notes that the *discourse principle*, which merely specifies what is implied by the impartial grounding of any norm, must be more sharply distinguished from the *moral principle* than was the case in his earlier writings (ibid.: 108–9). The *moral principle* must be distinguished from the *principle of democracy*, which specifies 'a procedure of legitimate lawmaking. Specifically, the democratic principle states that only those statutes may claim legitimacy that can meet with the assent (*Zustimmung*) of all citizens in a discursive process of legislation that in turn has been legally constituted' (ibid.: 110). In differentiated societies, law itself provides a necessary complement to morality, especially a post-conventional and in this sense a critical one (ibid.: 117).

How then does law get made? Not through a direct or 'unmediated' application of discourse ethics (ibid.: 158, emphasis omitted), but through a mix of 'pragmatic', '[e]thical-political' and 'moral' questions, concerned respectively with what is suitable, good and just (ibid.: 159–61, emphasis omitted). Mentioning Gadamer and Alasdair MacIntyre, he suggests that hermeneutic issues arise particularly in relation to 'ethical-political questions' (ibid.: 169 and 533–4,

n. 29). Political will-formation thus takes the following typical logical form (though often in different sequences):

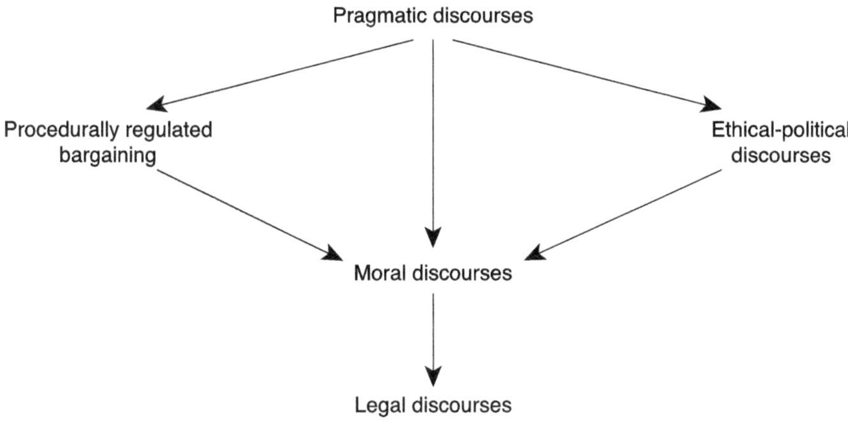

(Ibid.: 168)[7]

This becomes peculiarly complicated in the case of negotiations and other procedures (ibid.: 178–9).

Habermas directly addresses juridical hermeneutics in Chapter 5 of the book, headed 'Indeterminacy of Law and Rationality of Adjudication'. He distinguishes three 'paradigms of law': (1) bourgeois formal law; (2) welfare-state materialized law; and (3) proceduralist law. This third paradigm is – in Habermas's case – based on his discourse theory of law and politics and incorporates the other two. 'Legal ideologies', such as the first two paradigms, reduce the complexity of judgments; where, however, two or more paradigms conflict, one is forced, as in the case of conflicting moral principles, into a second-order examination of their interrelations. In the case of law, this involves a 'proceduralist conception' of 'reflexive law' which relates these models to 'political conflicts' between alternative models of society (ibid.: 395).

The term 'proceduralist' may seem to suggest, à la Luhmann, the unreflective operation of institutionalized procedures. Habermas means just the opposite: a process of *interaction*, as in the case of political structures, between formal institutions and 'the communications of [a] [. . .] public sphere rooted in the core private spheres of an undisturbed the lifeworld' (ibid.: 408). The emphasis is not so much on the competences of actors and institutions as on 'the *forms of communication* in which an informal and noninstitutionalized opinion-and-will formation can develop' (ibid., emphasis original).

> The reference to the communicative relations from which political power arises, the reference to the forms of communication on which the generation of legitimate law depends and through which it is reproduced – this reference

> directs our attention to those structures of mutual recognition that, as preserved in the legal order, are stretched like a skin around society as a whole. A legal order *is* legitimate to the extent that it equally secures the co-original private and political autonomy of its citizens; at the same time, however, it *owes* its legitimacy to the forms of communication in which alone this autonomy can express and prove itself. [. . .] This is the key to a proceduralist understanding of law.
>
> (Ibid.: 409, emphasis original)

This conception, Habermas believes, provides a way of rethinking long-standing controversies in legal theory over how to reconcile the requirements of consistency and rational justification. The three answers he examines are those of legal hermeneutics, realism and legal positivism. Hermeneutics goes beyond the simplistic model of judicial decision as subsuming a case under a rule. Here, Habermas mentions Gadamer and the way in which his conception of pre-understanding was embraced by Josef Esser (1970).[8] This is, however, open to realist objections:

> Legal hermeneutics already softened up the inner logic of law by embedding it in tradition and thereby relativizing it. That logic now completely disappears in a 'realistic' description of the causal process of adjudication.
>
> (Habermas 1992b: 201)

Yet realism cannot explain how someone who took this radically sceptical view could function in a legal system. Positivists (in law as in social science) brush aside hermeneutic complexities in favour of a simplified and autonomous formalism, which has as a consequence a decisionist conception of legal judgment.

Dworkin's alternative is a recourse to fundamental principles, which 'gives the hermeneutic approach a constructivist turn' (Habermas 1992b: 207; Dworkin 1986: 52–3), but his Hercules image admits to a certain unrealism of this heroic conception of the judge, who is also, Habermas stresses, conceived as acting monologically. This is the point at which Habermas introduces his discourse model, which 'might not solve this problem, but it at least takes it seriously' (Habermas 1992b: 226). This approach 'relies on a strong concept of procedural rationality that locates the properties constitutive of a decision's validity not only in the logicosemantic dimension of constructing arguments and correcting statements but also in the pragmatic dimension of the justification process itself' (ibid.: 226). To cut a long story short, Hercules is replaced by a legal and political community and its diverse and structured forums of communication.

> Legal discourses do not represent special cases of moral argumentation that, because of their link to existing law, are restricted to a subset of moral commands or permissions. Rather, they refer *from the outset* to democratically

> enacted law and, insofar as it is not a matter of doctrinal reflection, are themselves legally institutionalized.
>
> (Ibid.: 234, emphasis original)

Constitutional law is the sphere in which legal and democratic principles are perhaps most likely to come into conflict. Habermas focuses on the competence of constitutional courts in relation to basic norms. This is particularly important in the case of Germany where the Federal Constitutional Court reads the constitution as a set of ethical principles rather than as a formal system of rules (ibid.: 254). Controversies in the USA and Germany reveal conflicting conceptions of the democratic process, notably in the contrast between liberal (passive) and 'republican' (active) models of the citizen. Once again, a proceduralist conception of constitutional law is concerned primarily with the quality of democratic discussion; this, of course, raises serious empirical questions about the nature of the public sphere under modern conditions (ibid.: 285–6). A theme in Chapter 9 of the book, which is of obvious relevance to the European case, is that of the extension of law – for example, in the welfare state in relation to social rights conceived as a form of property.[9] Here again, broadening the focus to the political communication community as a whole may resolve some of these dilemmas.

Although *Faktizität und Geltung* is focused very much on the national state, this is also the period when Habermas was directing his attention more systematically to Europe, and his essay of 1990 on 'Citizenship and National Identity' is appended to the book. Here he argues that 'the democratic processes constituted at the level of the nation-state lag hopelessly behind the economic integration taking place at a supranational level' (ibid.: 491) and that 'democratic citizenship need not be rooted in the national identity of a people' (ibid.: 500), although it does presuppose socialization into a common political culture. Law makes possible a more 'abstract' (ibid.: 505) and less nationally limited conception of the autonomy and rights of citizens.

This brings me to a paradox. Having published a major book on law, and addressing with enormous care and growing passion issues of European democracy, including an article published in the journal *Ratio Juris* (1996a), Habermas might have been expected to focus more substantially on the development of EU law, especially as his colleagues and friends in Germany have been particularly prominent in addressing the political implications of legal developments. Although he did argue strongly for the need for a European constitution from 1995 on, and commented on the 1993 'Maastricht Judgment' of the *Bundesverfassungsgericht* (Habermas 1996b), he did not, as far as I know, say much about the ongoing work of the European Court of Justice, now Court of Justice of the European Union.

Whatever view one takes of the Court's activity over the second half of the twentieth century, it is clear that it often operated, sometimes decisively, as the pacemaker of the European integration process.[10] This was somewhat overlooked by both politicians and citizens (who might have freaked out if they had realized that they had acquired a federal supreme court), as well as by political scientists; meanwhile, experts on European Community law tended not to stress the political dimension (Armstrong and Shaw 1998; Joerges 1996; 2009). Although one can find analyses by both insiders and outsiders stressing the voluntaristic pursuit of integration underlying this judicial activism (Lecourt 1976; Maduro 1998), and its use of the legal concepts of 'effet utile' and 'implied powers' (Brunkhorst 2014b: 72–3), it is probably more accurate to regard it as a set of accommodations to specific situations (Everson and Eisner 2007), albeit shaped by what the future judge Thomas von Danwitz aptly called a pro-European '*Vorverständnis*' (1996: 140).[11]

This is, I think, quite an exciting story and certainly one of interest from the angle of legal hermeneutics and legal history (Keiser 2005), but perhaps not exciting enough to attract Habermas's interest even when he was working on his book *Faktizität und Geltung*.[12] The relatively harmonious (Dembour 1996) development of European law became eclipsed in the 1990s by constitutional issues which were of more obvious relevance, especially to someone like Habermas who had argued in favour of a new constitution for a reunified Germany (Arato 2009: 265–6). Andrew Arato and Thorsten Thiel provide critical retrospectives on Habermas's interventions, which, to some extent, contradicted his own principle that law is only legitimate when its addresses could in principle also see themselves as its authors (Thiel 2008: 176). In Thiel's nice image (ibid.: 173), the abortive constitution, despite the thorough and public deliberations of the Convention, did not emerge from or initiate a political process but was presented to the European citizens as something for them to 'grow into'. In the referendums that led to the abandonment of the constitution, Europe's 'democratic deficit' bit back.

In the early years of this century, the European Court began to extend its traditional role in liberalizing trade and mobility in a more starkly neoliberal direction, with a string of judgments including *Volkswagen* and, most dramatically, *Viking* and *Laval* in 2007. In the absence of any coordinated European labour law or social policy, the Court took the alternative route of 'making national welfare systems compatible with the internal market' (Habermas 1998a: 146; 1998b: 96, translation modified).[13] It seems to be this, rather than any more ideological preference for neoliberal strategies on the part of the Court (Höpner 2014: 13–14), that explains the turn.[14]

All this hardly made the headlines, unlike the second crisis, which broke out in these years, as the global economic crisis eventually revealed the weaknesses of the political management of the Eurozone.[15] The result was what Habermas, following Philipp Dann (2002) and Stefan Oeter (2003), called 'executive federalism', adding the adjective 'post-democratic': 'Executive federalism, already implicit in the Lisbon Treaty', threatened to 'expand [. . .] into a form of intergovernmental rule by the European Council, moreover, one which is at odds with the spirit of the treaty'. According to Habermas, '[i]n this way, the heads of government would invert the European project into its opposite. The first transnational democracy would be transformed into an arrangement for exercising a kind of post-democratic, bureaucratic rule' (2011a: 81; 2011b: 52).[16] 'The alternative', he went on, 'is to continue the democratic legal domestication of the European Union in a consistent way' (ibid.: 52–3).[17]

In this and other recent texts, Habermas has settled on the principle (2011b: 28–9 et seq.), which seems to be derived from Armin von Bogdandy (2009: 48–9),[18] that we have a kind of double mandate as citizens of national states and as citizens of Europe (and also, one might add, as citizens of cities, regions, etc. – extending this status to a triple, or even more multifaceted, mandate), rather as the covers of our EU passports list the Union and (in a larger font in the case of the UK) the name of our member state.[19] Thus, in May 2014, I could vote in the European election for Labour in the South-East England constituency and thereby also for Martin Schulz as likely Commission President, as well as, in a separate poll, for local councillors (and, if there had been a general election as well, for a Member of Parliament, likely Prime Minister and UK representative on the Council). If instead I had favoured Jean-Claude Juncker, however, there would have been no way to express this preference in my vote.

Once again, Habermas introduces this dualism, represented by Parliament and the Council, in the form of a rational reconstruction of a constitutionalizing process, which in reality was much untidier. Although this dual mandate conception seems the right starting point, Habermas concedes that the detail remains to be addressed (2013a: 81; 2013b: 59–60).[20] As he wrote in an essay published with Derrida in 2003, although the European identity that is currently being developed may feature a 'constructed' or 'fabricated' dimension, it is not capricious. In the two philosophers' own words, '[t]he political-ethical will that drives the hermeneutics of processes of self-understanding is not arbitrary' (Habermas and Derrida 2003: 295). And, as Habermas argued ten years later, '[t]o renounce European unification would also be to turn one's back on world history' (2013a: 98; 2013b: 17). It is sad, to put it mildly, that this now seems to be the path taken by the UK.

I am extremely grateful to Christian Joerges and Simon Susen for a number of helpful suggestions. Thanks also to Esteban Castro, Chris Rumford and Chris Thornhill for their encouragement.

Endnotes

1 Gadamer later said in a 1980 interview with the *Kölner Stadt-Anzeiger*, 'I do not understand that Habermas still expects everything from "emancipation"' (Müller-Doohm 2014: 137).
2 See generally Günther (2009: 72–4).
3 See Habermas, *The Theory of Communicative Action* (1981b; 1981c). See also Luhmann, who distinguishes between the 'function' and the 'performance' of law (Sciulli 1994: 49–50).

4 See Betti (1955) and, more recently, Alexy (1978a; 1978b) and Günther (1987).
5 On Habermas's relation to historical materialism, see Rapic (2014). An abbreviated version of my contribution to the book is on the *Theory, Culture and Society* website: http://theoryculturesociety.org/william-outhwaite-on-habermas-and-historical-materialism (accessed 30 June 2016).
6 On law, see Eder (1988); Guibentif (1994). Habermas was not yet seen as a sociologist of law. For example, a comprehensive survey fails to mention him (Tomasic 1985).
7 MIT Press and Polity Press granted permission to reprint this figure.
8 In fact, Günther suggests that he anticipated Gadamer's concept of '*wirkungsgeschichtliches Bewußtsein*' (1987: 327).
9 Habermas cites Henry Steiner in relation to the United States. For debates around *Faktizität und Geltung*, see Rosenfeld and Arato (1998). For a good recent overview, see Baxter (2011).
10 Seikel describes the role of the Commission and the Court as a 'strategic tandem' ('*strategisches Tandem*'), with the Commission steering in front and the Court pedalling faster or slower (2013: 82). See also the excellent analyses by Höpner (2011; 2014), to whom I owe this reference (Höpner 2014: 17), and the overview of the Court's history by Alter (2008).
11 In a fuller discussion, this account of the factors behind the development of European law could be related to the integration process as a whole. For an interesting overview of the latter, see Parsons and Matthijs (2015). See also Höpner (2014: 11); Bogdandy (2001: 23–4). In addition, see the classic discussion in Cappelletti, Seccombe and Weiler (1985) and the retrospective collection edited by Augenstein (2012).
12 He did, however, address these issues in general terms in a short tribute to Rudolf Wiethölter (Habermas 1989). In a recent paper, he modestly disclaims adequate competence in European law (Habermas 2014a: 184), but declares his 'admiration' for the way in which it has developed (ibid.: 175).
13 This is one of Habermas's relatively rare mentions of the European Court of Justice.
14 Höpner argues that the difficulty of changing EU law at the political level, with the need for treaty amendments, and the divergent interests of member states, combine to make retrospective resistance ('court curbing') improbable (2014: 17–20). Some national constitutional courts, notably the German *Bundesverfassungsgericht*, have attempted this approach, but they have proceeded on a rather weak basis, which would hardly be acceptable in the longer term for a Union of 30 or more members. The same principle applies in the case made long ago by Robert Lecourt on the primacy of European Community law: 'What would the Community become if, no sooner had the common rule been enacted, the judge filled its interstices with the provisions from each national law'? ('*Que deviendrait la Communauté si, aussitôt la règle commune édictée, le juge en comblait les interstices avec les dispositions de chaque droit national?*') (1976: 239). On this point, see also Habermas (2012: 20–8).
15 As Brunkhorst notes, with the introduction of the euro the Union 'has not only a court but also a currency without a government and a parliament' (2014b: 153). He suggests that with luck the European Parliament may come to play a more active role (ibid.: 164–5). See also Brunkhorst (2014a).

16 This analysis parallels that of Giddens, who similarly distinguishes between what he calls *EU1*, the formal institutions of the Union, and *EU2*, the *ad hoc* grouping of heads of state or government in the leading member states, 'where a lot of the real power lies, exercised on a selective and informal basis' (2014: 6). Brunkhorst, borrowing an image from Koskenniemi (2007), also writes of Europe's 'double face' and its slide towards 'deliberative Bonapartism' (Brunkhorst 2014b: 105). For other recent overviews of the legal context, see Everson (2013), Joerges and Ungureanu (2011) and Joerges (2015; 2016).

17 Joerges suggests the alternative that, given the inability of national states to include in their decision-making processes those affected by their decisions, 'instead of asking the EU to correct its democracy deficit, we should develop the potential for European law to compensate for the structural democracy deficits of its member states' (2015: 86). On this point, see also Innerarity (2014; 2015). At present, as Christophe Degryse notes, European legislation is on the defensive: www.socialeurope.eu/2015/07/refit-incipient-european-outbreak-legislative-anorexia (accessed 30 June 2016).

18 Habermas cites Bogdandy's suggestion that one should 'conceive of the individuals, who are national as well as Union citizens, as the only subjects of legitimacy' (Bogdandy 2009: 49). The emphasis here is on individuals only, rather than a holistic subject such as a nation. Bogdandy, however, adds that 'this theoretical position can only be used very carefully for the development of the law' (ibid.).

19 A Belgian passport, by contrast, lists both names in the same font, in the three national languages.

20 See, for example, Habermas (2014a; 2014b) and the critique by Scharpf (2015). A fuller account, which I cannot attempt here, might emphasize the relevance of the social thinkers with whom Habermas engaged, and others such as Bruno Latour and Luc Boltanski, for our understanding of the legal and political challenges facing contemporary Europe (Outhwaite and Spence 2014).

Bibliography

Alexy, R. (1978a) *Theorie der juristischen Argumentation*, Frankfurt: Suhrkamp, 1983.

—— (1978b) *A Theory of Legal Argumentation*, trans. R. Adler and N. MacCormick, Oxford: Oxford University Press, 1989.

Alter, K.J. (2008) 'The European Court and Legal Integration: An Exceptional Story or Harbinger of the Future?', in K.E. Whittington, R.D. Kelemen and G.A. Caldeira (eds) *The Oxford Handbook of Law and Politics*, Oxford: Oxford University Press.

Arato, A. (2009) 'Europa und Verfassung', in H. Brunkhorst, R. Kreide and C. Lafont (eds) *Habermas-Handbuch*, Stuttgart: J.B. Metzler.

Armstrong, K.A. and Shaw, J. (1998) 'Integrating Law: An Introduction', *Journal of Common Market Studies*, 36: 147–54.

Augenstein, D. (ed.) (2012) *'Integration through Law' Revisited: The Making of the European Polity*, Farnham: Ashgate.

Baxter, H. (2011) *Habermas: The Discourse Theory of Law and Democracy*, Stanford, CA: Stanford University Press.

Berger, P.L. and Luckmann, T. (1966) *The Social Construction of Reality*, London: Penguin.

Betti, E. (1955) *Teoria generale della interpretazione*, 2 vols, Milan: Giuffrè.
Bogdandy, A. von (2001) 'Beobachtungen zur Wissenschaft vom Europarecht: Strukturen, Debatten und Entwicklungsperspektiven der Grundlagenforschung zum Recht der Europäischen Union', *Der Staat* 40: 3–43.
—— (2009) 'Founding Principles', in A. von Bogdandy and J. Bast (eds) *Principles of European Constitutional Law*, 2nd edn, Oxford: Hart.
Borradori, G. (ed.) (2003) *Philosophy in a Time of Terror: Dialogues with Jürgen Habermas and Jacques Derrida*, trans. L. Guzman, P.-A. Brault and M. Nass, Chicago, IL: University of Chicago Press.
Bourdieu, P. (1986) 'La force du droit. Éléments pour une sociologie du champ juridique', *Actes de la recherche en sciences sociales*, 64: 3–19.
Brunkhorst, H. (2014a) *Critical Theory of Legal Revolutions: Evolutionary Perspectives*, New York: Bloomsbury.
—— (2014b) *Das doppelte Gesicht Europas*, Berlin: Suhrkamp.
Cappelletti, M., Seccombe, M. and Weiler, J.H. (eds) (1985) *Integration Through Law: Europe and the American Federal Experience*, 5 vols, Berlin: W. de Gruyter.
Cooke, M. (1994) *Language and Reason: A Study of Habermas's Pragmatics*, Cambridge, MA: MIT Press.
Cicourel, A.V. (1973) *Cognitive Sociology: Language and Meaning in Social Interaction*, Harmondsworth: Penguin Education.
Dann, Philipp (2002) 'Looking Through the Federal Lens: The Semi-Parliamentary Democracy of the EU', Jean Monnet Working Paper, No. 5/2002. Online. Available at www.jeanmonnetprogram.org/archive/papers/02/020501.html (accessed 17 October 2016).
Danwitz, T. von (1996) *Verwaltungsrechtliches System und Europäische Integration*, Tübingen: Mohr Siebeck.
Dembour, M.-B. (1996) 'Harmonization and the Construction of Europe: Variations away from a Musical Theme', Florence: European University Institute, Department of Law.
Dworkin, R. (1986) *Law's Empire*, Cambridge, MA: Harvard University Press.
Eder, K. (1988) 'Critique of Habermas's Contribution to the Sociology of Law', *Law & Society Review*, 22: 931–44.
Esser, J. (1970) *Vorverständnis und Methodenwahl in der Rechtsfindung: Rationalitätsgarantien der richterlichen Entscheidungspraxis*, Frankfurt: Athenäum.
Everson, M. (2013) 'The Fault of (European) Law in (Political and Social) Economic Crisis', *Law Critique*, 24: 107–29.
—— and Eisner, J. (2007) *The Making of a European Constitution: Judges and Law Beyond Constitutive Power*, London: Routledge.
Finlayson, J.G. and Freyenhagen, F. (eds) (2011) *Habermas and Rawls: Disputing the Political*, London: Routledge.
Gadamer, H.-G. (1967), 'Rhetorik, Hermeneutik und Ideologiekritik: Metakritische Erörterungen zu "Wahrheit und Methode"', in K.-O. Apel and others (eds) *Theorie-Diskussion: Hermeneutik und Ideologiekritik*, Frankfurt: Suhrkamp, 1971.
—— (1986) *Truth and Method*, trans. J. Weinsheimer and D.G. Marshall, 2nd rev. Eng. edn, New York: Continuum, 2004.
Garfinkel, H. (1967) *Studies in Ethnomethodology*, Cambridge: Polity Press, 1984.
Giddens, A. (2014) *Turbulent and Mighty Continent: What Future for Europe?*, Cambridge: Polity Press.

Guibentif, P. (1994) 'Approaching the Production of Law through Habermas's Concept of Communicative Action', *Philosophy & Social Criticism*, 20(4): 45–70.
Günther, K. (1987) *The Sense of Appropriateness: Application Discourses in Morality and Law*, trans. J. Farrell, Albany, NY: State University of New York Press, 1993.
—— (2009) 'Juristische Diskurse', in H. Brunkhorst, R. Kreide and C. Lafont (eds) *Habermas-Handbuch*, Stuttgart: J.B. Metzler.
Habermas, J. (1967a) *Zur Logik der Sozialwissenschaften*, Frankfurt: Suhrkamp.
—— (1967b) *On the Logic of the Social Sciences*, trans. S.W. Nicholson and J.A. Stark, Cambridge, MA: MIT Press, 1988.
—— (1968a) *Erkenntnis und Interesse*, Frankfurt: Suhrkamp.
—— (1968b) *Knowledge and Human Interests*, trans. J.J. Shapiro, Cambridge: Polity Press, 1987.
—— (1970) 'On Hermeneutics' Claim to Universality', trans. K. Mueller-Vollmer, in K. Mueller-Vollmer (ed.) *The Hermeneutics Reader*, New York: Continuum, 1985.
—— (1971a) 'Zu Gadamers "Wahrheit und Methode"', in K.-O. Apel and others (eds) *Theorie-Diskussion: Hermeneutik und Ideologiekritik*, Frankfurt: Suhrkamp.
—— (1971b) *Theory and Practice*, trans. J. Viertel, Boston, MA: Beacon Press, 1973.
—— (1976a) *Zur Rekonstruktion des Historischen Materialismus*, Frankfurt: Suhrkamp.
—— (1976b) *Communication and the Evolution of Society*, trans. T. McCarthy, Boston, MA: Beacon Press, 1979.
—— (1981a) 'The Dialectics of Rationalization', trans. L. Adelson and others, in P. Dews (ed.) *Autonomy and Solidarity: Interviews with Jürgen Habermas*, 2nd edn, London: Verso, 1992.
—— (1981b) *Theorie des Kommunikativen Handelns*, Frankfurt: Suhrkamp.
—— (1981c) *The Theory of Communicative Action*, trans. T. McCarthy, vol. II, Boston, MA: Beacon Press, 1987.
—— (1989) 'Der Philosoph als wahrer Rechtslehrer: Rudolf Wiethölter', *Kritische Justiz*, 22: 138–46.
—— (1992a) *Faktizität und Geltung: Beiträge zur Diskurstheorie des Rechts und des demokratischen Rechtsstaats*, Frankfurt: Suhrkamp.
—— (1992b) *Between Facts and Norms: Contributions to a Discourse Theory of Law and Democracy*, trans. W. Rehg, Cambridge, MA: MIT Press, 1996.
—— (1996a) 'The European Nation State. Its Achievements and Its Limitations. On the Past and Future of Sovereignty and Citizenship', *Ratio Juris*, 9: 125–37.
—— (1996b) '*Inklusion – Einbeziehen oder Einschließen? Zum Verhältnis von Nation, Rechtsstaat und Demokratie*', in *Die Einbeziehung des Anderen*, Frankfurt: Suhrkamp.
—— (1998a) *Die postnationale Konstellation*, Frankfurt: Suhrkamp.
—— (1998b) *The Postnational Constellation*, trans. M. Pensky, Cambridge: Polity Press, 2001.
—— (2011a) *Zur Verfassung Europas*, Berlin: Suhrkamp.
—— (2011b) *The Crisis of the European Union: A Response*, trans. C. Cronin, Cambridge: Polity Press, 2012.
—— (2013a) *Im Sog der Technokratie*, Berlin: Suhrkamp.
—— (2013b) *The Lure of Technocracy*, trans. C. Cronin, Cambridge: Polity Press, 2015.

—— (2014a) 'Zur Prinzipienkonkurrenz von Bürgergleichheit und Staatengleichheit im supranationalen Gemeinwesen. Eine Notiz aus Anlass der Frage nach der Legitimität der ungleichen Repräsentation der Bürger im Europäischen Parlament', *Der Staat*, 53: 167–92.

—— (2014b) 'Warum der Ausbau der Europäischen Union zu einer supranationalen Demokratie nötig und wie er möglich ist', *Leviathan*, 42: 524–38.

—— and Derrida, J. (2003) 'February 15, or What Binds Europeans Together: A Plea for a Common Foreign Policy, Beginning in the Core of Europe', trans. M. Pensky, *Constellations*, 10: 291–7.

—— and Luhmann, N. (1971) *Theorie der Gesellschaft oder Sozialtechnologie: Was leistet die Systemforschung?*, Frankfurt: Suhrkamp.

Harrington, A. (2000) 'Objectivism in Hermeneutics? Gadamer, Habermas, Dilthey', *Philosophy of the Social Sciences*, 30: 491–507.

—— (2001) *Hermeneutic Dialogue and Social Science: A Critique of Gadamer and Habermas*, London: Routledge.

Höpner, M. (2011) 'Der Europäische Gerichtshof als Motor der Integration: Eine akteursbezogene Erklärung', *Berliner Journal für Soziologie*, 21: 203–29.

—— (2014) 'Wie der Europäische Gerichtshof und die Kommission Liberalisierung durchsetzen: Befunde aus der MPIfG-Forschungsgruppe zur Politischen Ökonomie der europäischen Integration', MPIfG Discussion Paper 14/8, Cologne.

How, A.R. (1985) 'A Case of Creative Misreading: Habermas's Evolution of Gadamer's Hermeneutics', *Journal of the British Society for Phenomenology*, 16: 132–44.

—— (1995) *The Habermas–Gadamer Debate and the Nature of the Social*, Aldershot: Avebury.

Innerarity, D. (2014) 'What Kind of Deficit? Problems of Legitimacy in the European Union', *European Journal of Social Theory*, 17: 307–25.

—— (2015) 'Transnational Self-determination. Resetting Self-Government in the Age of Interdependence', *Journal of Common Market Studies*, 53: 1061–76.

Joerges, C. (1996) 'Taking the Law Seriously: On Political Science and the Role of Law in the Process of European Integration', *European Law Journal*, 2: 105–35.

—— (2009) 'Europäische Verfassung', in H. Brunkhorst, R. Kreide and C. Lafont (eds) *Habermas-Handbuch*, Stuttgart: J.B. Metzler.

—— (2015) 'The Legitimacy *Problématique* of Economic Governance in the EU', in Hertie School of Governance (ed.) *The Governance Report 2015*, Oxford: Oxford University Press.

—— (2016) 'The European Economic Constitution and its Transformation Through the Financial Crisis' in A. Södersten and D. Patterson (eds) *A Companion to European Union Law and International Law*, Oxford: Wiley-Blackwell.

—— and Ungureanu, C. (2011) 'Introduction', in C. Ungureanu, K. Guenther and C. Joerges (eds) *Jürgen Habermas*, vol. II, Farnham: Ashgate.

Keiser, T. (2005) 'Europeanization as a Challenge to Legal History', *German Law Journal* 6: 473–81.

Koskenniemi, M. (2007) 'Constitutionalism as Mindset: Reflections on Kantian Themes About International Law and Globalization', *Theoretical Inquiries in Law*, 8: 9–36.

Lecourt, R. (1976) *L'Europe des juges*, Brussels: Bruylant.

Maduro, M.P. (1998) *We, the Court: The European Court of Justice and the European Economic Constitution*, Oxford: Hart.
Mendelson, J. (1979) 'The Habermas–Gadamer Debate', *New German Critique*, 18: 44–73.
Müller-Doohm, S. (2014) *Jürgen Habermas: Eine Biographie*, Berlin: Suhrkamp.
Oeter, S. (2003) 'Föderalismus', in A. von Bogdandy (ed.) *Europäisches Verfassungsrecht*, Berlin: Springer.
Outhwaite, W. and Spence, D. (2014) 'Luc Boltanski in Euroland', in S. Susen and B.S. Turner (eds) *The Spirit of Luc Boltanski: Essays on the 'Pragmatic Sociology of Critique'*, London: Anthem.
Parsons, C. and Matthijs, M. (2015) 'European Integration Past, Present, and Future: Moving Forward Through Crisis?', in M. Matthijs and M. Blyth (eds) *The Future of the Euro*, Oxford: Oxford University Press.
Rapic, S. (ed.) (2014) *Habermas und der Historische Materialismus*, Freiburg: K. Alber.
Rosenfeld, M. and Arato, A. (eds) (1998) *Habermas on Law and Democracy: Critical Exchanges*, Berkeley, CA: University of California Press.
Scharpf, F.W. (2015) 'Das Dilemma der supranationalen Demokratie in Europa', *Leviathan*, 43: 11–28.
Schütz, A. (1932a) *Der sinnhafte Aufbau der sozialen Welt*, Vienna: Springer, 2013.
—— (1932b) *The Phenomenology of the Social World*, trans. G. Walsh and F. Lehnert, Evanston, IL: Northwestern University Press, 1967.
Sciulli, D. (1994) 'An Interview with Niklas Luhmann', *Theory, Culture & Society*, 11: 37–68.
Seikel, D. (2013) *Der Kampf um öffentlich-rechtliche Banken: Wie die europäische Kommission Liberalisierung durchsetzt*, Frankfurt: Campus Verlag.
Sorge, P. (1992) 'Habermas lascia Marx e si sposta a destra', *La Repubblica*, 21 October.
Susen, S. (2007) *The Foundations of the Social: Between Critical Theory and Reflexive Sociology*, Oxford: Bardwell Press.
Thiel, T. (2008) 'Braucht Europa eine Verfassung? Einige Anmerkungen zur Grimm-Habermas-Debatte', in M. Biegi and others (eds) *Demokratie, Recht und Legitimität im 21. Jahrhundert*, Wiesbaden: VS Verlag für Sozialwissenschaften.
Tomasic, R. (1985) *The Sociology of Law*, London: Sage.
Winch, P. (1958) *The Idea of a Social Science and its Relation to Philosophy*, London: Routledge, 2008.

Chapter 11

Law's disappearance

The state of exception and the destruction of experience

Cosmin Sebastian Cercel

In this chapter, I focus on philosopher Giorgio Agamben's challenge as regards the theoretical and historical understanding of law with a view to investigating the limits of legal hermeneutics. In particular, I reflect on the possibility of a radical rupture between law, violence and narrative that would be specific to the state of exception. By capturing the status of the law as it emerges from Agamben's theory of the exception and recovering its disruptive potential, I impugn the possibility of ascribing a meaning to the law – that is, I contest the assumption that lies at the very core of the hermeneutic enterprise.

The starting point of this exploration is a polemical observation according to which we are still far from assessing the significance of the state of exception for legal theory in a decisive manner. This analysis is, above all, historically situated: it takes place at a time when Agamben, the author to whom we owe the revival of the arcane politico-legal concept of the state of exception, announces the end of his genealogical reading of the history of law and power in the Western tradition (2014: 9–10). It is the end of a process which started almost twenty years ago by unearthing the secret *nomos* of modernity under the instantiation of the concentration camp (Agamben 1995), continued with a closer analysis of the legal and philosophical structure of the exception (Agamben 2003) and ultimately brought to light the concept of civil war as a central political paradigm (Agamben 2015). Given that this long and often convoluted exploration of the depths of European legal thought and political philosophy – to which the state of exception has been a central feature – has now come to an end, it is perhaps worthwhile to take a closer look at its intellectual legacy for the legal field. In particular, we need to ask to what extent we, as lawyers who are trying to make sense of the meaning and functioning of the law within our polities, are able to think the exception. With a view to a critical understanding of the law, the moment has come to underline the limits, the dangers and the opaque zones fostered by the concept of the exception. A thorough analysis requires to problematize both the exception's frail edges – that is, its recognized and unassumed restrictions – and its implications for other fields intimately related to the study of law such as history and political theory.

The standpoint from which I intend to map out the importance of the state of exception for legal thought is informed by a theoretical framework that puts history at the core of law's becoming. It is therefore a legal and historiographical understanding that infuses and sustains my project of reading the state of exception, both with and against Agamben, while keeping under a close scrutiny the ways in which the theory of exception points to a wider theoretical and intellectual framework that is part of our historical situation and affects the ways in which lawyers think, represent and relate to the law. My project is twofold. On the one hand, as a matter of intellectual history, it wishes to question the ways in which the re-emergence of the state of exception as a concept within legal thought is indicative of a wider sense of *malaise* with and within the law. On the other hand, as a matter of critical theoretical concern, it seeks to explore the hidden potentialities of the concept of the state of exception and to open the theoretical space for an authentic engagement with its consequences within jurisprudence and legal studies. I intend to do this by offering a reading of the concept of exception as used in Agamben's writings, while also relating to the intellectual constellation that infuses his work. Equally, I shall try to underline the ways in which Agamben re-enacts a series of intellectual topoi in order to approach the existing contemporary unfolding of a historical state of exception that he describes as being the advent of a both diffuse and looming '*global civil war*' (Agamben 2003: 87, emphasis added). As the state of exception appears to be the crucial dynamics befalling law in modern times while significantly undermining the articulation of the law as a self-referential system of signification, I seek to map further the conceptual background to which the exception refers and to assess its significance for understanding law as a historically inscribed structure.

In the context of my analysis, I will turn towards Agamben's earlier writings, and more specifically his essay on 'Infancy and History' (1978). Particular attention will be given to the concept of 'infancy' (ibid.: 11–63), which appears to encapsulate the paradigmatic Agambenian analysis of the relation between life and a structured system of signification such as language. In this way I intend to stress out the philosophical soundness of the thread linking the state of exception, understood here as an embodiment of the nexus between life and law, to the destruction of experience. Although I find this line of thought particularly important for underlining the limits of law's hermeneutics, I am critical of Agamben's use of '*transcendental history*' (ibid.: 50, emphasis original) as well as of the ambiguous place he ordains to history in his philosophical project. It is against this background that I emphasize a rather marginal and fleeting occurrence in his essay – that is, the political significance entailed by the modern dissolution of experience. I will argue that the state of exception could be read as precisely the politico-legal instantiation of the destruction of experience. Out of this argument, a series of historiographical, legal and memorial intricacies arise which need to be addressed in relation to the exception and the modern effacement of experience. I will conclude by suggesting some possible paths to escape the unhistorical temptations of Agamben's project while saving the initial critical potential that the concept of exception brings to the legal field.

A morphology of the exception

The state of exception is now part of the critical legal vocabulary and seems to become the more obscure the more it is presented and related to various contemporary readings of constitutional law (Humphreys 2006; Parsley 2010; McLoughlin 2012), international law and international relations (Johns 2005; Bikundo 2013) or simply to our contemporary political situation. This proliferation of the signifier 'exception' does not necessarily add much to the explanatory or exemplary value of Agamben's work for the legal field; rather it tends to confuse or to normalize the otherwise exceptional character of this concept for an understanding of our contemporary politico-legal landscape.

Apart from this overrepresentation of various tropes pertaining to the state of exception, there obtains, this time outside the ivory towers of scholarly investigation, a historical situation which can rightly be envisaged as an unfolding of the exception. This conjuncture appears under the guise of a series of ominous phenomena, which Agamben has astutely apprehended, either in his work addressing the state of exception at greater length (Agamben 1996: 3–49; 2009: 46–54) or on the occasions when he has embraced public positions in reaction to current political circumstances (Raulff 2004; Agamben 2008; 2013). Indeed, whether one is thinking of the status of international law in the post-Kosovo era, of 9/11 and the series of exceptional measures enforced and observed at both national and international level in relation to the threat of terrorism, of the financial crisis and the ensuing sovereign debt crisis with their own 'exceptional' financial measures, or of the rise of authoritarian movements, of the proliferation of various threats and of the overall discourse of looming catastrophes befalling our polities under various forms, it seems that the state of exception resonates secretly with a time of crisis, which is the 'now-time [*Jetztzeit*]' (Benjamin 1940: 395)[1] of our experience. To put it otherwise, 'now-time' is the time when the state of exception has once again 'enter[ed] into legibility' (Cadava 2001: 38).

Yet the semantic commerce at work between various discourses such as economy, politics, arts and the law seem to obscure and to some extent normalize the state of exception and its disruptive potential for challenging the (post)political disavowed consensus still dominant in the daily practice and theorization of the law. That is because the more the exception takes the guise of a ready-made cultural artefact apt to describe the diffuse malaise with our contemporary polities, the more it conceals its core, that of being a nonetheless legal theoretical matter. It seems thus perhaps too hasty to relate the exception to any instantiation of the suspension of the regular rules of a discourse without keeping in mind the ways in which the state of exception calls into question the foundations of our legal thought.

This is not to say that the state of exception is a purely formal legal problem or only a mere instantiation of the time-honoured debate around the autonomy of law in relation to politics. Of course, the emergence of literature on the exception bears the imprint of otherwise exceptional times, but one should be aware of the rather problematic historiographical framework that would enable us to link our contemporary status to the historical unfolding of the exception. According to Agamben's insights, as informed by Walter Benjamin's reading of history (1940), the exception is, and has always been, part of our modernity (Agamben 2003: 41–51). Moreover, the state of exception cannot be a purely legal phenomenon inasmuch as it points to law's indistinction in relation to violence and ultimately with unarticulated life. What should perhaps be emphasized is how the state of exception nests itself at the core of the law and as such undermines the symbolic structures of the political. It is in order to recover this initial critical thrust of the exception that its status within legal theory needs to be clarified. In order to embark into this process of conceptual clarification, I shall first propose a possible morphology of the state of exception before moving to a further situation of the concept within the work of Agamben as well as within the critical theoretical field.

It should be noted from the outset that the state of exception is a limit-concept for legal theory, inasmuch as it questions the basic assumptions of modern Continental legal thought and it blurs the pivotal distinction between the normative and the descriptive. Although its practice has nothing exceptional and responds to a long-lasting logic of unhindered state intervention in times of danger, the theoretical implications of such praxis are extremely compelling for legal thought and to some extent symptomatic for the Continental legal tradition. In short, the paradigm of the state of exception advanced by Agamben is a philosophical construct which, somewhat problematically, builds upon the constitutional practice and the normative statements existing in various modern constitutions consisting in either the suspension of constitutional guarantees or of the whole constitutional process, for a series of actions taken by state authorities for the protection of the constitution or of the constitutional order.

At this primary level we certainly face some difficult assumptions about the historical and cultural instantiations of the state of exception. To be sure, Agamben's preliminary investigation regards the state of exception as an essentially modern institution that becomes visible as a practice at the time of the French Revolution on the Continent (2003: 11–12)[2] and the Mutiny Acts at the outcome of the Glorious Revolution in Great Britain (Clode 1872: 64–76; Neocleous 2008: 42–4). Although to some extent aware of the distinctions between the various legal traditions, Agamben still notes 'the division – clear in principle, but hazier in fact – between orders that regulate the state of exception in a constitution or by a law and those who prefer not to regulate it explicitly' (2003: 9–10). However, as he concludes, this distinction is tenable only at the level of the formal constitution, since 'on the level of the material constitution something like a state of exception exists in all above-mentioned orders, and the history of the institution, at least since World War One, shows that its development is *independent of its constitutional and legislative formalization*' (ibid.: 10, emphasis added).

The state of exception seems to exist regardless of its environment, perhaps as a historical phenomenon outside the law, yet intimately connected to constitutional practice. What is important to capture at this juncture is the unstable topology of the state of exception in both historical and cultural terms. However, this does not prevent us from reading the state of exception as a structure which emerges within modern constitutional orders and which knows a specific process of proliferation in the times following World War I (ibid.: 7). More than a question of constitutional interpretation or even of historical truth, which perhaps it transcends, the state of exception emerges as both a symptom of high modernity and as a specific relation between law and politics within the framework of constitutional orders.

Indeed, drawing on Carl Schmitt's concept of '*Ausnahmezustand*' ('state of exception') (Schmitt 1922: 5), Agamben isolates the exception as a zone of indistinction in the structure of the law, a conceptual area where it is logically impossible to make any relevant distinction between law (as a normative category) and fact (as a descriptive one). It is through this suspension of the legal that a zone of indistinction between fact and norm, between force and form, is brought upon social reality. As he writes, '[s]ince "there is no rule that is applicable to chaos", chaos must first be included in the juridical order through the creation of a zone of indistinction between outside and inside, chaos and the normal situation – the state of exception' (Agamben 1995: 19).

In this sense, the suspension of the law creates an area between the stability traditionally attributed to legal normativity and its exterior: '[T]he situation created in the exception has the peculiar characteristic that it cannot be defined either as a situation of fact or as a situation of right' (ibid.: 18). One should not hasten to dismiss the state of exception as simply a marginal feature of modern legality. The paradox entailed by the state of exception is not a case of a mere *lacuna* in the law but purely and simply the status of the legal order. What the exception attests for is that the law acts

> as if the juridical order [*il diritto*] contained an essential fracture between the position of the norm and its application, which [. . .] can be filled only [. . .] by creating a zone in which application is suspended but the law [*la legge*], as such, remains in force.
>
> (Agamben 2003: 31)

In other words, in order to be effective the legal order has to be suspended for in itself it is pure normativity, estranged from life (ibid.: 40). The mechanism of the exception is functionally the only way out from law's pure self-reference. By the operation of the exception, law presupposes within its own texture an outside-of-the-law, a state of lawlessness that precedes and renders it conceivable, an outside awaiting to be colonized: 'Law is made of nothing but what it manages to capture inside itself through the inclusive exclusion of the *exceptio*: it nourishes itself on this exception and is a dead letter without it' (Agamben 1995: 22).

The territory of exception

It could be safely argued that in many respects the area mapped out by the concept of the state of exception is not an entirely new occurrence within the critical cartography of legal oddities. From the initial forms of positivism asserting the sovereign as a foundational character above the law (Bodin 1576; Hobbes 1651; Austin 1832: 166) to the realist experience looking at the law as social fact (Holmes 1897), to various forms of social theory informing our understanding of the law ever since the mid-nineteenth century (Marx 1844; Marx and Engels 1846; Weber 1922), the law's close relation to other configurations of knowledge or other social structures, which adopts many forms, is almost part of the established intellectual order of discourse.

Moreover, the fact that law is and can be related to unbridled exercises of force or to domination, control and instantiations of either mythical or historical violence is certainly no longer a radical stand even in our post-ideological context. Indeed, after the Marxist critique of law (Marx 1844; Marx and Engels 1846; Marx and Engels 1848: 1–30; Marx 1875: 208–26; Pashukanis 1924: 37–132) the onslaught launched by the Critical Legal Studies (CLS) movement against the quietism of legal orthodoxy (Gabel and Kennedy 1984; Fraser 1990) and the multitude of counter-discourses within legal studies which still fashion themselves as critical, radical or progressive, it seems that little can be added to the project of contesting the regimes of authority within the legal field and its complicity with domination. Even more, the choice of weapons might seem, at least at a first glance, somehow unfit as Agamben's sapping tools (Foucault 1975a: 105) include nonetheless the reflections of a conservative jurist in the person of Carl Schmitt not foreign to the very system of hierarchy that the critical legal field aims to contest and the legal institution *par excellence* under the guises of figures of ancient and medieval Roman law.

What is perhaps worth noting in Agamben's project is the method of reading and positively being able to propose a cartography of law's finitude which aims at circumventing and problematizing the intellectual legacy of modern political partisanship by going beyond the visited *topoi* of class struggle and domination. This is not to say that the project does not bear the imprints of a dialogue with a certain tradition of Marxism essentially carried out through the Benjaminian undertones present in the choice of theme and in his reading of history. However, it should not be forgotten that rather than discussing some of the obvious themes related to exception and sovereign power present in the *Eighteenth Brummaire of Louis Bonaparte* (Marx 1852) or the *Class Struggles in France* (Marx 1850) already indicating the role of dictatorship and exceptional measures in modern context (Carver 2004), Agamben's investigation takes as a starting point both Michel Foucault's concept of biopolitics (1976b: 14–36; 1976a: 175–211) and Hannah Arendt's theory of totalitarianism (1951).

Agamben's initial intention is to cover the gap between Foucault's apparent disregard for the totalitarian experience and Arendt's forgetting of the concrete exercise of power over human life. The analysis of the exception emerges thus as an exploration of 'this hidden point of intersection between the juridico-institutional and the biopolitical models of power' (Agamben 1995: 10–11). Instead of denouncing the legal system as ideology or an 'ideological state apparatus' (Althusser 1970: 67), Agamben's reading of the law unravels its critical points, those areas where the tension between the law and the sovereign power it is supposed to contain becomes visible. What the exception unravels is both law's limits as a system of signification and its very inscription in the registers of language. As he writes:

> Here the sphere of law shows its essential proximity to that of language, just as in an occurrence of actual speech, a word acquires its ability to denote a segment of reality only insofar as it is also meaningful in its own not-denoting (that is *langue* as opposed to *parole*, as a term in its mere lexical consistency, independent of its concrete use in discourse), so the rule can refer to the individual case only because it is in force, in the sovereign exception, as pure potentiality in the suspension of every actual reference.
>
> (Agamben 1995: 19, emphasis original)

More specifically:

> [J]ust as language presupposes the nonlinguistic as that to which it must maintain itself in a virtual relation [. . .] so that it may denote it later in actual speech, so the law presupposes the non-juridical as that with which it maintains itself in a potential relation of state of exception.
>
> (Ibid.)

The suspension of the law is thus not only an institution which founds the constitutional order and is essential to its survival, but something inscribed in the very possibility of articulating the law as and through language: '*The sovereign exception (as a zone of indistinction between nature and right) is the presupposition of the juridical reference in the form of its suspension*' (ibid., emphasis original). The slippage between law and language under the light of the relation of exception goes as far as to unravel a dual enigma traversing both language and law: that of constantly being beyond themselves insofar as '[l]anguage is the sovereign who, in a permanent state of exception, declares that there is nothing outside language' (ibid.: 20). As such, the intimate bond between law as normativity and language exposes the uncanny consequence of a constant equation blurring the distinction between meaning and power as 'to speak is [. . .] always to "speak the law"' (ibid.).

The first line of analysis entailed by this position opens up the possibility to read the state of exception in its political instantiation. Law as a bearer of the relation of exception does not contain the exercise of sovereignty and cannot limit the investment of life by forms of power. Rather, law under the seal of exception functions along the lines of the ban, the old Germanic term which defined at the same time the exclusion from the community and the insignia of the sovereign. Following Jean-Luc Nancy's theory of the ban (1983: 141–53), Agamben writes: 'we shall give the name ban [. . .] to this potentiality [. . .] of the law to maintain itself in its own privation, to apply in no longer applying. The relation of exception is a relation of ban' (1995: 23). To this stance of the law correspond two eerie historical figures. On one hand we find the *homo sacer*, the bearer of nude life who can always be killed, but never sacrificed, a life which is not protected by the law – rather through the law it becomes devoid of juridical meaning (ibid.: 52–62) – while on the other we face the concept of the camp, 'the most absolute biopolitical space ever to have been realized, in which power confronts nothing but pure life, without any mediation' (ibid.: 97). To be sure, it is this essential fracture inside the law which is placed at the centre of the historical unfolding of totalitarianisms within the history of the twentieth century and to the escalation of the control society (Foucault 1975b: 225) within the structure of our present.

At the end of this first exploration of the exception, some consequences become obvious for the writing of history, political theory and for legal thought. Perhaps the most audacious thesis is constructed around the blurring of the distinction between democracy and totalitarianism (Agamben 1995: 13). Indeed, Agamben's writing questions already at this point the possibility of drawing a clear dividing line between totalitarian terror and democratic stability. The emergence of biopolitics exercised through administrative practices, enacted through statutes and regulations, and sustained by the development of criminology, racial thought, social sciences, but also by legal thought and practice, are part of a drive which finds its roots in the Western politico-juridical thought before World War II and stretches beyond what we commonly refer to as pertaining to totalitarian experience. However, the centrality of the law within the framework of *Homo sacer* (Agamben 1995) is somehow obscured by the place of sovereignty and biopolitics which is either exercised in the indistinction opened by the exception or invests and divides the body politic as a consequence of the modern confusion between life and politics.

The exception stays as the background against which the biopolitical investment and the production of *homines sacri* takes place under the forms of ancient rituals still resisting in the fabric of the modern. It is not the rather tortuous path from exception to the relation of ban, to the *homo sacer* and then ultimately to the camps, which discusses at various lengths literature, linguistics, theology, historiography, ethics and politics, that hinders Agamben from fully engaging the exception and from addressing the cracks in the symbolic web of the law. It is perhaps the hasty slip into the realm of classic philosophy and his return to Aristotle in order to understand the meaning of life proper and that of a life devoid of meaning (*zóé*) (Agamben 1995: 1, 11–13), as well as his readiness to read into this distinction the seemingly timeless biopolitical significance of any exercise of political power (ibid.: 55, 65, 73, 100, 102). For where Foucault posited biopolitical power as a result of the interplay between practices, knowledge and techniques of power, strategies emerging at a historically confused yet still identifiable moment, in European history which we may call modernity (1976b: 214–5), Agamben assumes the modern to have already been infused with the biopolitical thought that the ancients have passed on to us through precisely political and legal vocabulary inasmuch as 'the history of Western politics is [. . .] the history of the shifting articulations of the functional bipolarity of the governmental power' (Zartaloudis 2011: 86).

Just why the exception and the ominous nexus between law and violence come to the fore particularly at the time of the interwar and continued to accelerate and proliferate through the experience of the camps, totalitarian regimes and putative democracies during the twentieth century, seems to stay one of the many enigmas entailed by the unfolding of the exception. Although this historical conundrum casts its shadow over Agamben's reading of the exception and calls into question its place within the horizon of the history of legal practices, some possible answers might be found in the continuation of its project.

Origins, traces and the temptation of the past

Whereas *Homo sacer* (Agamben 1995) follows the story of the biopolitical attributes of sovereign power and its disastrous consequences for our contemporary situation, the *State of Exception* (Agamben 2003) returns to the conditions of possibility of this new articulation of sovereign power and life. At this stage Agamben revisits the relation of exception and discusses at some length the intricacies opened by the exception within legal thought as well as the consequences entailed by these aporias. This analysis is followed by a new and at times arresting archaeological investigation into the origins of the exception.

Before tracing further Agamben's intellectual roots and mapping out some further consequences involved by the concept of exception for law, it is important to reassert the disruptive character of the exception. This essential fracture inside the law is fundamental for legal thought as it is the place where law is linked to biopolitical projects, the place through which the law suddenly steps down from being pure normativity and gives voice to the 'force of law' (Derrida 1992: 5; Agamben 2003: 32–41) underlining it. Rhetorically, the tension between law, understood as normativity, and 'force of law', unregulated historical violence (Felman 2002: 15–16), is crucial for the morphology of the exception he devises. The exception is an 'infancy' of the law (Agamben 1978: 11–63), the place where language fails and where the speaking being (Lacan 1975: 10) enters the scene of symbolization. Such a stance of the law calls into question its stable normative dimension as it undermines the political as such. By this displacement, politics and law are debased, adulterated forms of practices that are now doomed to fail.

Inasmuch as this poignant reading of the state of exception highlights the destitution of law and politics in contemporary settings, it is a continuation of a vocabulary and a rhetoric of fall and decline owed perhaps to Carl Schmitt's own attempt at making sense of the exception. Although critical of Schmitt's conclusion on the structure and the function of the exception, Agamben refers constantly to his work in a dialogue over time with the conservative lawyer. For his part, Schmitt holds that a legal norm cannot be conceived without presupposing the existence of a normal situation. Simply put, 'for a legal order to make sense, a normal situation must exist' (1922: 13). From this point of view, the place of sovereignty can be located in the act of deciding upon the existence of the normal situation. Otherwise said, the fundamental norm is itself subsequent to an act of decision of the sovereign, which means that there is, in effect, nothing 'fundamental' about it. In this sense, the law is exposed as being tainted at its very core by a continual permeability to the political. Not only, then, does the state of exception evoke a limit situation in the functioning of constitutional law, but it represents the paradigmatic structure of the legal. As 'the exception is more interesting than the rule' and since 'the exception proves everything' (ibid:. 15), it becomes the epitome of legal adjudication. In this manner, 'every concrete juristic decision contains a moment of indifference from the perspective of content because the juristic deduction is not traceable in the last detail to its premises and because the circumstance that requires a decision remains an independently determining moment' (ibid.: 30).

Accordingly, 'the exception in jurisprudence is analogous to the miracle in theology' (ibid.: 36) by linking the celestial realm of the law to the daily life of politics. While discovering the exception, Schmitt does not refrain from declaring fully that the exception reveals law's deepest nature, that it founds itself on a mere decision. Within its own intellectual project of legitimizing a conservative dictatorship (Balakrishnan 2000: 42–52) this limitation of the regulative power of the law is rather ambiguous. On the one hand, it opens the way to the ultimate destitution of the law under the strain of revolutionary forces, such as epitomized by the notion of sovereign dictatorship (Schmitt 1921: 112–31). On the other hand, as in the case of the commissarial dictatorship (ibid.: 1–33, 34–79, 132–47, 148–79), it enables the law itself to continue its life away from the dangers raised by the anarchic mob.

Both Schmitt and Agamben underline the impossibility of fully understanding sovereignty and the legal order without presupposing a relation with the non-legal, which can only take place through the state of exception. The state of exception – or the suspension of the legal – is the condition of the possibility of every instantiation of the legal discourse. Juridicity's secret lies in its non-relation with something that it necessarily escapes. In Agamben's words, 'the politico-juridical order has the structure of an inclusion of what is simultaneously pushed outside' (1995: 18). But whereas Schmitt ends up by celebrating the law's dissolution as enabling the assertion of the 'true' sovereign (1922: 7), Agamben dreads the way in which the opening of law colonizes life (2003: 64).

At this stage one tackles perhaps the most arresting part of Agamben's project which consists in shifting the focus from the troubled times of the interwar and the modern politico-legal implications of the state of exception towards the seemingly golden age of medieval legal reasoning as epitomized by *Decretum Gratiani*. In his own words, 'a recurrent opinion [. . .] posits the necessity as the foundation of the state of exception' (ibid.: 24). This shift functions here as an Ariadne's thread linking the French Decree of 1791 on the 'state of siege' to the European legal past of the *Corpus Juris Canonici*. It is now possible to enter into the Roman world of legal archetypes, for the *justitium*, an ancient Roman law institution, we are told, 'can in some ways be considered the archetype of the modern *Ausnahmezustand*' (ibid.: 41).

After a lengthy discussion of the significance of the *justitium* – that is, of the suspension or gridlock of the law – we learn that the state of exception is nothing but the production of the void within the legal system. Law's self-effacement thus appears as the central jurisprudential enigma that thinkers of dictatorship such as Schmitt, and perhaps intellectuals hailing from the Marxist tradition, are unable fully to understand. According to this reading, 'the state of exception is not a dictatorship [. . .] but a space devoid of law, a zone of anomie in which all legal determinations [. . .] are deactivated' (ibid.: 50). But this space is central to the law as it is only through its existence that law can be deployed. In hindsight, its mere existence, either as a historical possibility or as law's structural necessity, raises a crucial question for legal theory: if the law can fully disappear, what is the significance of acts which take place under the *justitium*? Or, in other words, what is a life without juridical meaning? In an attempt to render the theory of exception useful for an understanding of our contemporary situation, one must look back towards the silent dialogue between Benjamin and Schmitt over the meaning of the exception.

To put it simply, the exception read through *justitium* now seems to offer a new light into the stakes of this debate. Whereas Schmitt stubbornly insists on understanding the force brought by the void as still being part of the law, Benjamin sees in its unfolding the possibility of the existence of violence outside the law, which would be a pure violence unadulterated by the mythical forces of the law. According to the latter's reading, law is nothing short of a perpetual repetition of mythical powers (Benjamin 1921: 249). Indeed, the status of the law under the strain of the exception exposes law's original sin of being complicit with the forces that block history and demand sacrifice (ibid,: 250–2). Following Benjamin, Agamben tries to map not only the cartography of the exception but also its potential limits. Along this line of argument, nothing seems to resist the deployment of the exception, except a continual study of the law (Schütz 2011: 187) that would enable us to severe it from its ambiguous roots. As Agamben notes, 'the law – no longer practiced, but *studied* – is not justice, but only the gate that leads to it. What opens a passage toward justice is not the erasure of the law, but its deactivation and inactivity' (2003: 64, emphasis added).

But perhaps this unravelling of the limits of the exception is not enough, if not misleading. In opposing to the state of exception the search for a pure violence untainted by law (Benjamin 1921: 249), while shifting the register from politics to the theological and aesthetic implications of reading the suspension of the law, Agamben moves away from tackling the historical significance of the exception. Now, in his latest writings Benjamin shows the path in opposing the exception which has become the rule by precisely developing 'a conception of history that accords with this insight', while at the same time stressing that the 'amazement' at civilization's fall under the onslaught of fascism 'is *not* philosophical' (1940: 392, emphasis original). However, Agamben eludes these insights and turns towards Benjamin's reading of Kafka and its mystical overtones (Benjamin 1934). Whereas for Benjamin the way out of the unfolding of the exception was an understanding of history apt to sustain a 'real state of emergency' (1940: 392), which would sever the law from violence, Agamben focuses on the ontology of law and on the possibility of its deposition; in other words, he addresses philosophy, thus obscuring Benjamin's historical materialist inflections.

In order to further highlight the ambiguity at the core of the exception, read now through the lenses of *justitium*, another shift is added, this time moving further his own devised timescale from institutions of Roman law towards the anomic rituals and feasts specific to the Indo-European cultures. At the end of the day, the state of emergency is nothing other than 'the anomic drive contained in the very heart of the nomos' (Agamben 2003: 72). This temporal digression is illuminating inasmuch as it offers a possible answer to the causes that root the state of exception within the law. It is as if in the process of understanding the exception Agamben turns his eyes away from a purely historical reading towards a deeper structural and seemingly unhistorical feature of legality. Accordingly, law enables the exception within its framework insofar as the construction of legal thought and language in the Western tradition has been articulated around the radical ambivalence between chaos and order which is traversing the *nomos*. It is through the latent work of the *justitium* that jurists constantly conceal through their writings because they cannot think an outside-of-the-law that exception nests at the core of the law and constitutes itself as the real *arcana imperii*.

But the same gesture that evokes the times immemorial of the exception, thus turning it into a necessity that ceaselessly saps from inside law's pretences to predictability, order and clarity, also renders inoperable its disruptive features. It seems that from this standpoint, the state of exception risks turning itself into another argument supporting and comforting the cynical legal lethargy prevailing within the legal field. At the end of the day, law's constant self-transgression is nothing less than another chapter in an illustrious history of confusions from which there is no way out. Even more, this reading also confronts us with a central question. If the state of exception is the inner truth of the law, how can one still recognize the exception in its unfolding and how is it to be countered? Agamben's paraphrase of Alberico Gentilli opening his investigations of the exception asks why jurists remain silent on things that concern them, but the question cannot but resolve itself in the aporia of the fact that lawyers cannot but remain silent.

Redeeming the law

The answer that Agamben suggests comes in the form of a number of sibylline remarks concluding the *State of Exception*. As he writes, the task is 'to show the law in its nonrelation to life and life in its nonrelation to law' (2003: 88). Such a gesture 'means to open a space between them for human action, which once claimed for itself the name of "politics"' (ibid.). There are also some hints pointing back towards the origins of the exception:

> [L]ife and law, anomie and *nomos*, *auctoritas* and *potestas* result from the fracture of something to which we do not have access than through the fiction of their articulation and the patient work that, by unmasking this fiction, separates what it had claimed to unite.
>
> (Ibid., emphasis original)

To fully grasp the consequences of this programmatic injunction for a critical reading of law, some further remarks appear necessary.

At first glance, Agamben's call seems to point towards a continual undoing of law's violence that can only be achieved by an unravelling of law's fictitious attempt to be both a container of life and sovereignty and a bridge between normativity and life. The aim of such a work of deconstruction would be to redeem the law under the form of pure language, reclaiming it from mythical violence and opening the space for an authentic politics beyond the law. However, the praxis of such a task remains obscure, inasmuch as law is built upon this structural limit that is the state of exception, as Agamben constantly reminds us. It is in this sense that a return to the origins of the Agambenian project might shed a new light over the tedious process of redeeming the law.

In his essay on the destruction of experience, Agamben provisionally visits some of the major themes of his work: the relation between language and life, the status of the contemporary subject and the stitching between the semiotic and the semantic. Using as a starting point Walter Benjamin's essay 'The Storyteller' (1936), Agamben identifies as one of the central features of modernity the 'destruction of experience' (Agamben 1978: 13). He then follows on by tracing the intellectual origins of this current expropriation of experience. According to his reading, there are two major threads determining the impossibility of articulating life within a significant experience. His indictment does not come as a surprise, as the modern 'poverty of experience' (ibid.) is the result of the work undertaken by modern science and the new status ascribed to the subject within this project. As he writes, 'the expropriation of experience was implicit in the founding project of modern science' (ibid.: 17). It is by displacing the inner authority of experience that modern science, whose symptom is the Cartesian subject, with its search for certainty, abolishes the traditional separation between living experience and knowledge (ibid.: 19) and posits the experience as only the empty space of method. Insofar as 'in its original pure state, the Cartesian subject is nothing more than the subject of the verb, a purely linguistic-functional entity [. . .] whose existence and duration coincide with the moment of its enunciation' (ibid.: 22), it is and cannot act as the subject of experience.

This postulation finds its descendent in the Kantian subject of 'the *I think*, a transcendental subject which cannot be given substance or psychologized in any way' and who cannot *know* an object, rather (s)he can only *think* it (ibid.: 31, emphasis original). Under this light, the Hegelian dialectics is indicative of the radical change of the modern relation to experience which now becomes 'something one can only undergo but never have' (ibid.: 34). By asserting the 'Science of the experience of consciousness', which is 'a *path* towards science, an experience which is itself science' (Hegel 1807: 56) in his project of overcoming the Kantian split between the transcendental and empirical I, the last remnants of traditional experience are washed away by simply being displaced as negative and unattainable (Agamben 1978: 34). The ensuing philosophical and scientific projects of the nineteenth century, passing from Engels' attempt to offer a dialectic of nature to the myriad of positivisms trying to construct science of conscious facts, do not aim at recuperating experience, but at obscuring its loss and its traces. At the antipodes, '[t]he entire "philosophy of life", as well as a good part of turn-of-the-century culture, including poetry, set out to capture this lived experience as introspectively revealed in its preconceptual immediacy' (ibid.: 35). In this sense, it appears that the philosophical origins of hermeneutics lie precisely in the impossibility of understanding experience unless 'it ceases to be "mute" and "obscure" to become "expression" in poetry and literature' (ibid.: 36). But if the work of expropriation of experience is to be undone, and the reconstruction of experience within the frames of the present is to be possible, it can only pass through approaching the question of an experience which is still mute, as an infancy, that is a state which 'cannot merely be something which chronologically precedes language and which [. . .] ceases to exist in order to spill into speech [. . .]; rather, it coexists in its origins with language – indeed, is itself constituted through the appropriation of it by language in each instance to produce the individual as subject' (ibid.: 48). It is not by mere coincidence that the exemplary instances of experience to which Agamben points are the famous accidents evoked by Montaigne and Rousseau heralding, both in their way concepts of unconscious as well as the impossibility of subjective experience as such.

That is because experience is a fleeting moment which the subject cannot assume otherwise than through trauma (that is, it cannot assume), inasmuch as it has been evacuated from the ambit of modern subjectivity. In its liminal form, as infancy it is precisely the slippage point between the speech and the speaking being. It is a point of discontinuity, which is already at work within the human being. As Agamben observes:

> The historicity of the human being has its basis in this difference and discontinuity. Only because of this is there history, [. . .] only because there

> is a human infancy, only because language is not the same as the human, and there is a difference between language and discourse, semiotic and semantic.
> (Ibid.: 52)

The expropriation of experience is intimately linked to a debasement of authority understood as inherent to the articulation of narrative. As Agamben writes, 'experience has its necessary correlation not in knowledge but in authority – that is to say, the power of words and narration' (ibid.: 14).

Seen through these lenses, the destruction of experience is not only, if it could have ever been, a phenomenon affecting *only* subjectivity, but a dynamics which slips beyond the status of the subject in the realm of politics and law. Now is the time when 'all authority is founded on what cannot be experienced, and nobody would be inclined to accept the validity of an authority whose sole claim to legitimation was experience' (ibid.). Deprived by the claim to experience, as it could never be restated as a form of legitimation, both law and politics, as constituted authorities narrating the being-together, become effaced themselves. The consequences are bleak and herald Agamben's later politico-legal pessimism inasmuch as they echo the totalitarian experience: '[H]umankind is deprived of effective experience and becomes subjected to the imposition of a form of experience as controlled and manipulated as a laboratory maze for rats' (ibid.: 16). The state of exception is indicative of this dynamics, inasmuch as it points to the remnant of a limit form of experience which cannot be articulated, rationalized or integrated within the framework of a law that has broken its links with the narrative. Indeed, the indistinction between law and fact and the overall temporary and spatial confusions brought by the state of exception all point in the direction of the exception being nothing short of an infancy of the law, the limit point where life relates to law and fails to articulate this relation. In this sense, it is apt to describe it as underlining a stand of the legal discourse in which the law has become 'the monument of its own disappearance' (Schütz 2008: 127, emphasis omitted). With the state of exception, not only do we witness the failure of the law as a system of signification but the continual re-enactment of this failure. It is central to observe that this failure resolves itself through recourse to violence, as in psychoanalytical discourse violence, under the form of a *passage à l'acte*, signals both a dysfunction in the Symbolic and the flight into the Real (Lacan 1963: 136). More importantly perhaps, this recourse to violence not only reconstructs the pre-juridical limits of the law by bringing to the fore law's mythical violence, but it partakes in exposing the historical deadlock in which law finds itself under the conditions of the modern. In this sense, the state of exception is a symptom of the legal subject, pointing towards its recent history of debasement. Its inner logic is that of the 'extimity', for the subject reveals through its own language its inherent excess beyond signification.

Such a reading of the state of exception understood as an instantiation of the disappearance of experience or as a rendition of law's infancy – of the pre-juridical roots still present within the structure of the law – enables us further to explore the jurisprudential intricacies and pitfalls revealed by this concept. However, when placed within the framework of the intellectual history outlined by Agamben, this interpretation cannot offer an account of the material origins of law's destitution within modernity. In this way, it preserves the enigma at the core of the state of exception – that is, it maintains law's failure to limit and articulate the excess of violence sustaining it. It follows that a thorough understanding of the state of exception necessarily calls for a historical gaze. This is because the state of exception is structurally tainted by force in the very process of its formalization, an extreme situation from the standpoint of legal hermeneutics. One does not have in mind the gaze that classic historiography can offer, for the exception is both within and outside the law. Rather, one is thinking of the perspective of a historian able to move between disciplinary boundaries and to inquire into the conditions that have expropriated out of the law and its subjects the ability to translate into experience the material conditions of modernity.

Endnotes

1 For a thorough analysis of Benjamin's understanding of historical time, see Hamacher (2005).

2 See Loi des 8–10 juillet 1791 concernant la conservation et le classement des places de guerre et postes militaires, la police des fortifications et autres objets y relatifs, *Collection générale des décrets rendus par l'Assemblée Nationale*, Paris: Baudouin, 1791 [July], pp. 79–134; Loi du 10 fructidor an V [27 August 1797] qui détermine la manière dont les communes de l'intérieur de la République pourront être mises en état de guerre ou de siège, *Bulletin des lois de la République française*, no. 139, Paris: Imprimerie nationale [1797], #1380, pp. 14–5.

Bibliography

Agamben, G. (1978) *Infancy and History: The Destruction of Experience*, trans. L. Heron, London: Verso, 1993.

—— (1995) *Homo sacer: Sovereign Power and Bare Life*, trans. D. Heller-Roazen, Stanford, CA: Stanford University Press, 1998.

—— (1996) *Means Without End: Notes on Politics*, trans. V. Benetti and C. Casarino, Minneapolis, MN: Minnesota University Press, 2000.

—— (2003) *State of Exception*, trans. K. Attell, Chicago, IL: University of Chicago Press, 2005.

—— (2008) 'Terrorisme ou tragi-comédie', trans. M. Rueff, *Libération*, 19 November. Online. Available at www.liberation.fr/societe/2008/11/19/terrorisme-ou-tragi-comedie_257959 (accessed 30 June 2016).

—— (2009) *Nudities*, trans. D. Kishik and S. Pedatella, Stanford, CA: Stanford University Press, 2011.

—— (2013) 'Que l'Empire latin contre-attaque!', trans. M. Rueff, *Libération*, 24 March. Online. Available at www.liberation.fr/planete/2013/03/24/que-l-empire-latin-contre-attaque_890916 (accessed 30 June 2016).

—— (2014) *L'Uso Dei Corpi*, Milano: N. Pozza.

—— (2015) *Stasis: Civil War as a Political Paradigm*, trans. N. Heron, Edinburgh: Edinburgh University Press.
Althusser, L. (1970) 'Idéologie et appareils idéologiques d'État', in *Positions*, Paris: Éditions Sociales, 1976.
Arendt, H. (1951) *The Origins of Totalitarianism*, Orlando, FL: Harcourt, 1973.
Austin, J. (1832) *The Province of Jurisprudence Determined*, W.R. Rumble (ed.), Cambridge: Cambridge University Press, 1995.
Balakrishnan, G. (2000) *The Enemy: An Intellectual Portrait of Carl Schmitt*, London: Verso.
Benjamin, W. (1921) 'Critique of Violence', trans. E. Jephcott, in *Selected Writings*, vol. I, M. Bullock and M.W. Jennings (eds), Cambridge, MA: Harvard University Press, 1996.
—— (1934), 'Franz Kafka: On the Tenth Anniversary of His Death', trans. H. Zohn, in *Selected Writings*, vol. II, M.W. Jennings, H. Eiland and G. Smith (eds), Cambridge, MA: Harvard University Press, 1999.
—— (1936), 'The Storyteller: Observations on the Works of Nikolai Leskov', trans. H. Zohn, in *Selected Writings*, vol. III, H. Eiland and M.W. Jennings (eds), Cambridge, MA: Harvard University Press, 2002.
—— (1940) 'On the Concept of History', trans. H. Zohn, in *Selected Writings*, vol. IV, H. Eiland and M.W. Jennings (eds), Cambridge, MA: Harvard University Press, 2003.
Bikundo, E. (2013) 'Saving Human Lives From Hell: International Criminal Law and Permanent Crisis', *Netherlands Yearbook of International Law*, 44: 89–109.
Bodin, J. (1579) *On Sovereignty*, Cambridge: Cambridge University Press, 1992.
Cadava, E. (2001) '*Lapsus Imaginis*: The Image in Ruins', *October*, 96: 35–60.
Carver, T. (2004) 'Marx's *Eighteenth Brumaire of Louis Bonaparte*: Democracy, Dictatorship, and the Politics of Class Struggle', in P. Baehr and M. Richter (eds) *Dictatorship in History and Theory: Bonapartism, Caesarism, and Totalitarianism*, Cambridge: Cambridge University Press.
Clode, C.M. (1872) *The Administration of Justice Under Military and Martial Law*, London: J. Murray.
Derrida, J. (1992) 'Force of Law: The "Mystical Foundation of Authority"', trans. M. Quaintance, in D. Cornell, M. Rosenfeld and D.G. Carlson (eds) *Deconstruction and the Possibility of Justice*, London: Routledge.
Felman, S. (2002) *The Juridical Unconscious: Trials and Traumas in the Twentieth Century*, Cambridge, MA: Harvard University Press.
Foucault, M. (1975a) '"Je suis un artificier"', in R.-P. Droit (ed.) *Michel Foucault, entretiens*, Paris: O. Jacob, 2004.
—— (1975b) *Surveiller et punir*, Paris: Gallimard.
—— (1976a) *Histoire de la sexualité*, vol. I: *La Volonté de savoir*, Paris: Gallimard.
—— (1976b) '*Il faut défendre la société*', F. Ewald and A. Fontana (eds), Paris: Gallimard, 1997.
Fraser, D. (1990) 'If I Had a Rocket Launcher: Critical Legal Studies as Moral Terrorism', *Hastings Law Journal*, 41: 777–804.
Gabel, P. and Kennedy, D. (1984) 'Roll Over Beethoven', *Stanford Law Review*, 36: 1–55.
Hamacher, W. (2005) '"Now": Walter Benjamin on Historical Time', in A. Benjamin (ed.) *Walter Benjamin and History*, London: Continuum.

Hegel, G.W.F. (1807) *Phenomenology of Spirit*, trans. A.V. Miller, Oxford: Oxford University Press, 1977.

Hobbes, T. (1651) *Leviathan*, N. Malcolm (ed.), Oxford: Oxford University Press, 2012.

Holmes, O.W. (1897) 'The Path of the Law', *Harvard Law Review*, 10: 457–78.

Humphreys, S. (2006) 'Nomarchy: On the Rule of Law and Authority in Giorgio Agamben and Aristotle', *Cambridge Review of International Affairs*, 19: 331–51.

Johns, F. (2005) 'Guantánamo Bay and the Annihilation of the Exception', *European Journal of International Law*, 16: 613–35.

Lacan, J. (1963) *Le Séminaire*, vol. X: *L'Angoisse*, J.-A. Miller (ed.), Paris: Éditions du Seuil, 2004.

—— (1975) *Le Séminaire*, vol. XX: *Encore*, J.-A. Miller (ed.), Paris: Éditions du Seuil, 1999.

Marx, K. (1844) *Critique of Hegel's 'Philosophy of Right'*, J. O'Malley (ed.), trans. A. Jolin and J. O'Malley, Cambridge: Cambridge University Press, 1970.

—— (1850) *The Class Struggles in France*, trans. F. Engels, London: M. Lawrence, 1934.

—— (1852) 'The Eighteenth Brummaire of Louis Bonaparte', in *Later Political Writings*, T. Carver (ed.), trans. T. Carver, Cambridge: Cambridge University Press, 1996.

—— (1875) 'Critique of the Gotha Programme', in *Later Political Writings*, T. Carver (ed.), trans. T. Carver, Cambridge: Cambridge University Press, 1996.

—— and Engels, F. (1846) *The German Ideology*, C.J. Arthur (ed.), trans. S. Ryazanskaya, New York: International Publishers, 1970.

—— (1848) 'The Communist Manifesto', in *Selected Works*, vol. I, F. Engels (ed.), trans. S. Moore, Moscow: Progress Publishers, 1969.

McLoughlin, D. (2012) 'Giorgio Agamben on Security, Government and the Crisis of Law', *Griffith Law Review*, 21: 680–707.

Nancy, J.-L. (1983) *L'Impératif catégorique*, Paris: Flammarion.

Neocleous, M. (2008) *Critique of Security*, Edinburgh: Edinburgh University Press.

Parsley, C. (2010) 'The Mask and Agamben: The Transitional Juridical Technics of Legal Relation', *Law Text Culture*, 14: 12–39.

Pashukanis, E. (1924) 'The General Theory of Law and Marxism', in *Selected Writings on Marxism and Law*, P. Beirne and R. Sharlet (eds), trans. P.B. Maggs, London: Academic Press, 1980.

Raulff, U. (2004) 'An Interview with Giorgio Agamben', trans. M. Goodwin, *German Law Journal*, 5: 609–14.

Schmitt, C. (1921) *Dictatorship*, trans. M. Hoelzl and G. Ward, Cambridge: Polity Press, 2014.

—— (1922) *Political Theology*, trans. G. Schwab, Cambridge, MA: MIT Press, 1985.

Schütz, A. (2008) 'The Fading Memory of *Homo non Sacer*', in J. Clemens, N. Heron and A. Murray (eds) *The Work of Giorgio Agamben: Law, Literature, Life*, Edinburgh: Edinburgh University Press.

—— (2011) 'Study', in A. Murray and J. Whyte (eds) *The Agamben Dictionary*, Edinburgh: Edinburgh University Press.

Weber, M. (1922) *Economy and Society*, 2 vols, G. Roth and C. Wittich (eds), trans. E. Fischoff and others, Berkeley, CA: University of California Press, 1978.

Zartaloudis, T. (2011) 'Government/Oikonomia', in A. Murray and J. White (eds) *The Agamben Dictionary*, Edinburgh: Edinburgh University Press.

Envoi

Chapter 12

The hermeneutic character of legal construction

Ralf Poscher

According to a prevalent distinction in legal scholarship, jurists apply the law either through interpretation or construction. Already in ancient Roman law, jurists made a threefold distinction between *adjudication secundum legem* (following the law), *praeter legem* (beyond the law) and *contra legem* (against the law).[1] The twofold distinction between interpretation and construction merged the last two categories of the threefold model into one and then differentiated internally between legitimate and illegitimate construction. This system probably originates with the methodological writings of Friedrich Carl von Savigny, the eminent nineteenth-century German legal scholar and founder not only of the historical school in private law but of modern German doctrinal scholarship in general. Savigny distinguished between interpretation and '*Fortbildung des Rechts*', the – doctrinal – 'development of law' (1840: §50, 262). In the US, the distinction between interpretation and construction was introduced by Francis Lieber in his famous essay 'On Political Hermeneutics' of 1837. Francis Lieber was a German immigrant to the United States, educated at German universities. There is no evidence that Lieber knew of Savigny's methodological teachings of the early nineteenth century, first published only three years after Lieber's famous essay. But Lieber's general hermeneutic stance probably drew on some of the same sources as Savigny's, and, in particular, on Friedrich Schleiermacher, the founder of universal hermeneutics, whom both knew and admired.[2] Lieber's twofold distinction corresponds to Savigny's in that it links legal interpretation to the intentions of the legislator, although Savigny's account is enriched by his idea of legal institutions that the legislator can draw upon (1840: §5, 8–9).

Although the distinction between legal interpretation and legal construction is not very clear-cut in the accounts of Savigny and Lieber, the general idea is that legal interpretation aims at a content associated with the law by its creator. By contrast, legal construction is needed when legal interpretation falls short and the law must be amended by the interpreter to make it applicable to a case at hand. This is not to say that legal interpretation and construction form two separate steps in our practice of adjudication, a point that Lieber already noted explicitly (1837: 81). Although they are distinguished in legal methodology, in the practice of adjudication legal interpretation is nested within legal construction in the form of legislative intent or the genetic argument as one of the classical canons of legal hermeneutics. But their nestedness in legal practice does not alter their fundamentally different nature. They are not distinct in purely quantitative terms, with one fading into the other, but in a sharp metaphysical sense, with one being an empirical, the other a normative enterprise; one being reconstructive, about finding the pre-existing law, the other creative or constructive, about amending the law (Marmor 2005: 24–5).

If legal construction involves amending the law, if it concerns the creation of law, how can it still be characterized as a hermeneutic activity distinct from the creation of a law by legislative bodies such as parliaments, city councils, administrative agencies or presidents, which are not regarded as hermeneutic? My thesis is that legal construction, although it amends the law, is nonetheless a hermeneutic activity because it follows the structural model of legal interpretation. Thus, I will initially offer an account of legal interpretation and of its structures of significance for the explanation of legal construction. Subsequently, I will demonstrate how legal construction mimics legal interpretation though lacking some of its constitutive features. In the course of this analysis, various characteristics of legal construction will become apparent, in particular its relation to rule-of-law values, its truth aptness and its character as a proper academic discipline. I want to emphasize at the outset that this contribution addresses the theoretical reconstruction of legal construction. As such, it is not concerned with the legitimacy of legal construction. Nor does it discuss the specific forms legal construction may adopt. Suffice it to observe that these are highly contested in some areas of the law – for example, within constitutional law (Solum 2010: 116–8; Barnett 2011).

I. Interpretation

1. Interpretation as intentional explanation

In the most general sense, interpretation is a form of explanation that relates to intentional phenomena – that is, to someone's beliefs, desires, intentions, hopes, wishes, actions, etc. – and their products such as tools and – in the hermeneutic tradition most prominently – texts. If we see someone picking up an umbrella, we explain his action by his belief that it is going to rain, his desire not to get wet and his intention to go outside; we thus interpret his action. But interpretation is not limited to actions; it applies to any kind of object that is connected to intentions. Thus – to take Heidegger's famous example (1927: §15, 68–70) – we interpret a piece of wood connected to a metal bar as a hammer, because someone created it with the intention of fulfilling this purpose. And if we believe in the objective spirit steering the course of history, we can interpret the course of history, because we conceive of the objective spirit as an intentional agent.

As mental phenomena, intentional phenomena supervene on non-intentional phenomena such as neurophysiological brain states and ultimately the interplay of subnuclear particles. Different kinds of explanation address different levels of these supervening phenomena, drawing on different regularities at the respective levels. But interpretations as intentional explanations do not just differ from non-intentional ones in the level of explanation – like biological explanations with respect to physics – but also in the standards involved (Davidson 1991: 215). Interpretation has been characterized as a normalizing type of explanation, because it presupposes rational standards (Pettit 1994: 162–6) such as the principle of charity, according to which we must generally interpret beliefs of an agent charitably with respect to their truth (Davidson 1991). When we interpret other intentional beings, we rely – special circumstances aside – on the rationality of the agent. Without presupposing a certain degree of rationality, it would be impossible for us to reconstruct the intentions of agents other than ourselves. Interpretation as an intentional explanation is thus distinct from other causal explanations because of the standards employed, which are based on rationality.[3]

2. *Meaning and intentions*

If interpretation is the specific form of explanation that applies to intentional phenomena and relies on rationality, then linguistic interpretation is a special instance of this more general kind of explanation. The interpretation of linguistic artefacts is simply a special sort of interpretation that shares the intentional and rational features of interpretation as a whole. So it comes as no surprise that the contrast between interpretation and mere causal explanations is mirrored in Paul Grice's distinction between natural and non-natural signs. Natural signs have 'meaning' because of non-intentional causal relations between an object and its environment. Smoke thus signals fire, because of the chemical reactions between the materials involved. Non-natural signs, by contrast, acquire their meaning through the intentions that a speaker or author connects with an utterance. Shouting the English word 'fire' may also signal fire. But it does so because we infer that the person shouting intends to alert us to a fire and is neither deceived nor deceitful. It does so only because of the intentions of the person shouting, not because of some causal relation between the sound of the shout and the fire.

Meaningful utterances are a special kind of intentional action. They intend to communicate propositional content and we make sense of them by inferring the propositional content that the utterer intends to communicate. As in the case of the umbrella, we explain – that is, interpret – the shout of 'fire' through the intentions, beliefs and desires of the agent. We explain it by the intention of the person shouting to communicate the proposition that there is a fire, based on her belief that there is a fire and her desire to warn us. Non-natural meaning is thus an intentional phenomenon. Meaning is tied to intentions. There is no meaning without at least the presupposition of intentions. The famous lines drawn in the sand by the waves (Knapp and Michaels 1982: 727–8)[4] that resemble letters have no meaning. We can assign meaning to them only by presupposing some kind of hypothetical speaker (Alexander and Prakash 2004: 977 n. 25). If the waves form the signs 'I love you', we might suppose some ordinary sort of context like a couple on a romantic walk and one of them stating her or his affection.

Grice has developed this insight into a model of communication that has been widely accepted despite some arguments over its details (1989).[5] The utterance 'Please close the window!' has its meaning because a speaker connected a communicative intention with the utterance, and because its addressee recognizes the utterer's communicative intention: that she wishes the window to be closed. Interpretation of linguistic artefacts works like reverse engineering. The interpreter develops a hypothesis with respect to the communicative intentions that the utterer connected with the non-natural sign.

The reliance on communicative intentions is neutral with regard to the internalism or externalism of their content. A speaker might well communicate with the intention of deferring to some external standard or authority. If she says 'I'll have what you're having' in a bar, she might not know what she is ordering, but intends to order whatever her companion has ordered or is about to order. Thus, the reconstruction of meaning on the basis of communicative intentions does not have to take a stance in the debate about semantic realism – its metaphysical viability or its scope. Semantic realism presupposes a certain kind of communicative intention – indexical, referential and deferential to experts – without which it would not get off the ground (Moore 2007: 252–3; 2016) even if the metaphysical presuppositions were not contested. As will become apparent in the discussion of legal construction, it could even be understood in line with externalist intentions on the part of the legislator, which defers the regulation of fringe, borderline or unforeseen cases to the courts. But the externalist content of the communicative intentions is also in principle an empirical question that is answered by the state of mind of the speaker.

The main clue for inferring what Grice called 'speaker's meaning' is what he termed 'sentence meaning' – that is, the semantic meaning of the linguistic expressions used in the utterance (Levinson 1983: 17–21). But semantic meaning, too, rests on the speaker's meaning – or pragmatic meaning, as linguistics would say. Semantic meaning follows from the intentions that speakers habitually or characteristically connect with an utterance type.

Most of the time, the speaker's and the semantic meanings are in harmony. By using the utterance 'Please close the window!', the speaker intends to communicate that she wants the window – and not the door – to be shut. But Grice's discussion of pragmatic implicature (1989: 24–40) and Donald Davidson's treatment of malapropisms (1986) have shown that this harmony is not a necessary condition for communication. In Grice's famous example in which a colleague – asked for academic references – writes that the candidate has an 'excellent command of English', the context of the utterance reveals that the communicative intention was quite different from the semantic meaning of the expression (1989: 33). In the same way, we know what is meant when in Thomas Mann's novel *Der*

Zauberberg (*The Magic Mountain*), Mrs Stöhr confuses the expression 'magnet' with the expression 'magnate' (1924a: 758; 1924b: I, 698). The same holds in the above example if all the windows in the room are closed but the glass terrace door stands open. Irrespective of the semantics of the expression 'window', the context allows us to infer that the request 'Please close the window!' refers to the open door.

Communicative interpretation involves developing a hypothesis about an empirical fact, the intention of a speaker supervening upon a mental state. As with any empirical hypothesis, interpretations can be true or false. The speaker either had the intention or not. The interpretative difficulties that may arise are of a purely epistemic nature. It may be difficult or even impossible to infer the communicative intentions of a speaker, but the potential epistemic transcendence of communicative intentions is a property that they share with all other empirical objects and events in the world. Interpretation does not raise any issues other than those that have to be answered by empirical investigations in general. 'We thus need have no special sort of activity, distinct from normal descriptive or explanatory activity of science, that requires justification. [. . .] The communicative model thus causes no ripples in the smooth waters of science' (Moore 1995: 5; see also Fish 2008: 1116).

Nevertheless, the empirical hypothesis that has to be justified in the process of interpretation is of a very specific kind. The justification of an interpretation must connect an utterance, its semantic meaning and its context to the intentions of a speaker. Not all hypotheses regarding the intentions of a speaker are interpretations. If we had a mind-reading machine somehow able to causally reconstruct the intentional content of the speaker's mind from her brainwaves, the results would not be an interpretation of the mind it monitors. The hypothesis must be justified by the utterance, its context and principles of rationality, not just by any causal explanation.

In principle, this is already possible through our everyday knowledge of the semantic meaning of the expressions employed. Sometimes, however – as in the example of the terrace door referred to as a 'window' – more complex justifications are necessary. But the justification must always be directed at a relation between the linguistic expression, the text and the context on the one hand and the communicative intentions on the other. Most importantly in our context, an interpretation of an utterance cannot be justified by the substantive qualities of a proposition; it must be justified by an argument supporting the hypothesis that the utterer wanted to connect a certain communicative intention with his utterance – whatever its quality in substance might be. The substantial adequacy of an interpretation can be circumstantial evidence for the intention of the utterer, but no more than that (Davidson 1973: 137). An interpretation cannot be justified by the substantial adequacy of its content alone. In our example, the hypothesis that the expression 'window' referred to the terrace door cannot be justified by the fact that – irrespective of the speaker's intention – there are good reasons for closing the door.[6]

3. *Legislative intent*

In law, we encounter communicative interpretation with respect to legislative intent (see generally Ekins 2012). In our hermeneutic approaches to the law, communicative interpretation, however, is not particularly prominent. This is due not only to the theoretical difficulties of coming to terms with the idea of a collective intention on the part of the legislator (Hurd 1990; Larenz 1991: 328–9; Waldron 1999: 119–46). As the philosophical literature on collective intentionality shows, there seem to be reductive accounts of collective intentions as overlapping and interconnected intentions of the individuals involved, which make it possible to avoid dubious ontological claims about collective minds and the like (Searle 1990; Bratman 1999: 109–30). Although these accounts must be normatively enriched with rules for the ascription of meaning to individual legislators on the basis of the text and the legislative context to provide for a collective intent of the legislator, the theoretical difficulties of explaining our discourse about legislative intent can in principle be overcome (Ekins 2012). This is evident in the pervasive reference to legislative intent across different legal cultures.

The reason why legislative intent does not figure prominently in many hard cases for resolving legal indeterminacy is empirical in nature. The legislator is usually only concerned with the paradigmatic cases covered by his regulations. These paradigmatic cases will also dominate the everyday practice of the law. However, these are not the cases that attract the attention of the hermeneutic doctrinal efforts of higher courts and legal scholars. Legal doctrine develops its concepts, principles, tests and answers against the background of paradigm cases, but it does so with a specific interest in borderline cases and other cases of indeterminacy, which are the only ones that require a deeper hermeneutic engagement with the law. If we had only paradigm cases of free speech, we would not have to develop legal doctrine for it. However, the question of whether the links provided by search engines fall under its protection engages lawyers in legal hermeneutics. But for borderline cases like this no viable hypotheses on the empirical intentions of the legislator are generally available: more often than not the legislator simply has not considered the borderline case at hand, or even if he has done so, this might not be documented in the legal materials or the legal materials may remain inconclusive on the matter. Only in very rare cases do the legislative materials provide sufficient substance to justify a communicative interpretation for a borderline case.[7] It is for this empirical reason that communicative interpretation is on the one hand essential for the overall practice of the law, but on the other does not play a very important role in the legal hermeneutics that higher courts and doctrinal academics are engaged in.

II. Legal construction

Should the intentions of the legislator exhaust themselves, the law cannot afford to leave matters at that as such decision would lead to a denial of justice. Indeed, legal hermeneutics has to assume that the law holds an answer in every case. Thus, legal hermeneutics has to reach beyond communicative interpretation. To what extent can it still be understood as a hermeneutic activity when the interpreter goes beyond the intentions of the legislator? Beyond the communicative intentions of the legislator, there is no pre-existing meaning to be had. Signs have non-natural meaning only if there are communicative intentions connected to them and only as far as there are communicative intentions connected to them. Without intentions, they are just like the lines resembling letters produced by the ocean waves. Thus, when legal hermeneutics moves beyond the regulatory intentions that the legislator has expressed with a certain norm formulation, it amends the law for a borderline or otherwise indeterminate case and moves into the field of legal construction. Legal construction in the form of adjudication creates new law applicable to cases for which the legislator had no intentions; in the form of academic legal doctrine, it works out respective suggestions. Legal construction is no longer in the business of inferring already existing regulatory intentions but creates a new regulation for the case at hand (Marmor 2005: 25). It is no longer an empirical endeavour aimed at reconstructing a preexisting intention, but a normative activity aimed at amending a regulation by precisification.

But how can the creation of law for cases that have not previously been regulated still be regarded as a hermeneutic activity? The authors of the Constitution could not have had any intentions with regard to the hyperlinks of search engines and their protection by freedom of speech. How can a legal construction that includes or excludes search engines and their results from this fundamental right still be a hermeneutic activity? How is it different from the activity of a legislator who becomes aware of the regulatory gap and answers the same question? Are standard positivist and legal realist accounts of legal construction not correct in equating it with legislation as, for example, in Hans Kelsen's theory of legal interpretation? According to Kelsen, legal interpretation establishes a frame of meaning, and legal construction within the framed area of indeterminacy ultimately consists in a creation of law by the interpreter that differs in scale but not in structure from legislation (1960a: 239–60; 1960b: 233–56; 1934: 70; see also Larenz 1991: 366). If this was true, legal construction would be no more a hermeneutic enterprise than legislation.

I. Legal construction as the interpretation of a text

Contrary to Kelsen and to similar accounts, legal construction differs from other ways of creating law and specifically from legislation. Moreover, it differs in a way that gives it a hermeneutic character. The aspect in which it differs is the kind of justification that it requires. Other regulatory activities must justify the content of their regulations solely with regard to their adequacy regarding the substantive issue at hand. The legislator who must decide whether to protect search engines and their results as free speech could opt for a solution that protects every search result; or only those featuring politically charged terms; or the data issuing from national, large or small search engines; or whatever he regards as politically appropriate. Irrespective of his decision, he must justify his choice only on the basis of the political or practical appropriateness of the new regulation. If he can account for the new regulation with reasons that testify to its appropriateness, he has done everything required.

Unlike any form of legislation, legal construction cannot be justified solely by its political or practical appropriateness. Even though the legislative intentions do not provide for a regulation in cases in which legal construction becomes necessary, legal construction cannot simply seek out the politically or pragmatically most appropriate decision or consult the social sciences or economics. Instead, legal construction must always be justified as an interpretation of the text. But how can the creation of law be understood as the interpretation of the text, let alone be justified as such an interpretation when its author did not connect any intentions with the text for the case at hand? Hermeneutics is concerned with discovering the meaning of a text. Unlike natural signs, non-natural signs receive their meaning only from intentional subjects connecting communicative intentions with them. But if the author of a text did not connect any intentions with an utterance, where do the intentions that give a text meaning come from?

The semantic meaning of the text seems an obvious candidate as it supervenes upon the intentions that are habitually or characteristically connected with an utterance token that belongs to an utterance type. Independently of the communicative intentions that the legislator will have associated with the text of the law, it seems possible to elicit communicative intentions that are discovered in a quasi-statistical manner, as is now done in computer linguistics, which develops semantics on the basis of large linguistic corpora (Vogel and Christensen 2013). But even the electronic enhancement of traditional methods of lexicography will hardly help with ascription of meaning in borderline cases and other instances of indeterminacy of the law that legal construction has to address. Borderline cases and other instances of legal indeterminacy are usually also ones where the semantics of the expressions employed are indeterminate. If a zoning law contains regulations on the window surfaces of facades, the semantics of 'window' is of little help in deciding whether glass bricks count as a window for the purposes of the zoning regulation.

If semantics cannot assist, the question remains: Where do the intentions that can be connected to the text within the process of legal construction originate? At this stage, the issue of how to justify legal construction as an interpretation of the text seems to become more perplexing. The problem is not the legitimacy of legal construction. Rather, the issue concerns the theoretical conceptualization of it as a form of interpretation, even though it creates the law it is supposed to infer from the text and from the text's context. In other words, the theoretical question precedes the legitimacy issue. How, then, can the creation of a new regulation by means of legal construction be regarded and practised as a hermeneutic activity if neither its author nor semantics has assigned the required meaning to it?

2. *Construction versus association*

Beyond communicative intentions, there is no pre-existing meaning to be had. Signs have non-natural meaning only if there are communicative intentions connected to them and only as far as there are communicative intentions connected to them. Without the communicative intentions connected to them, they are just like the marks resembling letters produced by ocean waves. In this, legal construction resembles other hermeneutic activities that attribute meaning to objects to which no communicative intentions have been ascribed such as cloud formations or dreams (Moore 1995: 7–13). Even if it is irrational to read cloud formations as predictions of the future, these interpretations must be justified by the actual cloud formation and its suggestive Gestalt, density or colour play, not by their predictive adequacy alone. In the same way, the interpretation of dreams has to be justified with respect to the actual dream sequences and not just by the fact that they adequately describe the psyche of the person under analysis. Psychotherapy has to justify a plausible relation between the actual dream and its analysis. It must be able to explain why the puppet play in the dream can be interpreted as a text attempting to reveal early abuse or some other childhood trauma. An adequate psychotherapeutic diagnosis alone is no more an interpretation of a dream than an adequate regulation of a case of legal indeterminacy alone is a legal construction. Both must be justified as the interpretation of a text – that is, according to criteria in their respective disciplines that establish a justified connection between a text and an interpretative hypothesis.

Hermeneutics aims at the justification of a derivative production of meaning. It has to conceptualize the meaning that it supports as a reconstruction of a meaning that predates it, that has already been connected with the text it interprets. This approach distinguishes interpretation from association. In the case of association, the object offers only an opportunity for the production of meaning by the person perceiving it. There is nothing but a causal relation between the object and the association. Although the object triggers it, it is not conceptualized as containing the association, or even as containing any meaning at all. The famous madeleine may trigger childhood associations, and these associations can be explained without ascribing these meanings to the madeleine. The madeleine causes the childhood associations, but it does not intend to do so. The same is true of a poem or a song that a mother recited frequently to her child and that triggers memories of childhood whenever the child hears it at a much later date. The poem or song does not have to be about childhood in order to trigger childhood associations. For a hermeneutic justification, a merely associative relation is not sufficient. Rather, the justification of a hermeneutic relation has to pertain to a meaning of the text that predates the act of interpretation. In contrast to association, the meaning connected to a text is not only the trigger but also the measure of the text's meaning. It is not enough for the connected meaning to cause a text's meaning, but the text's meaning must also be intended by the text and its author.

3. The fiction of an author

The interpreter has to justify the ascription of meaning to a text as the reconstruction of a meaning that has already been connected to it even in cases such as legal construction, cloud or dream interpretation in which no meanings have been connected with the text by an author. Hermeneutic construction must do both: it has to newly ascribe a meaning to a text and justify this ascription as the reconstruction of a meaning on the basis of the text and its context. The first element – the connection of intentions with the text – is needed to provide the justification for the construction of a point of reference in the text. For its part, the second element – the reconstruction as intentions already connected with the text – ensures that the ascription of meaning is truly a hermeneutic construction and not merely an association. At least implicitly, the second element presupposes the fiction of an author (Marmor 2005: 23).[8] Meanings can be ascribed to texts only by intentional subjects. Since in cases of legal construction the author of a text and semantics, which supervene on a collective practice of meaning ascription by individual language use, must be discarded, the ascription of meaning to an otherwise meaningless text implicitly presupposes the fiction of an author who connected communicative intentions with the utterance and thus gave the utterance the character of a text. The postmodern slogan of the 'death of the author' (Barthes 1968; Foucault 1969: 793–6) has its merits with respect to the real authors of a text. For structural reasons, however, the author cannot be discarded from hermeneutics; as interpretation, hermeneutics always relies on an author – albeit a fictive one – for its justification.[9] It is ironical that Hans-Georg Gadamer rightly insisted on the productive element inhering to legal hermeneutics in particular (1986: 321–36), even as the hermeneutic character of this productive element is only secured by a justificatory structure that relies on an intentionalist concept of interpretation in the Romantic tradition, which is precisely what Gadamer set out to fight in the first place (ibid.: 175–214).

Sometimes, the fictions involved in interpretation are made explicit – for example, in the case of the interpretation of dreams when the subconscious is referred to as their author. For legal construction, the text itself is sometimes put in the position of the author. The famous phrase that a legal text can be smarter than the legislator[10] personifies the text and gives it the role of fictive author.[11] More explicit is the fiction of the author in Ronald Dworkin's holistic maxim of interpretation, according to which the legal system should be understood as a 'single person' (1986: 225, 242) which strives for integrity. For Dworkin, the text to which the interpretation relates is not a single law but a legal order as such, which is explicitly personified in the cause of interpretation. But irrespective of how the text that is the measure of legal construction is compartmentalized – a single provision, a whole statute, a distinctive part of the legal order, or the legal order as such – and regardless of whether the fiction is made explicit, legal construction is only justified if it can be shown that the regulatory suggestion is a reconstruction of a meaning that a fictive legislator could have connected with the text. Thus, the dissociation of the interpreter and pre-existing meaning can be achieved: although the interpreter does both, she simulates a previous ascription of meaning by a fictive author and interprets the text as a text by this author.

If legal construction has to be justified as an adequate reconstruction of the communicative intentions of an implicit legislator, the justification of legal construction is a function of the implicit legislator. Depending on the properties attributed to the fictive legislator, different hypotheses of interpretation can be justified. One possibility would be to refer to the historic or present actual legislator. As a consequence, the justification of the ascription of intentions could be supported by political orientations. Especially in totalitarian regimes, fictionalizations of this kind may figure prominently in the reinterpretation of historic laws or in the pre-emptive interpretation of new laws as observed under Nazi rule in Germany when the civil code was reinterpreted to exclude Jews from legal transactions or when the new race statutes were dynamically interpreted to support and keep pace with the dynamics of persecution and elimination (Rüthers 2012: 160–1, 166–72). In the liberal tradition, however, such overt references to political fictions are not the norm for legal construction. Instead, the liberal tradition makes use of rationalizations. Legal construction presupposes a rational standard for the – implicit – fictive legislator.

Since the construction of the intention of a rational legislator must itself be justified rationally, there is a double rational standard at play. Legal construction aims neither at the rational reconstruction of an irrational intention nor at the arational reconstruction of a rational intention – for example, by way of intuition or luck – still less at the irrational reconstruction of an irrational intention. Instead, the justification of a legal construction aims at a (fictive) rational legislator and must be justified as a rational reconstruction of its rational intentions. The double rationality standard can be conceived as being distributed among different roles: the rationality of the fictive legislator amending the law and the rationality of the interpreter reconstructing the fictive legislator's intentions. However, taking into account Davidson's point to the effect that rational speakers cannot intend the impossible (1989: 147), rational speakers already have to reflect on the possibility of a rational reconstruction of their intentions. Thus, the rational interpreter is also already embedded in the rational implicit legislator. Whether conceived as distributed among different roles or as embedded, both rationality standards determine legal construction. The double rationality requirement distinguishes legal construction from legal interpretation on the one side and from legislation on the other.

4. Legal construction versus legal interpretation

Since the fictive legislator is conceptualized as rational, legal construction must aim at a rational amendment of the law for the borderline or otherwise indeterminate case at hand. Legal construction thus has to amend the law according to substantive and not merely epistemic normative standards. In this, legal construction differs from legal interpretation. Legal interpretation aims only at the reconstruction of an actual legislative intent. It does not concern itself with the substantive rationality of the intentions it tries to reconstruct. The actual legislator can be more or less rational. It is not the task of legal interpretation to make it as rational as possible. It just has the task of reconstructing it, whatever its merits.

The normative standards that apply to legal interpretation are at heart only epistemic. These epistemic norms and rules of attribution, however, only aim at the reconstruction of the actual legislative intent, independently of its merits. For legal interpretation, evaluative and instrumental criteria of rationality only come into play inasmuch as they prove empirically valid with respect to the actual legislator. They only come into play within the framework of an empirical analysis and only in so far as the empirical hypothesis that the actual legislator complied with them is empirically sound. Whereas legal interpretation is a basically empirical endeavour – that is, reconstructing the intentions of the actual legislator – legal construction is a normative enterprise, since it aims at a fictive fully rational legislator. The rules attributed to the fully rational legislator have to be fully rational in an instrumental and evaluative sense. There is no room for rational imperfection with the fictive legislator, as there is in the muddy waters of actual legislation. Legal constructions cannot be justified only according to epistemic standards; they have to engage in the substantive justification of the amendment to the law they propose. Whereas legal interpretation can result in more or less rational norms, legal construction has to justify its results as a substantively rational amendment to the law to cover the borderline or otherwise indeterminate case at hand. This gives rise to a couple of substantial rationality standards for legal construction.[12]

(a) Generality

Even though the necessity for legal construction only arises with respect to a specific borderline or otherwise indeterminate case, legal construction does not aim at deciding that specific case alone. Legal construction aims at the intentions of a fictive rational legislator. Its perspective is thus intrinsically one of generality. It aims at a general rule to amend the law and only in the second instance at a specific decision on the basis of the rule it constructs. It constructs the rule in light of the case at hand, but it is not only concerned with a decision on that case. Since it has to construct an intention of a fictive rational legislator, it must develop a solution that stands the test of generalization. A mere Kadi-decision of the case at hand would not be a legal construction, whatever its merits. Modern legal systems delegate this kind of dispute solution to court settlements and deals. As the fictive intent of a fictive legislator, legal constructions must be justified as generalizable amendments to the law.

(b) Consistency

The fiction of a rational author entails further consistency requirements for legal construction. The fictive legislator is conceptualized as a unity to which the regulations created in the process of legal construction can be ascribed as non-contradictory and consistent communicative intentions. Dworkin made this idea explicit with his concept of integrity (1986: 95–6, 216–75). Like a natural person, the fictive legislator is imagined as an author whose integrity relies on the consistency of the regulations created by legal construction. The crucial factor is not the political or practical adequacy of the legal construction, but whether it fits well with the actual regulative intentions of the actual legislator. Even should the whole system of emissions trading prove ineffective, it does not follow that in cases of doubt the scope of the emissions trading system has to be constructed narrowly. Whether an enterprise is included in the system will depend on the consistency of its inclusion in the – possibly ineffective – regulatory concept of the legislator.

The fiction of a unitary and integer legislator explains the importance of both systematic and teleological arguments in legal construction. Irrespective of the political or practical adequacy of a regulation, the concept of an integer legislator entails that its objectives and aims must be consistently followed – even should they prove to be wrong in substance. There is, however, some wiggle room in legal construction, because the text to which the consistency requirements apply can be tailored in different ways. It can be limited to a specific regulation, but, especially in a constitutional system, it can also include the constitution. Depending on how the text is tailored, the consistency requirements can play out differently. If the constitution is included, unconstitutional legal constructions can be discarded although they might fit well with the lower-level regulation. The canon of constitutional avoidance[13] testifies to this overarching consistency requirement.

(c) Instrumental rationality

The presupposition of rationality for the fictive legislator also guarantees the practical soundness of legal construction. A rational legislator would not devise a practically unsound regulation. Within the boundaries of consistency, legal construction must respect the requirements of instrumental rationality[14] and practical soundness. So, it comes as no surprise that in his seminal study on legal construction in common-law and civil-law systems Josef Esser regards practical soundness as one of the essential characteristics of adjudication (1972: 139–73). In a weaker – and probably excessively weak – version, the same idea is taken up in the absurdity doctrine, which bans legal constructions that are obviously practically unsound.[15] A legal construction leading to absurd results can be banned not only if the semantics of the regulation so recommends, but equally when it seems to require this prohibition. The demand for instrumental rationality is also interesting because it is a possible entry point for knowledge acquired in other disciplines such as the social sciences or economics. Indeed, other disciplines can inform legal construction as regards the practical soundness of a legal construction. They can help to develop a more practically sound doctrinal amendment to the law. This explains how even a hermeneutic understanding of legal construction can call for a stronger interdisciplinary engagement of legal doctrine (Jestaedt 2014: 12).

(d) Evaluative rationality

If legal construction must be justified as a communicative intention of a fictive rational legislator, it must prove not only its instrumental but also its evaluative rationality. Just as a rational legislator would not devise instrumentally unsound regulations, it would not devise normatively unsound regulations that contradict exigencies of fundamental justice.[16] The orientation towards evaluative rationality explains the connection between legal construction and justice. Under conditions of extensive national and international fundamental rights provisions, this orientation can be represented within the hierarchy of norms and be addressed as a matter of consistency in doctrines such as constitutional avoidance.

(e) The 'fusion of horizons'

Legal construction is an operation for the present. The law is confronted with a phenomenon, such as a case, with respect to which there exists no predetermined intention on the part of the legislator. The law must therefore amend the historical intentions of the legislator in order to provide a solution for the case at hand, as in the matter of the hyperlinks provided by a search engine and the issue of freedom of speech. The law has to amend the intentions connected with the provision guaranteeing freedom of speech by making reference to intentions that will allow a determination of the hyperlink case. It thus updates freedom of speech to address present needs. Through legal construction, historic legal texts accordingly remain relevant for the present. Legal construction thus enables hermeneutics to accomplish a 'fusion of horizons' within law (Gadamer 1986: 317).

5. Legal construction versus legislation

Just as the normative character of legal construction sets it apart from legal interpretation, its relation to the text sets it apart from legislation. If the instrumental and evaluative rationality requirements were the only requirements for legal construction, it would be akin to legislation. It would only – but also already – be distinguished from legislation by the consistency requirement, since the actual legislator can break with a legislative tradition in ways the fictive legislator embodied in legal construction cannot. The actual legislator who has become doubtful of his emissions trading system might opt to exclude a borderline case even though it would be more consistent to include it.

There is, however, another feature that sets legal construction apart from legislation, which it shares with legal interpretation. For legal construction – as for legal interpretation – specific epistemic criteria have to be met. These specific epistemic justificatory requirements give legal construction its hermeneutic character. Like communicative interpretation, legal construction must be justified as an intention that could have been connected with the text. Since the relation between non-natural signs and their meaning is not determined by the casual relations of a mind-independent reality but by the intentions of the utterer, an utterer can connect any communicative intention with any sign. Rational utterers, however, cannot follow a humpty-dumpty approach. Rational speakers and authors can only connect those communicative intentions with an utterance for which they believe that they give the interpreters at least a fair chance of inferring their intentions. It is not rational to attempt the impossible – that is, to try to communicate an intention that the utterer knows cannot be inferred by the addressee (Davidson 1989).

This is why the intentions of a rational speaker are always reflexively related to the addressee of the utterance in the Gricean model of communication. The speaker does not simply intend to produce a certain representation in the mind of the addressee. Instead, he intends the addressee of the utterance to infer the communicative intention from the utterance and recognize the communicative intention of the speaker as such.[17] A rational speaker can have such a complex intention only when he can presuppose that the interpreter of the utterance will be able to infer the communicative intention on the basis of the utterance and its context. Inversely, a rational hermeneutic construction with respect to a fictive rational legislator has to show that and how the text plus its context can lead to the fictive intention that it constructs by rational means.

The connection to the text is habitually supplied by its semantics. Legal constructions have to fall within the indeterminacy range of the semantics and its context. The ascription of intentions to the text can normally be rationally supported as long as they fall within the penumbra of the text. Semantics are of significant importance, since otherwise the connection with the text would be severed and the hermeneutic character of legal construction lost. The connection to the text, however, can be more indirect in legal construction, too. In cases of legal analogies, the connection to the text is established by an argument holding that a legislator, who has issued a law with such a text and such an intention, would also have had a corresponding intention for the corresponding (or analogous) case it overlooked.

The reliance on the text and its semantics also explains why the forms of argument employed in legal construction are the same as in legal interpretation. To justify that a legal construction can be assigned to a text, semantic, systematic, teleological and historical arguments have to be made that relate the communicative intentions of the fictitious legislator to the text just as hypotheses regarding the actual intentions of the actual legislator have to be supported by semantic, systematic, teleological and historical arguments. The similarity of the argumentative tools also explains why legal interpretation and legal construction are not neatly distinguished in the practice of adjudication. Once at work with one of the tools, the interpreter proceeds regardless of whether she is still in the domain of interpretation or has already reached the domain of construction.

6. Legal construction and the rule of law

The dirty little secret, however, is that the interpreter has a fair amount of leeway over how to delineate the text to which he ascribes the meaning with which he wants to amend the law. It could be the text of a single provision, a statute, the norms of a certain area of the law or even – as in Dworkin's holistic approach – the whole legal order. This leeway in choosing the relevant text explains the specificity of the *nulla poena sine lege* principle in criminal law. The specificity of the stricter principle of legal determinacy in criminal law consists in restricting the text to a single provision of the criminal code. This distinguishes the criminal-law principle of determinacy from the more general rule-of-law principle of determinacy that allows, within limits, for a broadening of the textual basis. The restriction to the text of a single provision or code is also sometimes taken to distinguish different kinds of legal construction, such as construction *intra legem*[18] and *praeter legem* or even *contra legem* – although the latter is considered illegitimate most of the time (Neuner 2005: 139–78).

But irrespective of how the textual basis is delineated, the necessary connection with the text cannot be explained by rule-of-law standards of legal predictability. Since legal construction only comes into play in cases where the intentions of the legislator have fallen short, the results of legal construction are more often than not unpredictable not only for the addressees of the regulation but even for legal experts. In light of the hermeneutic unpredictability of legal construction, the addressees of the law might even be better served by amending the law with a regulation that is simply the most politically or pragmatically appropriate one, which does not have to compromise appropriateness out of respect for the text. In cases of legal construction, the requirement that it be related to the text cannot be explained by rule-of-law considerations of predictability; it can only be explained by the fact that legal construction has to comply with a hermeneutic standard.

The normative reasons for relying on hermeneutic and not simply on pragmatic justifications for amending the law in cases for which the legislator has not developed any intentions are a separate issue. Here I will only mention a general trend of social differentiation. The hermeneutic character of legal construction ensures a certain distance from the substantive issues that are transformed into legal issues by the legal system. Thus, the law can provide for both: on the one hand, it can provide for authoritative decisions; on the other hand, it can keep the social discourse on the substantive issues open. The hermeneutic character of legal construction guarantees that the authoritative legal decision is a purely legal one.

7. Legal construction and truth

For legal construction, the fictionalization and rationalization of the regulatory intentions connected to the text ensure the dissipation of a potential tension between the epistemically justified and the true interpretation. In contrast to cases of communicative interpretation, legal construction is not confronted with a potentially epistemic transcendent empirical reality. In cases of communicative interpretation, the empirical fact of the communicative intentions of the actual author decides on the truth of a rational interpretation. In legal construction, however, the epistemically justified reconstruction of the fictive intentions of the fictive rational legislator and these fictive intentions are necessarily identical. Since the fictive rational legislator can only connect communicative intentions with the text that he knows the addressee is able to reconstruct, a rational reconstruction of the fictive intentions will always fit that bill. In the absence of an actual empirical intention on the part of the legislator, the rational reconstruction of the fictive regulatory intentions by the interpreter cannot miss a deviant reality.

This epistemic relativization of legal construction leads to a potential loss of definiteness. Mere epistemic rationality standards do not provide for definiteness even with respect to empirical facts. The empirical world is definite. Empirical events either obtain or not. This, however, does not mean that different hypotheses with respect to an empirical event cannot all satisfy the epistemic standards equally well. There is no rational privilege between competing epistemic hypotheses under these conditions; it is only the contingency of the world that qualifies one of them as true and all others as false. Thus different rational reconstructions of an empirical communicative intention can all be rational. The semantics of the expressions employed and the context may support the reconstruction of different intentions equally well. In cases of legal interpretation as communicative interpretation, it is the contingent empirical communicative intention of the author that determines the truth of one of several equally well supported epistemic hypotheses. In the case of legal construction, however, there is no empirical intention of an author. The truth equivalent can only be found in the fictive communicative intentions. Because of their reflexive rationality, however, they run parallel to the epistemic rationality that guides the interpreter. They thus cannot privilege one of the possible rational legal constructions like an actual communicative intention.

This might explain why the truth aptness of legal construction seems questionable. As far as epistemic transcendence and definitiveness are connected with the truth predicate, legal construction cannot satisfy these conditions for structural reasons. Further, if science is connected with the truth predicate, this could explain the classic doubts with respect to the 'scientific' and scholarly character of doctrinal work, which is at the core of law as an academic discipline (Kirchmann 1848).

The German Federal Constitutional Court, for example, defines science, which is protected as a fundamental right under article 5, paragraph 3 of the German constitution, as a 'serious, systematic search for truth'.[19] According to this definition, the scientific character of legal construction would have to be denied if the truth predicate in the definition relied on potential epistemic transcendence and definiteness. In light of the large number of traditional academic disciplines, however, that like jurisprudence have a hermeneutic character, it is questionable if such a tight concept of science makes sense. A more adequate concept of science and scholarship might be restricted to the serious, systematic elaboration and rational justification of hypotheses.[20]

III. Summary

The reconstruction of the hermeneutic character of legal construction rests on the intentional character of non-natural meaning. Any ascription of linguistic meaning must rely on the connection between the communicative intentions of a speaker or author and an utterance. This also holds true for legal construction, which is required in cases where there are no communicative intentions connected to an utterance preceding the act of interpretation. As a hermeneutic discipline, however, legal construction has to presuppose a preceding communicative intention of an author. The rationality requirements connected with the – mostly implicit – presupposition of a fictive legislator explain not only a series of properties of legal construction but also what characterizes legal construction as a hermeneutic discipline and what distinguishes it from legal interpretation on the one hand and legislation on the other.

Endnotes

1 The distinction is occasionally traced to D.1.1.7.1. However, this source seems dubious as it concerns the legislative function of the *praetor*.
2 On Lieber's admiration for Schleiermacher, see Binder (1995: 2171); Freidel (1947: 21–2); and Holdheim (1995: 2155–6, 2164).
3 This might not exclude the 'interpretation' of qualia if it is conceded that there can be reasons for feelings. On reasons for feelings, see Skorupski (2010: 370–98).
4 The argument has been applied to law by Alexander and Prakash (2004). See also Fish (2008).
5 For Grice and the history of his reception, see, for example, Neale (1992). For the reception of Grice by the later Davidson, see, for example, Avramides (2001) and Cook (2009). Davidson warns against understanding this approach as a reductive theory of meaning (Cook 2009).
6 On the 'Principle of Charity' as a prerequisite for language and its understanding, see Davidson (1973: 137). For a discussion, see Glüer (2011: 112–52). See also Grice (1989: 27).
7 For an example in German constitutional law, see Schlink and Poscher (2000).

8 Even if Moore resists the fiction of an author, he has to admit that interpretation that goes beyond the intentions of the actual author is accompanied by the fiction of intentional content (1995: 16–7). Intentional content, however, implicitly presupposes an author, since only intentional subjects can provide intentions. Implicitly, Moore's fictions thus presuppose the fiction of an author, too.
9 See Marmor (2005: 24), who mentions 'the grammar of interpretation'.
10 See already Bülow (1885: 35). On the history of the idea, see Meder (2004: 106–8).
11 The same holds for the so-called objective method of interpretation, which tries to substitute the subjective meaning ascription by the legislator with an objective meaning of the law. For the objectivist tradition in the German methodological tradition, see Poscher (2015: 457).
12 Considerations of rationality can be of importance for the reconstruction of the actual legislator's intent to the extent that the assumption of rationality can support a hypothesis regarding his intention, which means that it must not be defeated by other evidence.
13 *Ashwander v Tennessee Valley Authority*, 297 U.S. 288 (1936), pp. 347–8 (Brandeis J., concurring); *Bond v United States*, 572 U.S. ___ (2014). See Barrett (2010: 138–43).
14 On the distinction between epistemic, practical and evaluative reasons, see Skorupski (2010: 33–55). Even if the three kinds of reasons are not considered irreducible in the way Skorupski suggests, the distinctions nonetheless provide for a useful typology.
15 *United States v Kirby*, 74 U.S. 482 (1868), p. 487; *Burns v United States*, 501 U.S. 129 (1991), pp. 136–7; *Clinton v City of New York*, 524 U.S. 417 (1998), p. 429; Bennion (2013: 969–1008); Dougherty (1994); Staszewski (2006). For a critique, see Manning (2003).
16 For Esser, the 'rightness' of interpretation always comprised normative rationality in an evaluative sense (1972: 162–71).
17 For the so-called 'Gricean mechanism', see Grice (1957: 383–6).
18 In traditional methodologies, legal construction *intra legem* is often considered to qualify as interpretation with the typical caveat that there is supposedly a continuum between interpretation and construction (Larenz 1991: 350) – a thesis contrary to the one developed above.
19 BVerfG, 29.05.1973, BVerfGE 35, 79 (113); BVerfG, 01.03.1978, BVerfGE 47, 327 (367); BVerfG, 11.01.1994, BVerfGE 90, 1 (12–3).
20 There are more recent decisions that do not refer to the truth component of the definition. For example, see BVerfG, 26.10.2004, BVerfGE 111, 333 (344); BVerfG, 28.10.2008, BVerfGE 122, 89 (105).

Bibliography

Alexander, L. and Prakash, S. (2004) '"Is That English You're Speaking?" Why Intention Free Interpretation is an Impossibility', *San Diego Law Review*, 41: 967–95.

Avramides, A. (2001) 'Davidson, Grice, and the Social Aspects of Language', in G. Cosenza (ed.) *Paul Grice's Heritage*, Turnhout: Brepols.

Barnett, R.E. (2011) 'Interpretation and Construction', *Harvard Journal of Law and Public Policy*, 34: 65–72.

Barrett, A.C. (2010) 'Substantive Canons and Faithful Agency', *Boston University Law Review*, 90: 109–82.

Barthes, R. (1968) 'La mort de l'auteur', in *Œuvres complètes*, É. Marty (ed.), vol. II, 2nd edn, Paris: Éditions du Seuil, 2002.

Bennion, F.A.R. (2013) *Statutory Interpretation*, 6th edn, London: LexisNexis.

Binder, G. (1995) 'Institutions and Linguistic Conventions: The Pragmatism of Lieber's Legal Hermeneutics', *Cardozo Law Review*, 16: 2169–89.

Bratman, M.E. (1999) *Faces of Intention*, Cambridge: Cambridge University Press.

Bülow, O. (1885) *Gesetz und Richteramt*, Leipzig: Duncker & Humblot.

Cook, J. (2009) 'Is Davidson a Gricean?', *Dialogue*, 48: 557–75.

Davidson, D. (1973) 'Radical Interpretation', in *Inquiries into Truth and Interpretation*, 2nd edn, Oxford: Oxford University Press, 2001.

—— (1986), 'A Nice Derangement of Epitaphs', in *Truth, Language, and History*, Oxford: Oxford University Press, 2005.

—— (1989) 'James Joyce and Humpty Dumpty', in *Truth, Language, and History*, Oxford: Oxford University Press, 2005.

—— (1991) 'Three Varieties of Knowledge', in *Subjective, Intersubjective, Objective*, Oxford: Oxford University Press, 2001.

Dougherty, V.M. (1994) 'Absurdity and the Limits of Literalism: Defining the Absurd Result Principle in Statutory Interpretation', *American University Law Review*, 44: 127–66.

Dworkin, R. (1986) *Law's Empire*, Cambridge, MA: Harvard University Press.

Ekins, R. (2012) *The Nature of Legislative Intent*, Oxford: Oxford University Press.

Esser, J. (1972) *Vorverständnis und Methodenwahl in der Rechtsfindung*, Frankfurt: Athenäum.

Fish, S. (2008) 'Intention Is All There Is: A Critical Analysis of Aharon Barak's Purposive Interpretation in Law', *Cardozo Law Review*, 29: 1109–46.

Foucault, M. (1969), 'Qu'est-ce qu'un auteur?', in *Dits et écrits*, D. Defert and F. Ewald (eds), vol. I, Paris: Gallimard, 1994.

Freidel, F. (1947) *Francis Lieber: Nineteenth-Century Liberal*, Baton Rouge, LA: Louisiana State University Press.

Gadamer, H.-G. (1986) *Truth and Method*, trans. J. Weinsheimer and D.G. Marshall, 2nd rev. Eng. edn, New York: Continuum, 2004.

Glüer, K. (2011) *Donald Davidson: A Short Introduction*, Oxford: Oxford University Press.

Grice, H.P. (1957) 'Meaning', *Philosophical Review*, 66: 377–88.

—— (1989) *Studies in the Way of Words*, Cambridge, MA: Harvard University Press.

Heidegger, M. (1927) *Being and Time*, trans. J. Stambaugh, 2nd Eng. trans., Albany, NY: SUNY Press, 2010.

Holdheim, W. (1995) 'A Hermeneutic Thinker', *Cardozo Law Review*, 16: 2153–67.

Hurd, H.M. (1990) 'Sovereignty in Silence', *Yale Law Journal*, 99: 945–1028.

Jestaedt, M. (2014) 'Wissenschaft im Recht: Rechtsdogmatik im Wissenschaftsvergleich', *JuristenZeitung*, 69: 1–12.

Kirchmann, J.H. von (1848) *Die Werthlosigkeit der Jurisprudenz als Wissenschaft*, Berlin: Springer.

Kelsen, H. (1934) *Introduction to the Problems of Legal Theory*, trans. B. Litschewski Paulson and S.L. Paulson, Oxford: Oxford University Press, 1992.
—— (1960a) *Reine Rechtslehre*, 2nd edn, Vienna: Deuticke.
—— (1960b) *Pure Theory of Law*, trans. M. Knight, 2nd edn, Berkeley, CA: University of California Press, 1967.
Knapp, S. and Michaels, W.B. (1982) 'Against Theory', *Critical Inquiry*, 8: 723–42.
Larenz, K. (1991) *Methodenlehre der Rechtswissenschaft*, 6th edn, Berlin: Springer.
Levinson, S.C. (1983) *Pragmatics*, Cambridge: Cambridge University Press.
Lieber, F. (1837) 'On Political Hermeneutics, or on Political Interpretation and Construction, and Also on Precedents', *American Jurist and Law Magazine*, 18: 37–101.
Mann, T. (1924a) *Der Zauberberg*, Frankfurt: S. Fischer, 2001.
—— (1924b) *The Magic Mountain*, trans. H.T. Lowe-Porter, 2 vols, London: M. Secker, 1927.
Manning, J.F. (2003) 'The Absurdity Doctrine', *Harvard Law Review*, 116: 2387–486.
Marmor, A. (2005) *Interpretation and Legal Theory*, 2nd edn, Oxford: Hart.
Meder, S. (2004) *Mißverstehen und Verstehen: Savignys Grundlegung der juristischen Hermeneutik*, Tübingen: Mohr Siebeck.
Moore, M.S. (1995) 'Interpreting Interpretation', in A. Marmor (ed.) *Law and Interpretation*, Oxford: Oxford University Press.
—— (2007) 'Can Objectivity be Grounded in Semantics?', in E. Villanueva (ed.) *Law: Metaphysics, Meaning, and Objectivity*, Amsterdam: Rodopi.
—— (2016) 'Semantics, Metaphysics and Objectivity in the Law', in G. Keil and R. Poscher (eds) *Vagueness and Law*, Oxford: Oxford University Press.
Neale, S. (1992) 'Paul Grice and the Philosophy of Language', *Linguistics and Philosophy*, 15: 509–59.
Neuner, J. (2005) *Die Rechtsfindung contra legem*, 2nd edn, Munich: C.H. Beck.
Pettit, P. (1994) 'Towards Interpretation', *Philosophia*, 23: 157–70.
Poscher, R. (2015) 'Hermeneutics, Jurisprudence and Law', in J. Malpas and H.-H. Gander (eds) *The Routledge Companion to Hermeneutics*, London: Routledge.
Rüthers, B. (2012) *Die unbegrenzte Auslegung*, 7th edn, Tübingen: Mohr Siebeck.
Savigny, F.C. von (1840) *System of the Modern Roman Law*, trans. W. Holloway, Madras: J. Higginbotham, 1867.
Schlink, B. and Poscher, R. (2000) *Der Verfassungskompromiß zum Religionsunterricht*, Baden-Baden: Nomos.
Searle, J.R. (1990) 'Collective Intentions and Actions', in P.R. Cohen, J. Morgan and M.E. Pollack (eds) *Intentions in Communication*, Cambridge, MA: MIT Press.
Skorupski, J. (2010) *The Domain of Reasons*, Oxford: Oxford University Press.
Solum, L.B. (2010): 'The Interpretation–Construction Distinction', *Constitutional Commentary*, 27: 95–118.
Staszewski, G. (2006) 'Avoiding Absurdity', *Indiana Law Journal*, 81: 1001–65.
Vogel, F. and Christensen, R. (2013) 'Korpusgestützte Analyse der Verfassungsrechtsprechung: Eine Abwägung von Prinzipien findet nicht statt', *Rechtstheorie*, 44: 29–60.
Waldron, J. (1999) *Law and Disagreement*, Oxford: Oxford University Press.

Index